THE NEW
INFORMATION
INDUSTRY

RICHARD KLINGLER

THE NEW INFORMATION INDUSTRY

Regulatory Challenges and the First Amendment

BROOKINGS INSTITUTION PRESS
Washington, D.C.

Copyright © 1996
THE BROOKINGS INSTITUTION
1775 Massachusetts Avenue, N.W., Washington, D.C. 20036

Library of Congress Cataloging-in-Publication Data:

Klingler, Richard.
    The new information industry : regulatory challenges and the first
      amendment / Richard Klingler. p.   cm.
    Includes bibliographical references and index.
    ISBN 0-8157-4944-9 (cl : alk. paper).—
    ISBN 0-8157-4943-0 (pbk. : alk. paper)
    1. Information services industry—United States.
    2. Telecommunication—United States.   3. Information
services—Law and legislation —United States.
    4. Telecommunication—Law and legislation—United States.
I. Title.
    HD9999.I493U645   1996   95-41744
    384′041—dc20   CIP

9 8 7 6 5 4 3 2 1

The paper used in this publication meets the minimum requirements of
the American National Standard for Information Sciences—Permanence
of Paper for Printed Library Materials, ANSI Z39.48-1984.

Typeset in Times Roman

Composition by AlphaTechnologies/mps, Inc.
Charlotte Hall, Maryland

Printed by R. R. Donnelley and Sons Co.
Harrisonburg, Virginia

ⓑ THE BROOKINGS INSTITUTION

The Brookings Institution is an independent organization devoted to nonpartisan research, education, and publication in economics, government, foreign policy, and the social sciences generally. Its principal purposes are to aid in the development of sound public policies and to promote public understanding of issues of national importance.

The Institution was founded on December 8, 1927, to merge the activities of the Institute for Government Research, founded in 1916, the Institute of Economics, founded in 1922, and the Robert Brookings Graduate School of Economics and Government, founded in 1924.

The Board of Trustees is responsible for the general administration of the Institution, while the immediate direction of the policies, program, and staff is vested in the President, assisted by an advisory committee of the officers and staff. The by-laws of the Institution state: "It is the function of the Trustees to make possible the conduct of scientific research, and publication, under the most favorable conditions, and to safeguard the independence of the research staff in pursuit of their studies and in the publication of the result of such studies. It is not a part of their function to determine, control, or influence the conduct of particular investigations or the conclusions reached."

The President bears final responsibility for the decision to publish a manuscript as a Brookings book. In reaching his judgment on competence, accuracy, and objectivity of each study, the President is advised by the director of the appropriate research program and weighs the views of a panel of expert outside readers who report to him in confidence on the quality of the work. Publication of a work signifies that it is deemed a competent treatment worthy of public consideration but does not imply endorsement of conclusions or recommendations.

The Institution maintains its position of neutrality on issues of public policy in order to safeguard the intellectual freedom of the staff. Hence interpretations or conclusions in Brookings publications should be understood to be solely those of the authors and should not be attributed to the Institution, to its trustees, officers, or other staff members, or to the organizations that support its research.

Foreword

SINCE 1990 technological and service developments have enormously restructured the various industries that control and use electronic communications. Those changes in telecommunications, cable television, broadcasting, computer hardware and software, video entertainment, and the like have also called into question the efficacy of the traditional federal and state regulations originally designed to shape competition in these formerly distinct industries. Various studies have described the broader change in how our society uses and distributes information and the regulatory and legal issues that affect particular industries. In this book Richard Klingler focuses on how the restructuring of a new information industry broadly challenges the way government regulates across the various industry sectors and the way that regulation can remain consistent with our First Amendment values.

Regulation of electronic communication has traditionally been conducted through separate regulatory regimes designed to address the competitive and social problems arising in what used to be separate and relatively stable industries. Broadcasting regulation was for the most part distinct from common carrier regulation, which developed largely independently from cable television regulation. Still different regulatory rules and processes applied to telephone companies' provision of video services and to the progeny of the Bell System. General antitrust law applied to all these regulated entities. The Telecommunications Act of 1996 maintained these divisions. Now, however, the lines separating businesses and services subject to different regulations have blurred, and the competitive assumptions generating the regulations have often changed or disappeared.

vii

Klingler traces the development of these regulatory regimes and their evolution in light of competitive changes. He contrasts these regimes and their underlying assumptions regarding competition and regulators' competencies with the dynamic, uncertain, and quickly changing nature of competition and service provision in the new information industry. He analyzes how the manifold structure of regulation has often failed to respond to recent developments and in many respects has outlived its usefulness. He also describes how developments in this new industry raise far-reaching First Amendment issues, and he outlines how First Amendment protections can and should be extended while preserving to regulators certain powers to redress failures of competition.

Klingler began this project as a guest scholar in the Center for Law, Economics, and Politics at Brookings in 1993-94. He is grateful to readers for their comments and suggestions. The manuscript was edited by Janet Mowery and Deborah Styles. Gerard Trimarco verified its factual content; Trish Weisman proofread it; and Julia Petrakis prepared the index.

Richard Klingler is an attorney with Sidley & Austin in Washington, D.C. He has participated in several of the regulatory and judicial proceedings narrated in the book and has, since 1994, worked in Australia with Telstra Corporation, most recently as regulatory counsel.

The views expressed in this book are solely those of the author and should not be ascribed to any business, to the people whose assistance is acknowledged above, or to the trustees, officers, or staff members of the Brookings Institution.

MICHAEL H. ARMACOST
President

May 1996
Washington, D.C.

Contents

1. The Transformation of Electronic Communication   1

2. Regulating Electronic Communication   13
    Common-Carrier Regulation *15*
    Regulation of Broadcasting and Other Wireless Communication *24*
    Cable Television Regulation *27*
    Telephone Company Provision of Video Programming *32*
    Regulation of Former Bell System Entities *37*

3. New Forms of Communication   44
    Provision of Information Services, Video Programming, and
       Advanced Video Products *45*
    Integration of Carriage Service and Distribution of Information
       Products *59*

4. Structural Reform of Regulation   69
    The Disparity between Emerging Information Networks
       and Traditional Regulatory Regimes *71*
    Strategic Responses to the Mismatch of Regulatory Structure
       and Market and Technological Developments *81*
    Challenges to Disparate Regulatory Regimes Posed by
       an Emerging Information Industry *93*

5. Extending First Amendment Protections   116
    Extending First Amendment Protections to All Electronic
       Media *118*

The First Amendment and the Regulation of Competition
   in the New Information Industry   *139*
Conclusion   *162*

Notes   164

Index   203

Tables
3-1. Local Exchange Carrier Proposals, 1992–95   50
3-2. The Vertical Connection between Major Programming
   Services and Cable System Operators   64
3-3. Illustrative Telecommunications Acquisitions and
   Mergers, 1994–96   67

CHAPTER ONE

The Transformation of Electronic Communication

IN LATE MARCH 1995, Nobuyuki Idei, the Sony Corporation's incoming president, outlined his company's strategic vision. Sony had already spent billions of dollars to add a principal Hollywood studio and music label to its core home electronic equipment businesses. Now, Sony announced, it would focus on information transmission, principally through cable television and satellite delivery in the United States because U.S. regulations allowed greater flexibility. "My dream is to fill a gap between content creation and content consumption," he said. "In the long range, the big opportunities lie here."[1]

This dream has disturbed the sleep of more than a few executives since the early 1990s. Information distribution is no longer the dull end of established newspaper, motion picture, and television businesses, and electronic transmission is no longer the preserve of dusty telephone monopolies. Now, how information is transmitted electronically and who controls that transmission will determine the fortunes of industries that were formerly distinct and how citizens receive, produce, and use that information. How the government chooses to regulate information transmission will significantly shape those outcomes.

Changes in the nature and regulation of information transmission threaten—and promise—a vast corporate reordering as a new and unified information industry emerges. Local telephone and cable television companies eagerly eye one another's core revenues and seek to integrate their transmission capabilities with content production and reception. At the

1

same time, novel transmission systems—from upstart telephone systems to satellite systems to private networks and the Internet—are multiplying and redefining the means available for the most basic personal and commercial communications. Television and motion picture industries seek to ensure that they both continue to be more than providers of content and preserve the preeminence of content—and their role in its provision. The computer software industry might simply become one of many suppliers of components to the emerging networks, or it might assume control of them through the importance of software products controlling access to the networks and through increased demand for computer applications made available over networks. The computer and consumer electronics industries, too, are on a collision course as they compete to provide the boxes that connect each home to the network, and their fortunes depend also on whether the network's intelligence is located at its core or its periphery. The newspaper, magazine, and book publishing industries struggle to exploit the opportunities afforded on these new networks to producers and packagers of content and, in their own terms, to avoid being confined to the margins of the emerging information industry. Finally, even greater change may come to industries that lie even farther from the core of the electronic networks—for example, advertising, document transport (including public and private mail systems), retail distributors, educational institutions, directory and booking services, data processing, libraries, gambling, and image processing (including text and photographic reproduction).

Changes in popular understanding of the uses and functions of information, and its relation to transmission, match this corporate reordering. In a disjointed fashion, it is widely perceived that our society is undergoing enormous changes in how information is produced, transmitted, received, and used. Print media—vulnerable to these changes as they are—have been quick to report the latest communications devices, new video products, mergers among communications companies, and related legislative and regulatory battles. The "information superhighway" has become a cliché in search of a policy, and "multimedia" a label attached to each new video product. Speculation about the uses and effects of these new technologies has acquired the tone of science fiction and has sent each interest and industry in search of opportunity or consolidation of gains. Anxiety is as rife as wonder.

However overstated at times, a communications revolution is under way. Its essence is the transformation and increasing importance of electronic distribution of information, and the ongoing migration of traditional forms of communicating to the emerging information networks. Until recently, electronic distribution of information assumed only a few distinct forms. Those basic forms in turn limited the uses of electronic networks and determined—and were determined by—how the government regulated information transmission. Now, powerful and overlapping new distribution systems are emerging that do not conform to the traditional means of distributing information or the regulation of them. The outline of these developments can be described briefly.

Consider the distribution of information before 1975. The structure of regulatory regimes continues to reflect the postwar technology that delivered, and to a considerable extent continues to deliver, information in the three essential forms that existed then. First, wireless, point-to-multipoint broadcasting constituted most electronically delivered mass information products. These broadcast communication products could be in voice form (radio) or video (television programming). Apart from motion pictures and an infant cable television industry, television broadcasting dominated by three major networks delivered nearly all video products. Second, switched, wire-based communications systems served principally to carry point-to-point voice communications, and those networks generally offered only those carriage services and not information or media products originated by the carrier. That is, the Bell System or independent telephone companies transmitted messages originated by customers and directed by those customers for delivery to other persons. Third, "packaged," or nonelectronically delivered, information products constituted most of the sources of information available to individuals. Some information was communicated personally, for example through performances, speeches, and especially retail transactions. Most information products were in print form and could be delivered through retail outlets (such as bookstores), private delivery systems (such as newspaper delivery), or public carriage systems (such as mail delivery of magazines). Video products of this type also existed in the form of theater distribution of motion pictures.

As described in greater detail below, initial regulatory policies largely tracked and reinforced these divisions. For the first delivery type, wireless transmission, broadcasting regulation developed through the Federal Communication Commission's (FCC's) implementation of Title III of the Communications Act of 1934.[2] The FCC established a system of broadcast licenses, allocated those licenses among competing applicants, and regulated licensees' conduct. In contrast, an elaborate regime of common-carriage regulation governed the second delivery type, wire transmission of third parties' messages. The FCC implemented Title II of the Communications Act, which embodied the traditional common-carrier duties initially developed for railroad regulation.[3] In addition, the FCC imposed a range of rate regulations, limitations on entry, and service regulations designed to "manage" competition or, ostensibly, to reduce ill-defined competitive abuses. Finally, relatively few regulatory requirements applied to the third delivery type, packaged information products, especially in print form. Antitrust actions and other government measures were occasionally directed against the motion picture industry.[4] Copyright and defamation laws applied to print products, and some laws governed use of the mails. Even so, the lack of the print media's control or use of electronic facilities, the long tradition of relatively limited regulation of print products, and the First Amendment protections that applied to them precluded application of more extensive regulations.

This tripartite system of delivering information flourished for a surprisingly long time but came under increasing pressure beginning in the late 1970s and early 1980s. Commercial offerings of satellite-delivered video programming developed in the late 1970s, with service directly to homes beginning soon thereafter. Regulatory restraints on cable television systems were substantially relaxed in the late 1970s, triggering tremendous growth in the scope of areas served and products offered.[5] Two developments in computer technology began to transform information delivery: computers were increasingly integrated into the telecommunications network, allowing provision of various "enhanced" or information services;[6] and the development and increased use of personal computers dramatically expanded the communicative uses of the telecommunications network.

Even so, the traditionally divided regulatory regimes initially accommodated these developments. Broadcasting and common-carrier regulation addressed aspects of satellite services. Broadcasting regulation formed the initial basis for regulating cable television systems, and a separate but closely related regulatory regime developed especially for those systems.[7] The FCC used common-carrier regulation to address many computer services, which were largely deregulated and have since often been treated as packaged products (for example, retail distribution of computer programs).[8]

The functions and variety of electronic communications had increased dramatically by 1990. Cable television systems and satellite systems delivered a far greater variety of video programming and increasingly delivered television broadcast signals to the home. Correspondingly, the increased use of video cassette recorders and personal computers expanded the range of available packaged products. The proliferation of personal computers in homes and computing ability in industry generated a range of new uses and services employing the telecommunications network, including services provided by carriers. Text, including electronic versions of traditional print and other mass-media products, could be made widely available in this manner. Carriers increasingly integrated wireless transmission capabilities into the telecommunications network, allowing a range of mobile services. Through toll-free 800-number services and telemarketing, even commercial retail information was often communicated electronically, either directly or in conjunction with mailed information such as catalogues.[9]

Since 1990 these developments have intensified and have been matched by new forms of electronic delivery of information. Cable television systems and satellite delivery systems have continued to expand in capacity and programming offerings, and new wireless video transmission systems are emerging. The development of database technologies and of the Internet have shown the importance of the merger of personal computing and the telecommunications network. Wireless telecommunications services multiply, and telecommunications competition in several long-distance and local markets has increased.

The most important recent developments have rested on technological advances that hold out two crucial possibilities: integrating the switching capacity typical of the telecommunications network with the ability to deliver increasing streams of data, often enough to display pictures or even video programming, and integrating computing and networked communication capabilities in a manner that would allow consumers to direct and ''interact'' with the information they wish to receive. The first development underlies the entry of telecommunications carriers into traditional cable television and other information services, as well as the possibility that cable television systems will perform telecommunications functions. The second prompts the possibility of an array of new video and text services that allow consumers to receive information they want when they want it, whether that information is traditional video programming, text or video information contained in vast databases and made available according to consumer requests, or videotelephony communication. The Internet is a prominent example, but more formal or closed networks emerging from cable television systems, resold telecommunications facilities, and private computing facilities are similarly providing users with access to entertainment products, retail transactions, computer applications, and new forms of personal communication. These services could complete the migration of commercial products and information to the electronic network, in the sense that the principal media products and sources of retail information and transactions could be conducted over that network. These capabilities could also allow individuals to become important producers of information, including video products, with enormous consequences for the development of personal communication, the arts, and politics.

Even as the structure and nature of information provision has changed dramatically, the structure and content of regulation of these services has remained relatively constant. The focus of regulators' activities has shifted with these market changes, but regulators continue to refine outdated regulations and to use powers designed for competitive problems that are long past. The Telecommunications Act of 1996 was in this sense a missed opportunity: although of tremendous commercial significance, the act only marginally revised the basic structure of regulation and in some respects exacerbated the difficulties created by the distinct regulatory regimes.

The following chapters describe these developments in greater detail and focus on several of the important legal and regulatory issues posed by this transformation of communication. Many of the most interesting legal issues are beyond the scope of this discussion. For example, the growing importance and forms of electronically communicated information present enormously difficult legal issues related to privacy, national security, law enforcement, intellectual property (including copyrights and patents), government disclosure obligations, international trade policies, and the coordination of technical standards.

Instead, this book focuses on how government regulates the industries that are most important to the development, operation, and provision of services over this emerging electronic information network. One basic theme is that regulators for historical and ideological reasons have focused on entities that physically control traditional electronic networks, which are an increasingly small and often indistinguishable constituent of an integrated and dynamic information industry. For several types of information service providers that are somewhat at the periphery of these networks, traditional regulation of electronic transmission may affect them greatly but will often do so indirectly. For example, newspaper and book publishers and the Hollywood television and movie studios determine what information will be transmitted and how it will be marketed and received, but they only indirectly participate in developing the emerging information network itself. Computer equipment manufacturers, manufacturers of consumer electronics equipment, and software producers do participate in that development process, but those industries have not been subject to extensive government regulation, will likely remain relatively competitive, and do not, or at least do not yet, directly operate and control the principal network facilities that transmit information. These industry sectors pose many of the most difficult policy and regulatory issues, and those issues arise and are resolved beyond the scope of traditional, industry-specific regulation through another regulatory regime of general antitrust law enforcement.

The prominent regulatory regimes instead address one corner of the new information industry: corporations that directly operate or control the facilities used to transmit information. These include television broadcasting companies, cable television system operators, and telecommunications carriers of various types. Four commercial broadcast networks dominate television broadcasting. Each directly owns multiple licensed broadcast stations in major metropolitan areas, and each produces and acquires programming formed into a common schedule to be broadcast over those owned and operated stations as well as by stations across the nation that are affiliated by contract with the networks. In addition, public television and commercial stations throughout the nation that are independent of the major networks remain important outlets for broadcast programming, and additional networks are emerging from those commercial stations. Individual cable television systems operate in small areas licensed by local governments, but several companies own multiple systems that together serve most cable television households and hold interests in much of the most popular cable television programming (apart from the generally more popular network television programming that cable systems retransmit). The most important telecommunications carriers for purposes of the emerging information network control facilities used to provide local telephone services, although niche local service competitors, cellular carriers, and long-distance carriers are also important. The most important local carriers are the "Baby Bells," or regional companies, which control the local telephone facilities divested from the Bell System in the early 1980s, and important local telephone companies that were independent of the Bell System, such as GTE. In addition to these three industries, there are operators of emerging networks. Producers of information content (including the mass media, both print and electronic) and producers of software and computer equipment may also fall within the ambit of these core regulations whenever they ally with these principal network operators.

Through their roles in shaping the emerging information network and supporting other elements of the new information industry, these corporations present the greatest competitive opportunities and dangers and are subject to exceptionally extensive government regulation. One of the greatest legal challenges, and a principal focus of this book, is to evaluate the continued relevance of various regulatory regimes that have developed over decades in response to distinct and now bygone competitive circumstances. The structure of many of the most important regulatory regimes and rules developed when communications industries were disparate. Separate regulatory regimes developed for radio communications (and specifically for television broadcasting), for common-carrier telecommunication of voice messages, and for cable television systems. Additional, distinct regulatory systems emerged that limited the ability of local telephone service providers to enter related markets (for example, long-distance services or distribution of video programming). Chapter 2 traces the origin and development of the principal regulatory regimes governing these core services and focuses on how regulators have built on and reshaped their regulations within distinct and separate regulatory structures in response to competitive changes affecting particular regulated industries. On a somewhat grander scale, the Telecommunications Act of 1996 repeats this pattern of essentially marginally revising and perpetuating the established, separate regulatory structures. This is hardly to suggest that regulators have generally aligned regulation to foster competition; they have at least as often responded to protect regulated companies from competitive changes or to protect politically powerful competitors from those regulated companies. (Indeed, as developed later, the very maintenance of these industry-specific regimes often serves these ends.)

The transformation of communication now poses a more fundamental challenge to existing regulatory structures. Until recently, most changes could be addressed from within each of the principal regulatory regimes. With some difficulties, policy issues could be plausibly categorized and addressed as separate broadcasting or cable television or telecommunications issues. No longer. The most pressing issues now cut across those categories and arise, for example, because telecommunications, broadcasting, and cable companies can now compete in established services and seek to compete in emerging services at the boundaries of traditional regulatory structures—or because companies in each of the industries seek to integrate their services and facilities with those subject to widely varying regulations. Chapter 3 traces some of the technological and market developments, particularly in the delivery of video services, that pose the greatest challenge to the traditional divisions among regulatory structures. It outlines how an array of emerging and often overlapping delivery systems has created a network and set of service providers capable of performing combinations of functions and transmitting types of information that traditionally have been subject to separate regulatory systems—or, because not previously delivered electronically, not regulated at all.

Chapter 4 begins to identify and address the central regulatory issues presented by this collision between a novel, emerging information industry, marked by dynamic network and information product development, and fragmented regulatory regimes resting on increasingly outdated competitive assumptions. It first surveys the extent of the transformation of information facilities and services and underscores the uneasy relation between the new and quickly evolving networks and segmented regulatory regimes oriented toward marginal adjustments within distinct industries. The chapter also examines several strategic and general regulatory issues presented by recent technological and market developments—including the circumstances (if any) requiring administrative regulation of the information industries to prevent anticompetitive conduct, the need (if any) to continue administrative regulation for reasons unrelated to competition, and potential adjustments to the traditional administrative model that might reduce the costs of regulating these industries through administrative proceedings. Finally, the chapter considers the particular challenges that the emerging information industry poses for each established regulatory regime, and modifications of each that might better respond to the emerging information networks and services. The essential point throughout is that recent developments now justify wholesale reexamination of the principal industry-specific regulatory structures that have developed over the past decades—rather than only the important but ultimately marginal adjustments to particular restrictions that have been the focus of recent political and policy disputes. And in many cases, that reexamination should lead to elimination or dramatic paring of current regulation.

The technological and market developments outlined in chapter 3 pose similar difficulties for the potentially most powerful limitation on government power in this industry, the First Amendment. Established First Amendment doctrine reflected and sprang from the same separation of communications services that originally produced distinct regulatory regimes. For communications that did not require electronic transmission, whether through newspapers or from street-corner speakers, the greatest First Amendment protections applied and government had the least latitude in enacting regulations. For broadcast television and radio (which until recently constituted nearly all electronically delivered mass media), a lesser type of First Amendment protection applied. This lesser protection was justified on the basis of the unique characteristics of broadcasting and permitted a limited but important range of government regulation, including regulation designed to affect the balance or content of communications. Telecommunications was believed to present almost no First Amendment issues, and telecommunications carriers were subject to the most extensive government oversight. The changes described above have dramatically undermined those assumptions. Speech, including traditional print products such as newspapers, may be electronically transmitted without use of broadcast technology, and the cable television operators and telecommunications carriers subject to the greatest regulation are already becoming among the most important providers of information and services protected by the First Amendment. Chapter 5 examines the implications of these developments. It suggests that recent developments have eliminated the basis for according broadcast and other electronically delivered information any lesser First Amendment protection, and for permitting administrative regulation on that basis. It also outlines an extension of traditional First Amendment principles that advances the libertarian values underlying First Amendment doctrines while confirming the government's ability to pursue certain regulatory objectives—especially those related to abuses of market power—that are not designed to shape the balance or content of communications. Here, too, the underlying point is that the changes shaping the new information industry challenge the limitations assumed to confine our First Amendment principles. Our nation has a vibrant and valuable tradition of limiting government's control over communications, and we have the opportunity to redefine and recommit ourselves to that tradition by extending it to the electronic communications at the core of the emerging information industry.

Although the following chapters directly explore issues of administrative law, regulatory policy, and constitutional doctrine, those issues cannot be divorced from larger questions of social organization. The technological and market developments that constitute the communications revolution raise fundamental issues about the sources of social control, the capabilities of governance, and the prevalence and benefits of competition. On the one hand, these developments present the danger that government will increasingly assert control over the means and content of public debate and that regulators and entrenched corporations will throttle new entrants or impede destabilizing market developments. Many established interests are seeking and will seek to increase regulation to reduce the inevitable dislocation caused by such profound social change. Our nation's libertarian tradition in matters of communication, embodied most prominently in the First Amendment, has had a checkered history when applied to electronic communication and will likely be sorely tested in the years to come. Enormous pressure already exists to regulate to reduce the legitimate competition that underlies the communication revolution, and that pressure will increase. Such disruptive competition often (perhaps usually) prompts corrective political and social responses, and the unknown future benefits of competition might give way before the all-too-certain costs of the change those forces are bringing.

At the same time, the fears of anticompetitive control over the information and services available to citizens are not fanciful. As information services and the opportunities for communication become more dependent on electronic transmission, any entity able to serve as a gatekeeper to and from the home could wield increasing power over the form and pricing of products available to individuals, as well as over individuals' opportunities to transmit their own communications. The emerging information networks may contain several sensitive points vulnerable to this type of control—for example, the wire link of home to network; the box that allows reception, selection, and transmission of information; the software format determining the connections of consumer to information sources; or the functions of the electronic gateways and menu services that allow access to competing information service providers. The need for carriers and service providers to establish a brand-name relationship with consumers may provide a few corporations with a degree of market power. If regulators can resist incumbent operators' importunings, measure costs of regulation, and accurately determine when market power will persist, even traditional economic theory would support regulatory efforts to check market power where it clearly exists and leads to these results, as well as more mundane distortions of pricing and service offerings.

These dystopias hardly exhaust the possible outcomes of the communication revolution. The market and technological developments also hold out the possibilities of democratic renewal, a cornucopia of advanced information products and services, a vastly more efficient retail and commercial market, heightened industrial productivity, active citizen engagement in the production of information, and the creation of edified communities of like interests and pursuits. Whether the communication revolution produces one of the dystopias or these benefits depends in part—perhaps in large part—on how we structure government regulation of the core transmission industries and the content and information services associated with them. The transformation of the information industries also provides an unusual opportunity to reconsider the bounds of our libertarian tradition of limited government oversight of the nature and form of public debate, and to reconsider the uses and capabilities of administrative powers to shape dynamic markets. The initial step in those tasks, in turn, is to trace the development and evolution of existing regulatory regimes that govern this new information industry.

CHAPTER TWO

Regulating Electronic Communication

AS OUTLINED in the previous chapter, the hallmark of current communications competition is the actual or potential overlapping of services and facilities among previously separate and separately regulated industries. There are increasing means of providing data services and delivering video programming. Entities other than traditional telecommunications common carriers are providing networked data and telephony service. Industries and corporations with greatly divergent core businesses are seeking to develop the content and delivery systems for the emerging interactive, computer, and video services. At the same time, the core businesses of the regulated industries have changed and collided dramatically since the mid-1980s.

The regulations that govern how these different entities may provide services remain quite distinct and generally arose far before this transformation, overlapping, and collision of markets, services, and technologies. Five principal regulatory regimes may apply to the provision of advanced and more traditional electronic communications. Common-carrier regulation was designed for telecommunications carriers, principally telephone companies, and was enacted as part of the Communications Act of 1934. It embodies a tariffing and public-utility model of regulation developed in the late nineteenth century in the course of regulating railroads. A separate regulatory system applies to wireless communications, and a more specialized set of regulations within that regime governs broadcasting. That, too, was part of the Communications Act of 1934. More recently, a separate statutory and regulatory system has developed for regulating cable television service; those regulations were initially developed through administrative actions to shield broadcast services from competition, but the Cable Acts of 1984 and 1992 have established a separate portion of the Communications Act for cable service alone. In addition, a distinct set of statutory and administrative requirements governs how local telephone companies may provide video services. Telephone company provision of video programming to subscribers in the local telephone service area was originally broadly prohibited, but first FCC regulations and more recently the Telecommunications Act of 1996 have greatly expanded the opportunities for local exchange carriers to provide video services. Finally, as a result of antitrust suits leading to the divestiture or "breakup" of the Bell System, a consent decree until 1996 governed the activities of both AT&T and the seven (at that time) regional companies, or "Baby Bells." The Telecommunications Act of 1996 enacted modified versions of the decree's restrictions and transferred their administration from a federal court to the FCC.

All of these regulatory regimes have changed considerably in response to competitive changes, especially since the mid-1980s. For the principal regimes, change has come largely through administrative interpretations of open-ended statutory commands. For common-carrier and broadcasting regulation, nearly all relevant regulatory requirements spring from elaborate rules developed by the Federal Communications Commission rather than directly from the Communications Act itself. The Cable Acts are more detailed, but they, too, are being implemented in large part through administrative elaboration. All of these administrative regulations, in turn, have evolved in rough response to prevailing regulatory models and fashions. For the regimes that the Telecommunications Act of 1996 significantly changed—local telephone company provision of video services and regulation of former Bell System carriers—the particular requirements continue to reflect the regulatory battles of the preceding fifteen years and will be implemented only through elaborate administrative proceedings. With the partial exception of cable television regulation, there has been a sea change from regulation designed to "manage" or stabilize competition to measures designed in part to foster competitive entry and to reduce regulatory requirements (at least where the absence of market power is demonstrated). As described below, many of these recent regulatory developments are contrary to and call into question the assumptions that generated the structure of the regulatory regime. These changes have been most pronounced for common-carrier regulation but have also extended to telephone company provision of video services and to aspects of wireless communications (especially for new services, but for traditional broadcasting services as well).

The following sections trace the origin, evolution, and operation of each of these regulatory regimes. In particular, they focus on the shifting administrative strategies pursued within each regulatory regime, and on recent changes that are often in considerable tension with the competitive assumptions that generated and continue to define each system of regulation. At the same time, the permanence and distinctness of each regulatory regime remain cardinal features. Each system of regulation defines specific activities that fall within its purview and specific practices deemed to require government oversight, and regulation then proceeds from within that regulatory model. Increasing attention may be devoted to delineating the boundaries between those regulatory regimes, but those systems' evolution has rarely extended to rationalizing or coordinating their operation and the divergent sources of regulation. The Telecommunications Act of 1996 was in many respects a missed opportunity. With the potential exception of treatment of telephone company provision of video and local services, the act principally clarified the relation between certain regimes, provided marginal regulatory relief for several pressing commercial difficulties, and left largely untouched the basic regulatory framework designed for formerly distinct industries and the competitive concerns of times past. For the principal regulatory regimes, recent responses to competition through administrative action have been only partially successful or have pursued divergent regulatory objectives. The result in these cases is either regulation set against itself, with both highly regulatory and relatively light-handed regulations operating on the same or closely related practices, or unresponsive restrictions, with regulators and industry participants unable to respond fully to current conditions because they are limited by frameworks designed for other eras.

Common-Carrier Regulation

The Communications Act of 1934, as amended, remains the principal source of regulation of most interstate telecommunications services, broadcasting, and cable television. The act established the Federal Communications Commission and provides it with broad powers over these services. Title II of the act regulates interstate "common-carrier" telecommunications services.[1] A "common carrier" is one that makes a general offering to the public to carry their messages by wire or air (usually without altering or originating those messages), and the messages may take the form of voice, data, or video.[2] Common-carrier regulations principally govern the activities of telephone service providers, including resellers, and thus include local telephone companies, long-distance companies, cellular service providers, and others. Radio and television broadcasters, carriers of strictly intrastate local communications, private telecommunications networks, and cable television systems are generally excluded from this type of regulation.[3]

The Structure of Telecommunications Regulation

Given the enormous complexity of common-carrier regulation, Title II of the Communications Act itself imposes surprisingly few specific obligations on common carriers. Instead, it principally sets forth general mandates for the FCC to elaborate and implement in particular adjudications and administrative rule-makings. For example, carriers must furnish service "upon reasonable request."[4] Their charges and practices must be "just and reasonable" and cannot amount to "unjust or unreasonable discrimination" among customers.[5] Carriers must place on file a generally available, tariffed rate offered for communications services and cannot reduce that rate for favored customers through rebates or discounts.[6]

Common-carrier regulation principally takes place through various opportunities for the FCC to review and regulate carriers' practices. Traditionally, the most important was the tariff filing and review scheme. Before providing service, carriers file tariffs describing their services and the charges they are thereafter obligated to assess for them.[7] Customers, competitors, and others may then initiate challenges to the services, alleging that the rates are too high (or too low) or that services are improperly provided. The FCC may on its own suspend and investigate the filed tariffs, or it may await a formal complaint before considering the reasonableness of a carrier's practices.[8] In addition, the act provides the FCC with authority to prescribe appropriate carrier practices, which extends to mandating certain offerings and determining appropriate rates, and to oversee the initiation and discontinuance of new communications facilities.[9] Other statutory provisions, including one empowering the FCC to "perform any and all acts . . . as may be necessary in the execution of its functions," have been interpreted as providing the FCC with tremendous discretion over the regulation of common carriers.[10] Since its formation, the FCC has employed these review processes to develop detailed rules and policies governing a broad variety of telecommunications rates and services within its jurisdiction.

This type of regulation and many of the economic assumptions underlying the FCC's oversight of the telecommunications industry can be traced, oddly enough, to the initial attempts to regulate the railroads in the late nineteenth and early twentieth century. The first modern administrative agency, the Interstate Commerce Commission (ICC), was created in 1887 to oversee competition and practices in the railroad industry, and the ICC expanded its powers considerably after passage of the Hepburn Act in 1906.[11] The Interstate Commerce Act (ICA), too, relied on a tariff-filing scheme to allow an administrative agency to oversee the rates and practices of an entire industry. The comprehensive nature of the intended regulation, and the extent to which competition was to be managed, stems from the crucial role that railroads—and regulating the railroads—played in both the American economy and politics at the turn of the century. Both elite reformers and populist politicians viewed constraining the railroads' practices, along with control of other industry "trusts," as essential to preserving traditional values as the nation underwent a particularly contentious phase in its initial industrial revolution.[12] The regulatory response was to displace competition in the entire industry—for both monopoly and non-monopoly services—and to entrust the industry's development instead to disinterested, expert administrators considered able to formulate policy in the "public interest."[13] They would elaborate a set of duties of reasonable conduct and nondiscrimination that carriers owed to the public simply by virtue of the public importance and character of their service.[14] These administrators, rather than politicians or industry executives or owners, would be charged with ensuring that rates and related practices were "reasonable," that railroad networks interconnected appropriately, and that railroads did not favor certain regions or classes of customers through pricing policies or by any other means.[15]

When regulating telecommunications, Congress pursued this same strategy of comprehensive commitment of an entire industry's practices to administrative control and oversight. Portions of the ICA had governed telegraph and certain telecommunications services from 1910 to 1934, and Congress used the ICA as the template for both the regulatory structure and specific statutory provisions of Title II of the Communications Act of 1934.[16] For both industries, the carriers' duties and the federal administrators' powers were nearly identical. As the Senate Report to the Com-

munications Act explained, "In this bill many provisions are copied verba-
tim from the Interstate Commerce Act because they apply directly to
communications companies doing a common carrier business, but in some
paragraphs the language is simplified and clarified. These variations or
departures from the text of the Interstate Commerce Act are made for the
purpose of clarification in their application to communications, rather than
as a manifestation of congressional intent to achieve a different objective."[17] This borrowing from the ICA was common. During the New Deal
era, Congress directly employed the ICA as a statutory model to craft the
regulations of the motor carrier, airline, natural gas, and electric power
industries as well.[18] For these industries, and for Title II of the Communications Act in particular, Congress believed it was replacing "the principle of
free competition" with regulation "involv[ing] the suppression of wasteful
practices due to competition, the regulation of rates and charges, and other
measures which are unnecessary if free competition is to be permitted."[19]

One departure from the ICA, the Communication Act's division of
regulatory authority between state and federal officials, continues to have
enormous policy implications. The Communications Act grants the FCC
authority over only interstate telecommunications service.[20] In practice, the
FCC's authority is quite broad, because it has been interpreted to extend to
regulation of local carriers to the extent that their networks complete
interstate calls or otherwise provide interstate telecommunications services
(as almost all do).[21] Even so, the result is a dual and overlapping regulatory
structure because state regulatory bodies can control the terms and conditions of intrastate service. State officials can and do erect entry barriers and
regulate local service rates and practices, although their powers have recently been curtailed in this respect.[22]

Two aspects of this division between state and federal regulatory
authority have proved particularly important. First, the FCC cannot
preempt certain state regulations in order to craft a uniform national
policy. Most federal agencies possess that power, derived from their
governing statute in conjunction with the Constitution's supremacy
clause, to set aside or preempt state regulation that interferes with
federal regulations and policies.[23] The FCC's power is not so broad. A
carrier that originates or terminates both local and interstate traffic may
maintain a single network but is subject to two sets of regulations. As
recently as 1986, the Supreme Court reaffirmed this limitation on federal
power in the Communications Act, and more recently an intermediary
federal appellate court invoked the limitation to set aside a broad FCC

rule designed to regulate carriers' provision of computer and advanced telecommunications services.[24]

The dual regulatory structure also established dual administration of rates. An early Supreme Court decision established that in traditional rate-making, the invested plant or rate base must be allocated for accounting purposes between that employed for intrastate service and that employed for interstate service.[25] Many of the policy disputes in the initial decades of the Communications Act's administration addressed this allocation, which had the increasing effect of requiring users of interstate telecommunications to subsidize local service rates (a distortion that in turn eventually contributed to long-distance entrants, such as MCI, which sought to undercut the Bell System's inflated rates on high-volume interstate routes).[26] Even now, carriers of both interstate and intrastate traffic may be subject to traditional, rate-of-return regulation by the state and federal ''price cap'' or incentive regulation for interstate services.[27]

Regulatory Responses to Competitive Pressures

In the initial decades after the passage of the Communications Act, the FCC's domestic common-carrier regulation principally addressed the activities of a unified Bell System, as well as the Bell System's dealings with independent telephone companies that generally served relatively rural areas. Apart from the difficulties presented by determining the relative roles of state and federal regulation (especially for rate regulation) and allocating fees among these entrenched carriers for joint services, few dramatic conflicts arose.[28] By the 1950s and through the 1960s, the FCC and the Bell System had, with minor exceptions, settled into a cozy, symbiotic relationship that resembled in many respects the operation of state-owned telecommunications monopolies that are only now eroding in many European nations. As long as the Bell System provided adequate, widely available basic service at rates that did not annoy any important constituency or generate unusually large profits, the FCC would demand no more than marginal adjustments in services.[29] The FCC provided little elaboration of the broad commands of the act and regulated with the presumption that telecommunications services were best provided by a single, monopoly carrier. The Bell System, in turn, aggressively structured its services and network to forestall competition and justified these actions as necessary to continue to provide comprehensive and reliable services.[30]

Two related developments during the 1970s transformed common-carrier regulation. First, significant competition in long-distance services emerged. Courts reviewing FCC decisions seized on the limited inroads that the FCC had allowed into the Bell System's end-to-end control of much of the telephone network. Using those decisions, and driven largely by a populist hostility to large corporations, the Court of Appeals for the District of Columbia Circuit directed the FCC in effect to pry open the Bell System monopoly and allow entry by long-distance competitors, particularly MCI.[31] At the same time, the Bell System's pricing of long-distance services virtually invited competitive entry. Rates bore little relation to costs. Regulatory policies had inflated long-distance rates to subsidize local service, and charges were barely related to traffic volume or the costs of constructing and operating particular routes.[32]

The second development was ideological. Influential administrators and other policymaking elites increasingly sought to integrate fundamental economic concepts into regulation. Competition was in vogue, precisely when the economic traumas of the mid-1970s created widespread doubt in agencies' ability to "manage" concentrated industries.[33] The result was to reverse the traditional regulatory role. Creating or fostering vigorous competition—rather than constraining it or managing monopoly behavior—became a principal policy objective. Alfred Kahn's tenure at the Civil Aeronautics Administration and the deregulation of the airline industry prominently reflected these changes.[34] Similar efforts to increase competition transformed regulation of the railroad, motor carrier, natural gas, electricity, and other industries—many of the very industries that, like telecommunications, had been regulated through the administrative structure derived directly from the Interstate Commerce Act.

Beginning in the 1970s and continuing even now, the FCC adopted a range of policies designed to increase competition and competitive pressures. In 1976 and 1980 orders, the FCC limited carriers' restrictions on the use of their services, thus allowing resale both by competing long-distance carriers and by carriers that sought to secure volume discounts and pass a portion of that discount on to smaller-volume customers.[35] For larger carriers, the FCC imposed extensive accounting and marketing restrictions that limit their ability to provide traditionally regulated services in conjunction with more competitive services.[36] Local carriers must equally provide access services to all long-distance carriers and make competing carriers' long-distance service available to subscribers on a nondiscriminatory basis.[37] For smaller carriers, the FCC in practice eliminated nearly all regulatory requirements—including tariff filing, entry restrictions, and rate regulation—through a series of proceedings in the early 1980s.[38] More recently, the FCC has initiated a broad set of pricing and antibundling measures designed to increase competition in the markets for various services provided by local telephone companies.[39] The resulting rules require local telephone companies to offer elements of their facilities and services separately and at rates closer to costs, with the ultimate goal of allowing entry by competitors into both local telephone service and the service of linking consumers with long-distance carriers.

Many of the FCC's recent efforts have cannibalized much of the Communications Act and relinquished all but the pretense of expert administrative oversight of a range of carrier and service provider practices. The FCC attempted to exempt entire classes of carriers found to lack market power from the act's tariff filing requirements and simultaneously effectively insulated them from challenge to or oversight of their rates, services, and practices.[40] For larger carriers, the FCC largely abandoned its efforts to assess "reasonable" rates in relation to costs, and instead allowed carriers to opt for a system of incentive regulation. This "price cap" system of rate regulation reduced most FCC oversight of carriers' costs, pricing, and rates of return, and increasingly made even the most regulated carriers subject to market risks and rewards.[41] Oversight of AT&T's offerings was "streamlined" for services in markets found to be substantially competitive and further reduced once AT&T was found "non-dominant" in most domestic markets.[42] In addition, the FCC loosened its interpretation of what constituted a discriminatory service offering in a manner designed to accelerate competition in the enormous market for sophisticated services customized to meet business customers' telecommunications requirements.[43]

Perhaps the most dramatic regulatory changes were the FCC's determinations that Title II of the act would no longer encompass broad classes of services. Instead of overseeing the development of large segments of the industry, the FCC determined to leave those services almost exclusively to market forces. For example, when confronted with the initial integration of computer services into the telecommunications network and products, the FCC declined to oversee these "enhanced" information services.[44] It simply declined to regulate them within the scope of common-carrier regulation. Similarly, the FCC declared that common-carrier regulation would no longer apply to the sale and manufacturing of telecommunications equipment designed to be used on customers' premises, or to the installation and maintenance of wiring inside customers' premises.[45] Whereas the Bell

System had traditionally been regulated from the standard black handset at one end to the Princess phone at the other, the FCC now ended its regulation of the telephone network at the customer's premises. Combined with the virtual deregulation of resellers of telecommunications services, these determinations narrowed the FCC's focus to the principal operators and owners of telecommunications facilities and insulated from regulation the private networks, network-based computer services, and personal computer services that are transforming how individuals receive and use information.

In limited respects, the Telecommunications Act of 1996 continued this deregulation of common-carrier activities. For example, the act granted the FCC broad powers to "forbear from applying" the Act's requirements to classes of telecommunications carriers or services, where the FCC concluded that enforcement was unnecessary and contrary to the public interest.[46] It also reduces tariff filing burdens for local exchange carriers and removes certain barriers that had limited electric utility companies' provision of telecommunications services.[47] Perhaps most important, the act preempted state and local regulations that "prohibit or have the effect of prohibiting the ability of any entity to provide any interstate or intrastate telecommunications service."[48] Although this provision seeks to end the local grants of monopoly powers and other preferences that have protected incumbent local service providers, its practical effect will likely remain uncertain for some time because the act also preserves and in some respects may enhance the powers of states and local governments to regulate local carriers' activities.

On balance, however, the 1996 Act greatly increases the FCC's role in regulating common-carrier activities. The act establishes a process to define and to meet "universal service" goals.[49] Two related parts of the act impose a series of obligations on local exchange carriers that are designed to increase competition, especially facilities-based competition in local services. One requires that local exchange carriers provide certain interconnection, facilities-sharing, and other services that might aid competitive entry and establishes a complex enforcement regime administered by both state commissions and the FCC.[50] A second part, described in greater detail below, specifically addresses the activities of the local exchange carriers that had been part of the Bell System.[51] It makes their entry into certain prohibited activities (for example, long-distance calls originating in the carrier's local exchange area) dependent on undertaking limited measures designed to increase local service competition and reduce the potential for anti-competitive activities.

Despite the FCC's important deregulatory initiatives, common-carrier regulation remains a baroque accretion of obligations set down to meet each decade's perceived imperative but then built on rather than removed by each successive set of administrators. The model of administrative action, the form and scope of the FCC's powers, and many of the most important substantive obligations still derive from the original Communications Act of 1934. Title II's division of regulation between federal and state officials persists, creating conflict between relatively deregulatory and often highly regulatory policies in overlapping jurisdictions—especially for rate and entry policies. So, too, do Title II's tariffing and nondiscrimination requirements, which often impose significant constraints on carriers' competitive pricing and service offerings and provide ample opportunities for competitors to employ the regulatory process to slow and restrict a competitor's offerings. And the FCC has often pursued its policies designed to foster competition not by constructing policies to address the issue at hand but by focusing the full burden of Title II's regulatory scheme on established carriers. Nearly every effort to bolster competitors in traditional monopoly markets or to create competitive submarkets for telecommunications services has been attempted through increased regulation on the largest, entrenched carriers. Just as the FCC opened the long-distance market through restrictions on Bell System offerings, so has it crafted enormously complicated regulation of local telephone carriers to allow competing service providers to use the local carriers' facilities.[52] Extensive regulations govern how large carriers may provide regulated services as well as enter unregulated markets that the FCC seeks to make more competitive.[53] Complicated accounting, cost allocation, and marketing restrictions confront large carriers that seek to depart from their core businesses.[54] These regulations are designed principally to prevent cross-subsidies through cost shifting from unregulated activities to rate-regulated activities, to buttress price cap regulation, to foster interconnection and access, and to prevent entities with market power, and often control over essential facilities, from favoring their affiliated enterprises. The most recent legislative revisions, too, both further complicate the dual administration of telecommunications by state and federal authorities and create yet another elaborate set of industry-wide prescriptions designed to address certain of the competitive difficulties created by the incumbent local service providers.

Regulation of Broadcasting and Other Wireless Communication

Radio transmissions are used not only for what the name immediately suggests—the familiar AM and FM radio broadcasting—but also for any type of wireless electromagnetic communication, whether generally broadcast to recipients over a large area or intended for a particular destination. Thus radio, or "wireless," transmission is employed by satellites, television broadcast stations, cellular telephone systems, paging systems, microwave relays, wireless cable services, various local and federal government communication systems, and a range of emerging personal communication technologies. A distinct regulatory structure—Title III of the Communications Act—empowers the FCC to regulate who may offer which of these services and how they may be provided.[55]

Certain provisions of Title III apply generally to these services that use the electromagnetic spectrum. The spectrum may be thought of as the three spatial dimensions of the "airwaves," plus added dimensions of time and wavelength frequency. Even in the same geographic area, radio signals of sufficiently different frequencies can be transmitted simultaneously without interfering with the reception of other signals. For all commercial radio services, the FCC allocates licenses, which are permits for a user to broadcast signals at a certain frequency within a particular area for a certain period (usually several years, with likely renewal). Title III, and the FCC rules developed under that authority, govern the permitted uses, frequency, geographic scope, allocation, and conditions attached to the use of those licenses.[56] Other regulations and Title III provisions apply specifically to broadcast services, a subset of wireless communications.[57] Broadcasting encompasses wireless transmissions that are designed for general, unfettered reception and is typified by AM and FM radio and television services.[58] It does not include subscription services and other wireless systems designed to transmit communications to a particular recipient or recipients.

Traditional regulation of broadcast services reflects a fiduciary or "trusteeship" model: the government temporarily commits its resources (the spectrum) to the care and use of particular licensees, who are correspondingly charged with broadcasting in the public interest and subject to extensive government oversight designed to protect the public interest.[59] To select among applicants for broadcast licenses, the FCC devised comparative criteria for use in selecting the licensees most capable of discharging this role—deemed by the FCC to be applicants with demonstrated ties to the community, broadcast experience, integration of ownership and management, lack of financial interest in other licenses, and membership in designated minority groups.[60] Successful applicants for television and radio broadcast licenses pay no fee to the government for their license or use of the spectrum. The government also has devoted and continues to devote considerable resources, both in direct outlays and especially in allocation of valuable licenses, to public television and radio broadcasting.[61]

In addition to charging the licensees with general obligations to conduct its broadcasting in the "public interest," the FCC developed extensive regulations designed to shape the content of the licensees' broadcast programming. These regulations extended to obscenity and indecency, children's programming, overall programming formats, various aspects of political advertising, and, through the "Fairness Doctrine," the sufficiency and balance of programming devoted to issues of public controversy.[62] The FCC also has pursued less direct, structural regulation designed to alter programming content. These include rules limiting ownership of multiple television and radio broadcast stations (on a national and local level) and rules designed to prefer members of minority groups and new entrants into the broadcasting industry.[63]

In part to ensure that broadcasters could meet their public-interest obligations, the FCC initially shielded licensees from significant competition. The FCC's allocation of licenses ensured that there would be little competition among licensees in particular geographic areas and little threat to the established national television networks.[64] In addition, the FCC until the mid- to late 1970s significantly restricted video technologies—especially cable television and satellite broadcasting—that threatened significant competition with traditional broadcast licensees. Similarly, cross-ownership rules barred owners of newspapers and cable television systems from engaging in television broadcasting in their local markets.[65] At the same time, the FCC sought to diffuse control of licenses. The FCC restricted both control of multiple licenses on a national basis and control of multiple licenses within a particular geographic area.[66] Within a local service area, a single owner generally could not acquire attributable ownership interests in two licenses of the same type or in two separate types of licenses (for example, a television broadcast license and a radio broadcast license).[67]

Much of this regulatory structure remains, but regulation of wireless services has shifted in important respects in response to competitive changes. The most dramatic change has been in the allocation of licenses for new services. As set forth in greater detail in chapter 5, the FCC's allocation policy has proceeded in three stages: first, it awarded licenses without compensation through comparative proceedings to determine the applicant best able to employ the license in the public interest; second, especially in the early 1980s and most prominently for cellular telephony licenses, the FCC often distributed licenses without compensation through a lottery system; increasingly, the FCC has conducted auctions for spectrum allocated to new licenses and services and has, in conjunction with the National Telecommunications and Information Administration (NTIA), redesignated large portions of the electromagnetic spectrum for commercial uses.[68] In addition, the FCC has reduced several of the most prominent aspects of its regulation of the content of broadcast programming.[69] Most controversially, the FCC repudiated its Fairness Doctrine after concluding that its policies likely violated the First Amendment and were counterproductive (because the potential for regulatory proceedings, including loss of licenses, often caused broadcasters to reduce their coverage of controversial issues).[70] There are indications, however, of renewed congressional and FCC interest in increased regulation of the content of broadcast programming.[71]

Separately, the FCC also has eliminated or reduced many of the particular restrictions that it had justified on the basis of the unique or dominant market role of broadcasters, particularly in the delivery of video programming. For example, the FCC has dramatically relaxed the regulations governing the financial and syndication interests that television networks may acquire in the programming they broadcast, has scheduled the elimination of rules limiting the broadcast of network programming, has permitted common ownership of a greater number of broadcast licenses (on both a national and a local market basis), and has eased certain cross-ownership restrictions.[72] In early 1995 the FCC undertook a broader reexamination of its broadcast license ownership rules in light of increased competition. Responding to an internal report that questioned the continued need for certain regulations when multiple providers of video programming existed as well as to recent increases in the delivery systems that supplied that programming, the FCC continued to reexamine its rules that limited ownership of multiple licenses on a national basis, ownership of different types of licenses in a local market, and ownership of the same type of license in the same market.[73] This inquiry served as a prelude to reexamination of rules governing networks and their relationships with affiliated stations; separate inquiries addressed minority ownership issues and what types of interests constituted ownership for purposes of the rules.[74]

The Telecommunications Act of 1996 only marginally altered the Communications Act's structure and form of regulating broadcast licensees, but it contained several commercially important amendments. The act largely eliminated the cross-ownership restrictions between the broadcast and cable television industries: it permits a television licensee to own cable television systems in its local service area and directs the FCC to "permit a person or entity to own or control a network of broadcast stations and a cable system."[75] The act also increases the number of licenses that a single entity can control. The act directs the FCC to eliminate restrictions on the number of AM and FM licenses that may be owned on a national basis and to relax restrictions on ownership of multiple licenses in particular markets. For television licenses, the FCC is to relax restrictions on the national ownership of television licenses (newly limited to a reach of 35 percent of national households), as well as to permit greater cross-ownership of television and other licenses in a single market.[76]

The act also increased the interests established by a broadcast license by permitting licenses to be granted or renewed for a longer period (eight years, for both radio and television licenses) and by focusing the license renewal process simply on whether the license has met a basic standard of service (including whether "the station has served the public interest, convenience, and necessity").[77] Another provision of the act governs the FCC's treatment of licenses for advanced television services. Current licensees who receive any such new licenses must continue "to serve the public interest, convenience, and necessity" and pay fees, as determined by the FCC, designed in part to reflect "the value of the public spectrum resource."[78]

Cable Television Regulation

Cable television systems remain the nation's principal means of delivering video programming. Cable television systems "pass," or are capable of providing service to, 95 percent of the nation's households with televisions, and nearly two-thirds of all households with television subscribe to cable service.[79] Title VI of the Communications Act, which comprises the Cable Acts of 1984 and 1992, governs what constitutes cable television service, who may provide that service, and certain terms and conditions of the service.

This distinct regulatory regime encompasses only "cable service," the familiar set of television-like programming channels that traditional cable systems provide to subscribers. The cable statute and related regulations address only "one-way transmission . . . of video programming" and other programming services over wires to subscribers, along with limited two-way signaling occasionally used to select those channels.[80] Congress intended to regulate services that directly competed with broadcasting, and the 1984 Cable Act defines "video programming" as "programming provided by, or generally considered comparable to programming provided by, a television broadcast station."[81] Logically enough, the FCC has concluded that the act, and cable regulations generally, address services like those that television stations provided in 1984.[82]

Although cable television systems were designed to provide this type of cable service, and generally continue to do so, cable television regulation does not address most of the additional and advanced services that cable systems are beginning to acquire the capabilities to provide. Until 1996, if a cable system (or telephone company, or other business entity) provided fully interactive, two-way services, that service was not a "cable service" and not subject to Title VI's requirements.[83] The Telecommunications Act of 1996 somewhat blurred this line, and some advanced services may now fall within cable television regulation.[84] If a cable system or other business uses a cable system's facilities to complete or initiate telephone calls, common-carrier regulation likely applies—and cable service regulation clearly does not.[85] The regulatory division works both ways: if a telephone company or other entity begins to use wires to provide one-way delivery of its own video programming to subscribers, and operates other than as a common carrier, cable television regulations (or the new "open video system" rules) will likely govern that service.[86]

Cable television regulation owes its peculiar form to governmental efforts to manage competition between cable system operators and the television broadcasting industry. Cable service originated as community antennae television, or CATV, which was principally a method of retransmitting broadcast television signals by wire to places that could not receive those signals over the air.[87] The FCC's regulation of cable television was initially asserted as a matter of "ancillary jurisdiction," based on the use of the broadcast signal and potential competitive effect of cable television on broadcast television, which clearly was within the FCC's jurisdiction.[88] Several Supreme Court decisions in the 1960s and 1970s set forth the boundaries of this type of jurisdiction and required the FCC to rest its actions on a sufficiently direct effect on broadcasting.[89] Initially, the FCC's regulation consisted largely of determining when cable television systems could—or, in some cases, must—retransmit broadcast television signals. Much of that regulation, persisting through the 1970s, sought to limit the competitive threat posed by cable systems to existing broadcasting stations, and in particular sought to preserve the established broadcast networks and affiliate systems.[90] Not until the FCC undertook broad deregulatory measures in the late 1970s did the cable industry begin to grow significantly in major urban markets.[91]

The 1984 Cable Act created a statutory basis for the FCC's regulation of the cable industry and established the essential elements of the current regulatory structure. The act divides regulatory authority between the FCC and local officials. Local municipal officials would continue to control entry into the cable television business through awards of "franchises," or licenses, required to provide service and use the rights-of-way over public property.[92] Through often elaborate contracts entered between the municipality and the cable operator as a condition of providing service, the franchise power brought with it broad powers to control the terms and, in circumstances limited by the 1984 act, the content of service.[93] These franchises often were initially granted as outright monopolies, and allegations of corruption often surrounded their award.

The 1984 act established a limited federal regulatory role. It protected cable systems from certain types of local regulation and imposed limited requirements that systems carry programming provided by unaffiliated entities.[94] The FCC acquired direct statutory authority to promulgate rules designed to protect broadcasting stations and to control the use of television programming. In 1988, after an eight-year hiatus, the FCC reinstated its "syndicated exclusivity" rules, which in most circumstances prohibited a cable operator from duplicating syndicated programming that was already broadcast by local stations.[95] The FCC also modified and reaffirmed its rules that limited cable systems' carriage of duplicative network programming.[96] Perhaps most controversially, the FCC repeatedly attempted to implement rules requiring cable television systems to carry the signals of certain local television stations. Reviewing courts just as often invalidated these rules as arbitrary or contrary to the First Amendment.[97]

In the years following the 1984 Cable Act, two broad market developments increased demands for greater regulation of the cable television industry. Both developments stemmed from cable operators' market power over delivery of video programming by wire to the local community—power either guaranteed by an exclusive municipal franchise or enhanced by the high costs of replicating the cable facilities.[98] Whatever the competitive outlook for delivery of video programming in the 1990s and beyond, the cable industry then faced limited competition for multichannel programming delivery. Even by 1991, less than one-half of 1 percent of the more than 11,000 cable systems faced competition from another cable television system.[99]

First, subscribers increasingly complained about the quality of cable television service and the increasing charges for that service. Portions of the rate increases could be justified by the expanding programming services of cable system operators and by increased charges for certain established cable programming. Nonetheless, substantial evidence of rate increases that could not be justified in this manner was presented to Congress in a series of hearings in the late 1980s and early 1990s.[100] Consumer groups and others argued that local municipalities had almost no control over rates and terms established by cable systems, and that little substitution among video products existed to create a market check on cable rates.

Separately, cable programmers and potential competitors to cable television systems also objected to cable operators' treatment of cable programming. Cable system operators affect programming in two pertinent ways: they select the programming that would be presented to their local community and often assume ownership interests in cable programming and thus influence its availability. There was and continues to be a high degree of integration of ownership of multiple cable systems and cable programming networks or sources, especially for the programming networks with the most subscribers and the largest audiences.[101]

Cable programmers unaffiliated with any cable system, or simply unaffiliated with the particular system to which they sought access, alleged that cable operators favored affiliated programming or assumed ownership interests as a condition of transmitting a cable programming network. Potential competing video delivery systems—for example, second cable systems or SMATV (single-mast antenna television) systems designed to serve concentrated areas such as large buildings—alleged that cable operators restricted their access to desirable programming.[102] Television stations, especially smaller, independent stations, claimed that operators would refuse to carry the station or would place the station on an undesirable channel.

In the 1992 Cable Act, Congress responded to both of these sets of complaints. An elaborate regime of rate regulation for nearly all cable systems was the most important response to consumer complaints. An expanded ''basic tier'' of cable channels would be subject to aggressive rate regulation, implemented by both the FCC and local authorities acting in accord with FCC regulations, as long as the cable system was not subject to "effective competition" in the provision of a comparable array of video programming.[103] The FCC chose to establish a benchmark rate, designed to reflect how rates would be set if competition existed, and cable systems would either have to begin to conform to those rates or show that their costs justified higher charges.[104] Members of Congress and others criticized the FCC's initial benchmark formula as reducing rates insufficiently, and the FCC revised its benchmark formula in a manner that it concluded would reduce cable systems' rates for basic services by approximately 17 percent from the rates charged in September 1992.[105]

The 1992 act also regulated cable system operators' control over programming. The act's "must carry" provisions required cable operators to carry the signals of certain local commercial and public television stations (the number depended on the size of the cable system and the nature of the stations) and was immediately subject to a constitutional challenge that was pursued before the Supreme Court (this challenge and its disposition directing further proceedings are discussed extensively in chapter 5).[106] The act separately limited the percentage of channels that a cable operator could devote to affiliated programming and limited the percentage of homes that could be served by systems under common ownership.[107] The FCC rules implementing this first requirement created significant loopholes, and a federal court promptly declared the second requirement to be unconstitutional.[108]

Perhaps the most significant limitation on cable operators' control over programming was the 1992 act's prohibition of discrimination in the distribution of programming owned in whole or part by cable operators. Such integrated programming had to be made available on equal terms to affiliated cable systems and to other delivery systems, including direct competitors.[109] Other provisions of the act also sought to limit operators' control over programming. The act imposed uncertain limitations on cable operators' ability to gain a financial interest in cable programming as a condition of carrying the programming (the operator was allowed to negotiate for such an interest but could not acquire the interest by "coercing" a programming distributor).[110] And the act attempted to buttress preexisting "leased access" requirements, which provided limited rights for unaffiliated programmers to gain access to a cable system but which even the FCC had concluded had been readily evaded.[111]

The Telecommunications Act of 1996 altered this regulation of traditional cable television systems only minimally, but it significantly clarified the relation between cable television regulation and regulation of other, related telecommunications services. For traditional cable television regulation, the principal change was to limit aspects of rate regulation.[112] As part of efforts to regulate violent and indecent programming (discussed in chapter 5), the act also required that cable operators scramble certain channels devoted to "indecent" programming and limited the "leased access" and PEG channel rights in relation to programming "which contains obscenity, indecency, or nudity."[113]

At the same time, the act clarified the limits of traditional cable television regulation. The act limits local franchising authorities' control over cable system operators' provision of traditional telecommunications services.[114] The extensive statutory provisions for telephone companies to provide programming directly to subscribers, discussed below, also limit the role of local franchise authorities.[115] Although those provisions are intended to provide for telephone companies' competition with traditional cable television systems, their departure from the Cable Act's reliance on local franchising may have broad, unintended consequences for the continued operation of traditional cable television regulation.

Telephone Company Provision of Video Programming

Another set of regulatory requirements, established by the Telecommunications Act of 1996, governs local telephone companies' provision of video programming in their local telephone service areas. These new provisions establish different ways for telephone companies to compete with cable television system operators, but they are informed by a long history of regulation of competition between the two industries. Telephone companies' provision of video services was once nearly entirely precluded by a statute prohibiting "any common carrier" from "provid[ing] video programming directly to subscribers in its telephone area."[116] FCC rules in the late 1980s and early 1990s considerably expanded opportunities for telephone company entry into video services, and telephone companies in 1993–95 successfully blocked enforcement of the statute itself on First Amendment grounds. The Telecommunications Act of 1996 repeals the statute, eliminates the FCC's rules, and establishes a new framework for telephone companies' provision of video services.

Broad limitations on telephone companies' provision of video services first arose in the late 1960s and early 1970s to protect what was then the emerging cable television industry from competition by telephone companies. Telephone companies had begun to offer "channel service" to carry the programming of cable television systems, which were often affiliated with the telephone carriers. The FCC concluded that the telephone companies' monopoly over local telephone facilities (especially pole attachments and conduits necessary to provide cable service) might stunt the development of independent cable television service providers.[117] It thus enacted an initial version of the video restriction in 1970.[118] Despite the growth of the cable industry and the development of measures designed to secure cable television operators' access to telephone poles, the FCC regulation remained intact. In the 1984 Cable Act, Congress, with little debate, slightly revised and codified the FCC regulation in the form described above.

Soon after the Cable Act became effective, the FCC initiated proceedings to determine whether the restriction should be adapted to changing competitive conditions.[119] The growth of the cable television industry and the FCC's conclusion that limited regulatory safeguards could prevent cross-subsidization and other anticompetitive conduct by the telephone companies led the FCC to conclude tentatively in 1988 that it should recommend to Congress that the categorical cable-telco restriction should be repealed.[120] In 1992 the FCC formally recommended repealing the restriction and allowing telephone companies to provide video programming "subject to appropriate safeguards."[121]

The FCC also narrowed the scope of the cable-telco restriction. For example, the FCC concluded that the restriction was designed only to prevent monopoly abuses of local exchange telephone facilities and applied only to carriers that possessed monopoly power.[122] Thus, the restriction did not bind long-distance telephone carriers and upstart competitors of the established local carriers. The FCC also adopted a relatively narrow definition of the "video programming" that local carriers were prohibited from providing: the restriction encompassed only programming that resembled television programs offered in 1984, but telephone companies could offer interactive and other "nonprogram" video services.[123]

In addition, the FCC seized on the statute's limitation to programming "provide[d] . . . directly to subscribers" and crafted elaborate "video dial-tone" rules that governed how telephone companies could, indirectly, provide *other parties'* video programming.[124] These rules allowed local telephone carriers to establish two-tier facilities in their local service areas to transmit video programming and other, more advanced video services.

One part, the "first level platform," would be an offering on a common-carrier basis of facilities that would transmit video programming and advanced services to customers, and the carrier would have to ensure that sufficient facilities were provided to unaffiliated service providers and programmers to meet the common carriage nondiscrimination requirement. The "second level platform," in contrast, could comprise the carrier's own interactive services and "gateways" to advanced services—although competitors offering those services would have to be provided nondiscriminatory access to the "first platform" transmission and switching facilities.[125] A carrier that offered "video dialtone" service would not have to secure local authorization as a cable operator or be subject to regulations applicable to cable television systems.[126] Even under these rules, however, the local carrier was still prohibited from providing its own video programming to subscribers in areas in which it provided local exchange telephone service.

The video dialtone rules presented only a general framework for limited telephone company entry into the provision of video services, and the FCC left many of the most difficult policy issues to be resolved through further rulemaking and case-by-case determinations. Cable television companies, in particular, used these proceedings to seek limitations or "safeguards" on the video dialtone services that threatened their core business. In the rulemaking proceedings, the FCC began to elaborate on the telephone companies' obligation to provide sufficient capacity on their systems for unaffiliated service providers, on a nondiscriminatory basis. These proceedings also addressed requirements designed to ensure that video dialtone facilities were not constructed using a cross-subsidy based on telephone charges, and that telephone companies did not practice anticompetitive marketing or use customer information secured through provision of telephone service.[127] Objections to the particular form of video dialtone offerings were to be considered through proceedings addressing individual applications, required by section 214 of the Communications Act, made by local telephone companies to construct facilities to provide video dialtone services. Local telephone companies promptly filed applications to provide technical and market trials, as well as service, that would potentially cover more than 8 million households and businesses. In the course of authorizing trials and limited service, the FCC continued to elaborate on how common-carrier obligations would apply to these traditional and emerging video services. The FCC's disposition of these applications was marked by lengthy delay, but authorizations increased considerably in late 1994 and early 1995. By spring of 1995 the FCC had granted eight applications for commercial service (for more than 1.5 million households) and ten applications for trials.[128]

This initial phase of video dialtone regulation permitted limited entry by telephone companies into video carriage and related information services but continued to prohibit most forms of direct delivery of programming selected by telephone companies over their own systems. That is, the restriction continued to prevent telephone companies from distributing their own video offering in the manner that cable television system operators did. In late 1993 and 1994 most of the largest local telephone companies secured a series of judicial decisions that barred enforcement of this prohibition on First Amendment grounds.[129] Although the judicial relief was relatively broad (the government could not enforce the restriction against the successful regional Bell companies and other local providers in their local service areas), the reasoning was fairly narrow. The courts set aside the cable-telco restriction on the ground that the particular, categorical statutory prohibition was insufficiently crafted to address the underlying competitive concerns that the government had identified in defense of it.[130] The decisions would thus likely not preclude more carefully tailored and reasoned limitations or safeguards on telephone companies' direct provision of video services in their local service areas.

After the telephone companies' successful judicial challenges to the absolute prohibition, the FCC commenced wide-ranging proceedings to address what regulatory restrictions should accompany telephone companies' provision of video programming directly to customers in their local telephone service areas.[131] The FCC questioned whether the statutory requirements and related regulations grounded in Title VI and applying to cable television operators applied as well to these activities, and whether the commission possessed the power to apply only certain cable television obligations—either under Title VI or, if cable regulations did not apply, pursuant to common-carrier regulation authorized by Title II of the Communications Act.[132] Separately, the commission outlined the regulatory safeguards it was considering imposing to prevent abuses of market power (including rules governing capacity allocation, acquisition of cable television systems in local telephone service areas, and limitations on joint marketing), as well as accounting and other rules designed to prevent funding of video services through charges for telephone service (apart from profits secured from that service).[133] It also suggested that its extensive regulations designed to limit the integration of carriage services with noncarriage information services would also apply to telephone companies' provision of video programming.[134]

In the Telecommunications Act of 1996, Congress broadly addressed the issues that had bedeviled the FCC and sought to ease telephone companies' entry into competition with cable television system operators. The act repealed the statutory cable-telco prohibition and terminated the effect of the FCC's video dialtone regulations.[135]

In their place the act provided four ways a local exchange company could provide video programming to subscribers. First, with minor exceptions, only Title III's requirements would apply to any entity, including a telephone company, that used radio communications to deliver video programming to subscribers.[136] That is, the licensing system rather than cable regulation would control these services. Second, and somewhat tautologically, Title II's common-carrier regime would govern "to the extent that a common carrier is providing transmission of video programming on a common-carrier basis."[137] Of course, the FCC's video dialtone proceedings had attempted to elaborate just these common-carrier requirements, but Congress simultaneously eliminated them. Third, telephone companies could simply establish and operate traditional cable television systems, subject to the full range of cable television regulation.[138] The act generally limited telephone companies' ability to acquire or enter joint ventures with cable television systems that operated in their local service areas.[139]

The fourth method of telephone company entry into this market, through an "open video system," departs considerably from previous regulation and, depending on regulations implementing the statute, may provide a highly advantageous form of entry. To qualify as an "open video system," a local exchange carrier's facility must comply with regulations, to be developed by the FCC, that ensure that video programming providers can secure carriage services on nondiscriminatory and reasonable terms.[140] System operators have substantial claims on system capacity for their own video services and may select among different programming providers for a portion of remaining capacity. Title II's obligations to obtain a section 214 certificate and make capacity available on a nondiscriminatory basis do not apply.[141] For open video systems, additional regulatory burdens are considerably less than those imposed on cable television systems. Certain cable television regulations apply (including those governing privacy, billing, and certain restrictive dealings), and the FCC is to develop and impose the equivalent of "must carry" obligations. At the same time, cable rate regulation and local franchising regulation do not apply to an "open video system" (although fees equivalent to franchise fees may be required).[142]

The result is a hybrid system that may provide significant competitive advantages for local exchange carriers and other entities that might secure its benefits. It allows telephone companies to avoid the principal burdens of cable system operation, to provide only limited access, and to secure the principal benefits of cable television systems—substantial control over system capacity to provide an integrated video programming offering and the absence of Title II obligations. Of course the practical benefits of the model will depend on the implementation of regulations and separate restrictions imposed on the marketing and terms of carriers' traditional telecommunications services offered in conjunction with video services.

Regulation of Former Bell System Entities

An additional, distinct regulatory regime applies to the activities of the telecommunications carriers that once formed the Bell System—and that still compose most of the nation's principal telecommunications carriers. Until the enactment of the Telecommunications Act of 1996, a consent decree limited the activities of AT&T Corp. and especially the seven original Baby Bells, or regional companies. That decree, resulting from the government's lawsuit that broke up the Bell System in 1984 and administered by a federal judge, restricted the regional companies' ability to provide long-distance service or manufacture telecommunications equipment as long as a substantial risk remained that those markets would be harmed by the regional companies' market power over facilities used to provide local telephone service.[143] These restrictions limited the local service companies' entry into a range of standard and advanced services that required communication between local exchange areas. The decree also imposed certain nondiscrimination requirements on those carriers.[144] With the Telecommunications Act of 1996, modified versions of the principal consent decree requirements assumed statutory form. The act also provided immediate, prospective relief from certain decree restrictions and established the FCC as the principal arbiter of when additional relief for the local exchange carriers would be appropriate.

Before January 1, 1984, a unified Bell System provided most telecommunications services in the United States. The Bell System was a single enterprise comprising twenty-two Bell operating companies (BOCs), Western Electric Company, and Bell Telephone Laboratories. The BOCs owned franchised monopolies that provided local exchange telecommunications service to approximately 80 percent of the nation's telephone subscribers, and these facilities also originated and terminated long-distance ("interexchange") calls. The BOCs and the Long Lines Department of AT&T owned the facilities used to provide intrastate and interstate long-distance services. Bell Laboratories conducted basic and applied research and engineered an integrated telecommunications network. It also designed telecommunications equipment, which Western Electric Company then manufactured for sale to the BOCs.[145]

This integration of equipment manufacturing, exchange monopolies, and long-distance services prompted antitrust suits by the United States in 1949 and 1974 and extensive private antitrust suits during the 1970s. This potential liability increased as FCC regulations fostered competitive entry into long-distance services. The basis for these suits was that the Bell System's local exchanges were not only natural monopolies but also "essential facilities" or "bottlenecks" that affected equipment manufacturing and interexchange services. The Department of Justice's suit leading to divestiture alleged that, as a "regulated monopolist, AT&T has had both the incentive and the ability, through cross-subsidization and discriminatory actions, to leverage the power it enjoys in its regulated monopoly markets to foreclose or impede the development of competition in related, potentially competitive markets."[146] The department had compiled extensive evidence that the Bell System had used its monopoly facilities to prevent competition in the provision of equipment used in the telephone network or equipment that might be connected to it. To protect its integrated system, the Bell System was alleged to have similarly employed those facilities to stifle alternative delivery systems, such as satellites or land-line competition that required interconnection with the Bell facilities.[147] The Bell System principally defended its conduct as authorized by regulations or justified by efficiencies provided through integrated service.

The resulting consent decree, entered in 1982, created a new structure for the provision of telecommunications services in the United States and a new set of regulatory restrictions.[148] The Justice Department and the Bell System settled the suit through a consent decree that incorporated the department's competitive theory, which sought "divestiture of the Bell operating companies from AT&T in a manner that would separate the local exchange functions of the operating companies from AT&T's interexchange, manufacturing, and other functions."[149] This separation, or divestiture, was designed to strip the local monopolists of the incentive to harm competition in those potentially competitive markets. For example, if the local carrier could not provide long-distance service, it would have no incentive to price its local access services or discriminate in interconnection in a manner that would favor any affiliated provider of long-distance service. The decree thus broke the Bell System into an entity (now AT&T Corp., which is further divesting itself of its manufacturing division) that provided long-distance service and telecommunications equipment manu-facturing, and the BOCs, which were organized into seven regional Bell operating companies ("regional companies" or RBOCs) and restricted to providing local telephone service within particular LATAs, or local access and transport areas.[150]

The decree's restrictions on telecommunications services also reflected the Justice Department's theory. To shield the competitive markets from market power abuses of local facilities, the decree imposed three principal "line-of-business" restrictions on the RBOCs: they could not carry signals between LATAs (that is, provide long-distance service), manufacture tele-communications equipment, or provide information services.[151] The RBOCs also were required to provide equal "exchange access" to any and all interexchange carriers that sought to connect to the local exchange for the purpose of carrying consumers' long-distance calls.[152] AT&T, corre-spondingly, was prevented from acquiring the assets or stocks of RBOCs as a means of recreating the proscribed combination of local bottleneck mo-nopoly and competitive services.[153]

The decree restriction on inter-LATA service also affected the regional companies' attempts to employ broadband facilities to deliver video and other products—from traditional cable service to interactive services and even voice and videotelephony. This issue arose particularly for regional companies' participation in cable ventures beyond their own regions—in-cluding Southwestern Bell's interest in the Hauser systems and US WEST's interest in the Time Warner Entertainment cable systems, some of which are being upgraded to "full-service networks." The decree's inter-LATA restriction had been interpreted as applying to reception and transmission of video programming to the cable system head-end for subsequent delivery to customers; to transmission from the head-end to customers in another LATA; and to transmissions between customers in one LATA and a server or network of servers in another LATA.

The decree contained two related mechanisms that permitted adjust-ments or alterations in response to competitive changes. Changes might come through case-by-case waivers—for example the many waivers of the interexchange restriction provided to accommodate the regional companies' cellular services—or through wholesale elimination of particular requirements. Regional company petitions for relief were first presented to the Department of Justice, which then communicated its position to Judge Harold Greene, who oversaw the decree's administration. If all parties to the decree—the Department of Justice, the regional companies, and AT&T—agreed to a proposed modification, it was granted almost as a matter of course. The decree underwent hundreds of adjustments of this sort. If a regional company sought relief that another party opposed, however, a more stringent, traditional antitrust standard applied.[154] The decree provided that, in those circumstances, the regional company must establish ''that there is no substantial possibility that it could use its monopoly power to impede competition in the market it seeks to enter.''[155]

The waiver or modification process often addressed requests that would provide significant relief from the decree's provisions. For example, the regional companies secured a waiver of the decree to provide long-distance service in conjunction with various types of cellular service.[156] US WEST secured waivers of the long-distance service restriction to provide various services through the ''full-service networks'' to be developed with Time Warner,[157] and RBOCs received extensive waivers to provide video services beyond their local service areas.[158] AT&T, too, secured a waiver of a provision of the decree in order to complete its merger with McCaw Communications, then the largest single provider of cellular service.[159]

The regional companies also sought wholesale elimination of all three of the decree's principal restrictions (on providing long-distance service, manufacturing telecommunications equipment, and providing ''information services''). The regional companies' initial attempts to remove the manufacturing and long-distance restrictions, undertaken in the late 1980s, proved futile. They were unable to convince either the courts or the Department of Justice that long-distance relief was appropriate, and the courts established that there had been no appropriate showing justifying relief from the manufacturing restriction, despite the department's endorsement of the regional companies' position. The courts concluded that the regional companies' bottleneck monopoly over local services remained nearly complete and that there had been no relevant change in the regional companies' ability and incentive to harm competition in related markets in the manner that prompted the Bell System breakup.[160]

The regional companies' efforts to remove the decree's restrictions on their provision of information services proved more successful. The Justice Department's antitrust case had not been based on a history of anticompetitive conduct regarding information services. No decree party opposed the regional companies' petition to remove the information services restriction, thus ensuring that the petition would be evaluated against the more forgiving public-interest standard.[161] Newspapers, which faced potential competition for classified and other advertising revenue that might migrate to electronic databases and other information services established by local telephone companies, vigorously opposed this relief—first in the courts and then before Congress. Nonetheless, and despite considerable resistance from Judge Greene, the decree was modified in 1991 to allow the local telephone companies to provide those services subject to other decree provisions.[162] Removal of this restriction contributed to the regional companies' efforts to provide video programming and advanced services, either directly or through acquisition of interests in ventures with cable television and other companies.

The Telecommunications Act of 1996 built on and modified this regulatory structure in three important respects. First, new statutory requirements rather than consent decree provisions would govern all postenactment activities of the entities that had been subject to the decree.[163] The consent decree continued to apply to claims that preenactment conduct violated the decree, but Judge Greene's oversight of the industry's development was effectively concluded.[164] Even pending claims for additional relief were not to be adjudicated at the trial court level.

Second, those new statutory requirements reflected modified versions of the decree's obligations and in certain respects provided substantial immediate relief to the affected entities. The act removed the relatively minor obligations that had been imposed on AT&T and no longer restricted certain affiliates of Bell operating companies (or successors engaged in wireless services).[165] The decree's nondiscriminatory access and interconnection obligations for local exchange carriers were incorporated by reference into the act, with a new exception for wireless services.[166] For interexchange services and manufacturing, the act preserved all relief that local exchange carriers had secured under the consent decree through the waiver and modification processes.[167]

The act codified the prohibition on a regional company's provision of interexchange services, defined as the consent decree had, with various exceptions. The act generally immediately permitted long-distance services that terminated calls or that originated in states where a regional company had no local exchange operations (as opposed to the ''in-region'' origination that posed particularly severe threats to competition), as well as various interexchange services that were ''incidental'' to certain services that would otherwise be prohibited because they crossed LATA boundaries.[168] For example, this exception in certain cases encompasses video and audio programming to subscribers, signaling, and mobile services.[169] Manufacturing of telecommunications equipment would be permitted for a restricted company once it secured any substantial relief from the core long-distance prohibition.[170] For the regional companies' provision of long-distance, manufacturing, and certain other services, extensive regulations requiring establishment of separate affiliates, marketing safeguards, and information disclosure would apply.[171]

Third, the act altered the standard that governs local exchange carriers' requests for additional relief from the core long-distance restriction (which, in turn, guides manufacturing relief) and charged the FCC with the initial determination regarding whether relief is justified. The consent decree standards derived from the antitrust laws no longer apply directly. For local exchange carriers' applications to provide long-distance services originating in their local service areas, the FCC is to grant such applications if it finds that the local carrier has complied with various requirements designed to increase competitive entry into local services and that ''the requested authorization is consistent with the public interest, convenience, and necessity.''[172] The Department of Justice's role is considerably reduced: the FCC is required to ''consult with the Attorney General'' and to give ''substantial weight to the Attorney General's evaluation.''[173]

This restructuring of the consent decree obligations reflects what the Conference Report characterizes as ''one of the underlying themes of the bill—to get both agencies back to their proper role and to end government by consent decree. The Commission would be carrying out the policies of the Communications Act, and the DOJ should be carrying out the policies of the antitrust laws.''[174] The new provisions governing the former Bell System entities reflect many of the difficulties with this approach: the restrictions now administered by the FCC reflect antitrust remedies; as with other laws, antitrust laws often are enforced through consent decrees; the core policy of the Communications Act involves regulating competition, which is also of course the policy of the antitrust laws; and it is unclear what policies other than regulation of competition the Communications Act legitimately advances. These broader issues are taken up in chapter 4, but in this context it is enough to note that Congress has revised and entrenched yet another, elaborate administrative regulatory regime that applies to the entities and services regulated by the other regimes described above.

CHAPTER THREE

New Forms of Communication

THE TECHNOLOGICAL and market changes since the mid-1980s present an increasing challenge to the basic regulatory structures outlined in the previous chapter. Many of the most important and highly publicized developments in information services and technologies are occurring at the periphery or beyond the scope of those regulatory structures, which principally restrict the owners and operators of traditional networks. For example, the Internet, on-line and networked database and retail services, computer applications distributed through networks, private networks, most other resold telecommunications services and facilities, and many satellite services largely escape all or at least the more intrusive forms of traditional regulation. A principal exception exists when carriers or network operators whose other activities subject them to established regulation undertake these same services.

Even as regulation of traditional networks becomes less relevant to the provision and shaping of principal information services, those old networks are being transformed in a manner that undermines and challenges the rationales of even the established regulatory regimes. Each regulatory regime was structured around a particular type of network with certain limited and peculiar capabilities, and all rested on the basic, tripartite division between carriage, broadcasting, and ''packaged'' or nonelectronically delivered products. Now, the capabilities, uses, and scope of existing networks are changing dramatically. As the following discussion elaborates, mass distribution of voice and particularly video information products has assumed an increasing range of forms no longer amenable to isolated and distinct regulatory regimes. Over-the-air broadcasting once

44

was a unique and overwhelming source of widely distributed video information, and cable television systems until recently principally extended the availability of that service. Now, multiple and increasingly overlapping programming delivery systems form a web of information transmission sources. These competing distribution systems still often support point-to-multipoint services, but those broadcast services are increasingly embedded in networks also capable of more sophisticated delivery—including point-to-point services, extending to traditional voice and data carriage. Not only are traditional telephony networks and wireless point-to-point networks providing video services, but traditional broadcast networks—over-the-air television stations as well as cable television systems—can also increasingly perform individualized communications functions.

The increasing capabilities of networks, as well as the fact that they overlap, also threaten to erode the distinction between carriers and content providers. As long as carriers' networks were confined to voice carriage, they had little incentive to provide services based on content. Now for video and text, only networks exist, and they all deliver content. It is increasingly difficult to separate the broadcaster or information service provider from the carrier.

A third challenge to the traditional forms of information delivery is the merger of packaged and electronically delivered information products. As information delivery networks become more sophisticated, carriage services are increasingly integrated with a broader variety of content services. Information may be delivered in any number of forms: a packaged product, print or otherwise, may be transmitted and made available in electronic form, and many of the features peculiar to packaged products increasingly can be replicated through electronic communications systems.

Provision of Information Services, Video Programming, and Advanced Video Products

The regulatory structure outlined above, and particularly Title III's requirements, rest in large part on the assumption that licensed broadcast stations are a unique and uniquely important source of electronically delivered mass-media products—especially for video information. This is no longer so. Broadcast stations are now one of many sources of video services, and new technologies could soon make them even less important as delivery systems.[1] This is especially so for interactive and other services that will allow individual subscribers to choose the information to be delivered. This transformation of video distribution, as described below, has taken two forms: many outlets other than broadcasting stations distribute video programming and related information to communities, and the number and type of those sources are increasing rapidly; and those outlets' increasing capacity ensures that broadcasting stations will be less important to distribution of mass media and advanced video offerings. Not only are broadcast stations no longer unique, but their bottleneck function is decreasing and likely has disappeared: programmers have a variety of outlets or means of access to citizens, and citizens may receive video information products from a variety of sources.

Cable Television Systems

Cable television systems are the principal means of delivering video programming in urban and suburban areas. Cable television systems "pass," or are capable of serving, more than 95 percent of the nation's 94.2 million households with television, and 61.7 million households (64.4 percent of television households) subscribed to a cable service in September 1995.[2] Cable systems' offerings generally include channels devoted to cable programming networks, the signals of local commercial and public broadcast television stations, the distant signals of nonnetwork "superstations," and channels devoted to public, educational, and government offerings. Households with cable service generally discontinue direct, over-the-air reception of broadcast television signals and rely instead on cable system delivery of that broadcast programming.[3]

Cable systems have also increased the sources and variety of video programming. There were 34 cable networks in 1982 and 100 by 1993.[4] Cable network spending on video programming in 1993 was estimated at approximately $3 billion ($1.8 billion for original programming), and basic and pay cable networks attracted 24 percent of the prime-time television audience in 1992.[5] The capacity of cable television systems is increasing rapidly. Older systems with twelve to thirty channels have increasingly been supplanted by systems capable of providing two to three times that many channels. Average active channels increased by nearly 40 percent from 1984 to 1989.[6] By the end of 1993, 77 percent of cable systems, serving 97 percent of cable subscribers, provided thirty or more channels, and the percentage of systems with 12 or fewer channels declined from 22 to approximately 7 from 1987 to 1993.[7] As the FCC has noted, "more than half of all households now receive 10 over-the-air stations and, when cable services are included, a total of 30 channels of television programming."[8] As digital compression technologies improve and systems are upgraded with fiber-optic cables (at least from the cable head-end into neighborhoods), system capacity may increase severalfold from current levels. For example, the advanced Time Warner cable system in Queens, New York City, is capable of providing 150 channels of programming.[9] Integration of switching capacity into cable systems would increase capacity considerably more, allowing some households to select from a vast array of video material as well as the next generation of interactive services. Fully switched service would essentially transform cable systems into telecommunications providers and remove "channel" capacity as the relevant constraint on available programming and other service offerings. For example, Time Warner and US WEST have announced plans to upgrade cable systems into full-service networks that would eventually provide the equivalent of switched capacity,[10] and cable system operators have announced plans for large-scale purchases that will begin to integrate switching capacity into their systems to support voice communications.[11]

Local Telephone Companies

Companies that provide traditional local telephone service (local exchange carriers, or LECs) are likely on the verge of providing widespread video programming and other video and text services. These services will be provided in much the same way that cable television services are provided: a central location will distribute video programming to individual households in distinct geographic areas. The principal differences are that the telephone companies' video programming offerings will often be provided in conjunction with traditional telephony and advanced information services, the channel capacity provided even initially will often rival or surpass the largest cable systems, and subscribers will potentially have tremendous control over which services and programming they receive.[12]

Telephone companies will provide video programming and related services by using four principal technologies. Certain Baby Bells (including Bell Atlantic, NYNEX, and Pacific Telesis) are investing in wireless video service provision, and others (especially Ameritech) are constructing traditional cable television systems.[13] With asymmetrical digital subscriber line (ADSL) service, telephone companies can use their existing, low-capacity copper plant that currently delivers voice transmissions. Bell Atlantic's trial in northern Virginia employs this technology.[14] More commonly (because ADSL limits picture quality and service offerings), telephone companies are upgrading their delivery plants through a combination of fiber-optic wire (from centralized locations to the curb, or neighborhood node) and coaxial cable (from the neighborhood node to the home).[15]

Before the Telecommunications Act of 1996, local exchange carriers' provision of video programming and advanced services to subscribers over common carrier facilities had to conform to the FCC's "video dialtone" rules, which governed the fourth type of delivery system.[16] Bell Atlantic, GTE, NYNEX, and Pacific Telesis indicated that they would separately construct these video dialtone systems in eleven markets in their respective local telephone service areas, and these systems could provide service to 2.5 million households.[17] Although the act replaced the video dialtone rules with other provisions designed to facilitate local exchange carriers' development of video services, it also ensured that the new provisions would not end previously approved video dialtone systems.[18]

Two applications to provide video dialtone service, approved by the FCC, illustrate the video services and facilities that LECs are developing. Ameritech initially proposed a video dialtone network that would extend to 1.3 million homes and businesses in five areas (Detroit, Cleveland/Columbus, Indianapolis, Chicago, and Milwaukee).[19] In each location, a fiber-optic network would extend to a "node," which initially could serve 500 households through further transmission through coaxial cable. As demand for switched digital service increased, that demand would be met by extending fiber deeper into the neighborhood, to serve 125 homes per node.[20] That network would provide 240 digital and 70 analog channels designed for general distribution of signals, and 80 "switched" digital channels that establish individual connections between information service providers and individual households (with one-way video programming distributed to households and two-way carriage of control signaling allowing selection among programming and services).[21] Each class of channels would be allocated among broadcasters, programming sources, and information service providers. Those information services could include interactive services, which allow customers to select the particular material (programming or other information) that would be made available to them and to shift continuously to receive other information, as well as other retail, programming, and text-based services. At least initially, telephone service would not be provided over the network. Despite securing authorization, Ameritech declined to proceed with construction of these networks.

Separately, NYNEX secured authorization for similar systems to be deployed in Rhode Island (for 63,000 homes and businesses) and Massachusetts (for 334,000 homes and businesses) and plans to roll out this network to half of its customers (which include most households in New York and New England) by 2010.[22] This system will also combine fiber-optic cable with coaxial cable and will provide broadcast and interactive services over 21 analog channels and 400 to 800 digital channels. Like the Ameritech system, the NYNEX networks are designed to provide advanced information services and programming from unaffiliated service providers, as well as enhanced information services from the operating carrier.[23]

As even these two video dialtone proposals indicate, the local carriers' plans are subject to revision as the carriers' general telephone infrastructure and video service strategies change. Table 3-1 sets forth the history and regulatory disposition of the local carriers' proposals and describes where permanent facilities are to be constructed. Certain of the carriers have not proceeded beyond technical or market trials, and others such as Ameritech have abandoned or suspended their initial proposed services. These plans will be revised in light of the Telecommunications Act of 1996, which both clarified when telephone companies can operate traditional cable television systems and replaced the video dialtone regulations with, principally, rules to be developed for "open video systems."[24] Those systems that are proceeding, however, will continue to present the potential for video networks that overlap with cable television systems and that could provide the infrastructure for the next generation of advanced telecommunications and information services.

The breadth of the LECs' potential offerings of video services is also reflected in their plans to deploy broadband facilities capable of eventually delivering video programming as well as switched voice and video services. Most of the regional Bell companies and other large providers of local telephone service have announced extensive plans to replace existing copper wire plant with broadband facilities. For example, Pacific Bell plans to spend $16 billion to upgrade facilities in this manner for 1.5 million homes by the end of 1996, and 5.5 million homes by 2000, with the remainder to be completed by 2015.[25] US WEST announced a similar broadband plan with slower deployment (.5 million subscribers annually from 1995 to 2000), estimated at $10 billion to $15 billion.[26] Bell Atlantic picked contractors and suppliers for the initial phase of its five-year, $11 billion broadband project.[27] GTE announced plans to provide broadband services to 7 million homes in 66 markets by 2004.[28] And Southern New

Table 3-1. *Local Exchange Carrier Proposals, 1992–95*

Date first filed	Telephone company	Location	Homes passed	Type of proposal	Status
10/21/92	Bell Atlantic VA	Northern Virginia	2,000	technical/ market[a]	approved 3/25/93; expanded 1/20/95
10/30/92	NYNEX	New York, N.Y.	2,500	technical	approved 6/29/93
11/16/92	New Jersey Bell	Florham Park, N.J.	11,700	permanent	pending
12/15/92	New Jersey Bell	Dover Township, N.J.	38,000	permanent	aproved 7/18/94
4/27/93	SNET	West Hartford, Conn.	1,600	technical/ market	approved 11/12/93
6/18/93	Rochester Telephone	Rochester, N.Y.	120	technical/ market	aproved 3/25/94
6/22/93	US WEST	Omaha, Neb.	2,500 or 60,000[b]	technical/ market	approved 12/22/93
12/15/93	SNET (amended)	Hartford and Stamford, Conn.	150,000	technical/ market expansion	approved 11/22/94
12/16/93	Bell Atlantic	Washington, D.C. LATA	300,000	permanent	see 6/16/94 filing
12/20/93	Pacific Bell	Orange County, Calif.	210,000	permanent	approved 7/19/95
12/20/93	Pacific Bell	So. San Francisco Bay, Calif.	490,000	permanent	
12/20/93	Pacific Bell	Los Angeles, Calif.	360,000	permanent	approved 7/19/95
12/20/93	Pacific Bell	San Diego, Calif.	250,000	permanent	approved 7/19/95
1/10/94	US WEST	Denver, Colo.	357,000	permanent	suspended by applicant 5/31/95
1/19/94	US WEST	Portland, Ore.	162,000	permanent	suspended by applicant 5/31/95
1/19/94	US WEST	Minneapolis- St. Paul, Minn.	357,000	permanent	suspended by applicant 5/31/95

Table 3-1. *(continued)*

Date first filed	Telephone company	Location	Homes passed	Type of proposal	Status
1/31/94	Ameritech	Detroit, Mich.	232,000	permanent	approved 1/4/95; abandoned by applicant 6/27/95
1/31/94	Ameritech	Columbus and Cleveland, Ohio	262,000	permanent	approved 1/4/95; abandoned by applicant 6/27/95
1/31/94	Ameritech	Indianapolis, Ind.	115,000	permanent	approved 1/4/95; abandoned by applicant 6/27/95
1/31/94	Ameritech	Chicago, Ill.	501,000	permanent	approved 1/4/95; abandoned by applicant 6/27/95
1/31/94	Ameritech	Milwaukee, Wis.	146,000	permanent	approved 1/4/95; abandoned by applicant 6/27/95
3/16/94	US WEST	Boise, Idaho	90,000	permanent	suspended by applicant 5/31/95
3/16/94	US WEST	Salt Lake City, Utah	160,000	permanent	suspended by applicant 5/31/95
4/13/94	Puerto Rico Tel. Co.	Puerto Rico	250	technical	approved 12/5/94
5/23/94	GTE-Contel of Virginia	Manassas, Va.	109,000	permanent	approved 5/2/95
5/23/94	GTE FL Inc.	Pinella and Paso Counties, Fla.	476,000	permanent	approved 5/2/95

Table 3-1. *(continued)*

Date first filed	Telephone company	Location	Homes passed	Type of proposal	Status
5/23/94	GTE CA Inc	Ventura County, Calif.	122,000	permanent	approved 5/2/95
5/23/94	GTE HI Tel. Co.	Honolulu, Hawaii	334,000	permanent	approved 5/2/95
6/16/94	Bell Atlantic (amended)	Washington, D.C. LATA	1,200,000	permanent	suspended by applicant 4/25/95; withdrawn 5/24/95
6/16/94	Bell Atlantic	Mid-Atlantic	2,000,000	permanent	suspended by applicant 4/25/95; withdrawn 5/24/95
6/27/94	BellSouth	Chamblee and DeKalb Counties, Ga.	12,000	technical/ market	approved 2/8/95
7/8/94	NYNEX	Rhode Island	63,000	permanent	approved 3/6/95
7/8/94	NYNEX	Massachusetts	334,000	permanent	approved 3/6/95
9/9/94	Sprint/Carolina Tel. & Tel. Co.	Wake Forest, N.C.	1,000	technical/ market	approved 12/28/84
11/16/94	US WEST	Cedar Rapids, Iowa	63,000	permanent	dismissed
11/16/94	US WEST	Colorado Springs, Colo.	161,000	permanent	dismissed
11/16/94	US WEST	Des Moines, Iowa	120,000	permanent	dismissed
11/16/94	US WEST	Albuquerque, N.M.	214,000	permanent	dismissed
4/28/95	SNET	Connecticut	1,500,000	permanent	pending

Source: Reprinted from Annual Assessment of the Status of Competition in the Market for the Delivery of Video Programming, Second Annual Report, App. D, CS Docket no. 95-61 (released December 11, 1995).

a. A technical trial tests the technical feasibility of a VDT network, usually without charging customers for access to the network. A market trial charges either programmer-customers, end-user subscribers, or both for access and is designed to test customer willingness to pay for that access. Both types of trials may be combined into one.

b. The technical phase of the trial was authorized to pass 2,500 homes; the market phase of the trial expanded the technical trial and is authorized to pass 60,000 homes (thus far US WEST reports serving 5,000 homes).

England Telephone adopted a $4.5 billion broadband development plan, to provide a combination of fiber and coaxial cable to much of its service area by 2010.[29]

These plans, in addition to ongoing trials and the applications presented to the FCC, appear to support industry claims that telephone companies will broadly enter the markets for carriage and, soon, direct provision of video programming, but the scope and pace of the development of these networks remains uncertain. Talk is cheap, and these companies have experienced considerable difficulties and delays in developing trials for both the broadband networks and advanced information services. Demand for these services is uncertain, although the developing competition for traditional telephone services—for which these networks are also, and particularly, designed—is far less speculative. Even so, the Telecommunications Act of 1996 is likely to accelerate telephone companies' provision of video services, at least once the FCC develops implementing rules. The act in limited circumstances increases telephone companies' ability to develop or operate cable television systems. Depending on the FCC's eventual rules, the act's "open video system" provisions may considerably reduce regulatory impediments to and increase the commercial attractiveness of developing innovative video systems.[30]

Satellite Programming Delivery

Direct-to-home (DTH) satellite service has, since its initial commercial availability in 1980, served as an important source of video programming to rural and less dense areas. With the recent initiation of higher powered services (which allow reception on smaller, 18-inch dishes rather than the traditional dishes of four feet or more), satellite delivery of programming will increasingly serve suburban and urban customers as well.

There are three principal types of DTH satellite services, distinguished by their allocated spectrum and associated power. Traditional, or C-band, satellite service was developed in 1976 and first made commercially available to homes in 1980.[31] As of 1994, this service offered 103 scrambled channels of video programming, 150 unscrambled video channels, and 75 audio services.[32] Estimates of households receiving the service often exceed 3.5 million (of which approximately 1.6 million are authorized subscribers to scrambled services).[33]

Several major cable television companies have interests in Primestar, which offers a medium-powered Ku-band service. Although some have alleged that the service is an effort to protect cable systems (and consent decrees have been entered to resolve antitrust claims to that effect),[34] Primestar may be poised for considerable growth. In mid-1994, slightly more than 70,000 subscribers received Primestar's initial service of 37 channels of programming (31 video and 6 audio), but subscribership has been projected to be 2 million to 5 million by 2000.[35] By spring 1995 service included 73 channels offered to 300,000 subscribers in the coverage area of 60 percent of the continental United States.[36] Its chairman predicted national service by the end of 1995, and the service had secured roughly 775,000 subscribers by September 1995.[37]

A third type of service, high-powered Ku-band, was initiated in June 1994 and has been particularly successful. Subscribers to this digital satellite system (DSS) choose between the offerings of two programming packagers, DirecTV and USSB (United States Satellite Broadcasting Company), which between them offer as many as 175 channels of programming (and expansion of the channels offered is likely). That programming includes substantial offerings of pay-per-view movies and sports, channels on cable television systems, and channels developed for this particular service. Local broadcasting channels are not included. By March 1995 consumers could purchase reception equipment at 11,000 retail outlets, and DirecTV had 400,000 subscribers to its programming service of as many as 150 channels—with 1.5 million subscribers predicted by the end of 1995.[38] Subscribers increased to 900,000 by September 1995.[39] USSB officials state that 100,000 new subscribers receive the DSS service each month, and predict between 12 million and 15 million subscribers by 2000.[40] The FCC notes that analysts' estimates of DSS subscribers by 2000 are generally closer to 10 million.[41] Nearly all DSS subscribers select programming from both DirecTV and USSB, and approximately half of the subscribers are drawn from areas also served by cable television systems.[42]

Satellite Master Antenna Television Systems (SMATVs)

SMATVs employ an antenna to receive satellite-delivered video programming and then distribute the signals to subscribers through wires. This type of system generally serves a relatively small area, such as apartment complexes.[43] The number of subscribers served through this technology has varied from approximately 1 million in 1983 to 500,000 in 1987, to 953,000 in 1993 (with service in mid-1994 provided by 5,000 systems).[44] Recent estimates have reassessed subscribership at the lower level of approximately 950,000 in 1995 but predict continued and substantial growth.[45] This distribution system has attributes of a cable television system and of satellite broadcasting. The system operates much like a cable system to the extent that both receive satellite-delivered video programming and retransmit that programming by wire to individual households. For SMATVs, however, there is generally no equivalent of the cable system head-end to control reception and origination of programming (or to allow ready upgrading of the system for advanced services), and the wireline delivery system is much less elaborate. SMATVs also resemble DTH systems in that the antenna operates essentially as a common receiving device, with the signal shared by a relatively small number of households.

Other Wireless Technologies

In addition to satellite broadcasting and traditional television broadcasting, two types of wireless cable systems are also capable of providing video programming and other video services to the home. One is formally known as multipoint multichannel distribution service (MMDS). Using allotments of spectrum, MMDS systems can provide 33 channels of programming, a capacity that may increase with the introduction of compression technology.[46] Again, this delivery system operates in much the same way that a cable television system does: it receives satellite-delivered video programming at a central location and retransmits it to subscribers. Unlike a cable television system, that retransmission employs electromagnetic spectrum. The FCC credits estimates of subscribership of 600,000 at the end of 1994, an annual increase of 51 percent, and the industry association estimates that 800,000 subscribers received service from 190 systems in mid-1995.[47] One analyst predicts more than 1.8 million subscribers by 1996 and more than 3.2 million subscribers by 2000.[48] Recent regulatory changes, especially requirements imposed on distribution of video programming in which cable systems have an interest, are likely to increase the growth of this type of distribution system.[49]

Another technology, employing exceptionally high frequency, point-to-point delivery, has the potential of providing two-way voice and data services in combination with multiple channels of video programming and related services. This service, local multipoint distribution service (LMDS), has been authorized in New York City (providing 49 channels of programming), and 900 applications for service in other locales have been filed.[50]

Those additional services have been delayed as the FCC resolves a dispute between LMDS applicants and satellite service providers regarding competing claims for use of the designated spectrum.[51]

Electric Utilities

An intriguing competitive possibility—but so far only a distant possibility—is that the network operated by electric utilities could provide an increasing array of traditional information services. That network, including considerable fiber-optic facilities, already provides a "third wire" into nearly every home. Computing facilities are already being integrated into this network (at the initiation and reception ends) to monitor, regulate, and record electricity transmissions. Initial trials are under way for communications services that will use the utility network, but these services concentrate principally on communications relating to monitoring energy usage and demand.[52] Utility advocates portray this network as capable of providing a broader range of services, perhaps including telephony and even video services.[53] The Telecommunications Act of 1996 amended statutory provisions governing public utilities in order to ease electric utilities' entry into telecommunications markets.[54]

Traditional Broadcasting

Even if broadcasters often rely on retransmission of their signals by cable system operators, traditional broadcasting remains a robust industry. Broadcast licensees and especially the television networks will almost certainly remain important—and perhaps the most important—suppliers and packagers of video programming. For present purposes, the relevant point is not whether broadcasting will survive but whether it will retain the overwhelming importance and dominance in electronically distributed video programming that led to the current regulatory structure.

In the longer term, the greatest potential disadvantage of and threat to broadcasting as a means of delivering video services is that it may be capable of providing service in only one of the two most significant video markets. Broadcasting obviously competes in the distribution of traditional video programming. However, several of the delivery systems considered above are considerably superior to broadcasting stations for provision of emerging video services (which include but extend beyond video programming).[55] Compared with broadcasting stations (which likely will never be able to provide some of these services), the facilities of cable television systems and local telephone carriers can be more readily upgraded to provide them.

Despite this general handicap, television broadcast technology is hardly stagnant. Two developments could boost the uses and capacity of traditional television broadcast services. The first is digital compression technology. This technology would allow multiple (perhaps four to six) channels of video programming to be broadcast over the spectrum currently allocated to the single channel of broadcast programming.[56] The additional channels would not necessarily have to be vested in the original licensee, but technological limits might require some degree of coordination in broadcasting. The second development allows limited interactive services to be provided in conjunction with traditional broadcast programming and facilities. Lengthy regulatory proceedings have addressed this service (interactive video and data service, or IVDS), and the FCC recently conducted auctions to allocate the spectrum necessary for it.[57]

Even with the potential expansion of the offerings associated with traditional broadcast television, the relative importance of that service has diminished and will likely do so considerably. As more stations serve particular communities, the importance of individual broadcasting stations as a programming source or delivery system has diminished. The number of traditional broadcast television stations has continued to increase rapidly: from 1976 to 1991 the number increased from 962 to nearly 1,500, increasing the number of communities with access to more than three television signals.[58] As noted, cable system delivery of broadcast signals has brought an average of ten broadcast station signals to more than half the country's households.[59] In addition, broadcasters depend on cable television systems for delivery of their signals: indeed, broadcasters' claims to this effect generated the 1992 Cable Act's requirement that cable systems carry and not reposition the signals of local commercial and public television stations.[60]

Programming available through cable television systems and other means of video distribution has also affected the importance of television broadcasters, as individual sources of information and collectively as an industry. Even without yet accounting for shifting viewing patterns resulting from introduction of MMDS, satellite, and telephone video services, broadcasters have lost market share to other sources of video programming. Time devoted to viewing television remained relatively constant from the 1970s through the 1980s,[61] and there is substantial evidence that other sources of delivered video programming are close substitutes for (and thus reduce viewing of) broadcast television programming, for purposes of both ultimate consumers and upstream suppliers, including advertisers.[62] In households with cable television, the principal networks' prime-time programming attracted 46 percent of viewers; 20 percent viewed programming retransmitted from independent stations (17 percent) and public stations (3 percent); the remaining households viewed programming originating from other, nonbroadcast sources.[63] National cable programming networks increased in number by 110 percent, to 99, from 1984 to 1994.[64] As the FCC concluded in 1990, even before the advent of significant competition from sources other than cable television systems:

> As viewer choices have increased, broadcast network audience shares and real advertising revenues have fallen significantly in the last decade. . . . For example, given greater sources of video entertainment for American consumers, the proportionate viewing of broadcast network programming has declined sharply, as the three-network prime-time share of households fell from 90 to 60 between 1975 and 1991. Meanwhile, network advertising revenues in real dollars reached a peak in 1984 and have continued to decline since. Network advertising has also fallen steadily relative to GNP since 1979, with the exception of 1982–84. Over the same period, cable advertising and total subscriber revenues have grown substantially in real dollars, far outpacing the growth of GNP.[65]

The FCC has since found that "the decline in network share is attributable, in large part, to the emergence of other viewing options . . . [which] represents not only a source of diversity for viewers, but also additional market opportunity for program producers."[66] Since 1990 broadcasting advertising revenues have rebounded, but the relative growth of advertising devoted to electronic media other than broadcasting reflects the underlying development. Advertisers' expenditures related to television networks increased by approximately 9 percent from 1990 to 1993, but national and local advertising expenditures related to cable television systems increased by approximately 68 percent during the same period (from a much lower base).[67] Increased competition among video programming distributors and programmers' easier access to audiences have prompted the FCC to reexamine or to relax a series of regulations governing broadcast station ownership and operation.[68]

Even if the relevant inquiry were limited to traditional broadcast facilities, that network, too, has changed significantly in a manner that undermines the importance of the three most established television networks. Wholly apart from cable and satellite delivery, four or more broadcast stations serve 144 of the industry's principal viewing markets ("Designated Marketing Areas") that encompass more than 93 percent of television households.[69] Commercial independent stations increased to 1,532 by January 1995 (from 862 in 1970).[70] The Fox Broadcasting Company has knit together 190 of these stations as affiliates and secondary affiliates to form a fourth television broadcast network, which now reaches more than 97 percent of U.S. television households.[71] In 1995, two additional networks began service: by mid-1995, United Paramount Network had 105 primary and secondary affiliates capable of reaching 86.5 percent of television households, and another network, WB, in early 1995 could reach 78 percent of households through forty-seven affiliates and distant retransmissions through cable systems.[72]

Integration of Carriage Service and Distribution of Information Products

For several decades following passage of the Communications Act in 1934, technology and market forces roughly corresponded with the distinction underlying the regulation of the principal information industries: electronic facilities for mass distribution of information (broadcasting stations) were distinct from facilities used to carry person-to-person communications (common-carrier telecommunications facilities).[73] Now, just as the uniqueness of licensed wireless facilities for the mass electronic distribution of video products has disappeared, so has this distinction between these two types of facilities. There is, instead, an increasing and accelerating integration of carriage and mass-media operations and facilities. That integration takes three forms. One is functional: facilities designed for one purpose (mass distribution or carriage) are increasingly capable of performing the other. Another is financial: for both types of integration, entities that control increasingly flexible distribution facilities also seek to provide information products suited to distribution by their own facilities. A final type of integration reflects the scope of the content that can be communicated electronically: increasingly, electronically distributed information encompasses information that is also available nonelectronically, including printed material.

Functional Integration

The functional integration of carriage facilities and mass-media distribution facilities has proceeded from both ends of the spectrum. Some distributors have or are poised to become more traditional carriers. Cable television systems are the most prominent example. Traditional cable television systems function primarily as broadcast stations, reflecting their origination as retransmission facilities for distant broadcast signals (much as an affiliated broadcast station could be viewed as essentially a retransmission facility for network programming).[74] In advanced systems, too, the system operator produces or otherwise secures programming and distributes it from a central point to subscribers. Even here, there is an important if limited element of carriage: the system operator generally chooses among programmers (some affiliated, many not) that desire access to the cable system's subscribers, and operators are required to make certain channels available to a variety of unaffiliated programmers.[75]

Developments since the late 1980s have greatly increased the carriage, and potentially the common-carriage, aspect of cable television systems. Requirements that cable operators provide programmers with access to their systems have been augmented, benefiting particular classes of information producers and requiring cable system operators to provide access to unaffiliated programmers.[76] The increasing capacity of cable television systems will separately increase access to cable systems' distribution facilities. As capacity increases, cable systems may increasingly serve as a readily available carriage conduit between programmers and subscribers, and their separate role as selector and provider of programming to subscribers could correspondingly diminish.

More significantly, the introduction of computing and switching capacity into cable television systems could allow them to function much as traditional telecommunications carriers do. Even without integration of particular cable systems into the general telecommunications network, servers—large computers giving subscribers personal access to databases of programming and other services—might allow cable systems to provide a range of interactive and gateway services (allowing access by subscribers to various products, including database information products) as well as programming. If cable systems are integrated into the telecommunications network through connections to switches, then they could in addition provide a range of traditional telecommunications services (including special access, switched access, and local exchange services).[77]

Similar functional integration is occurring for common-carriage facilities. Traditionally, common-carrier telecommunications facilities principally transmitted other parties' person-to-person communications. Satellite transmissions embodied one of the most important initial departures from this model. Before the 1980s domestic satellite transmission had served principally as an alternative transmission path for long-distance, common-carriage telecommunications. In the 1980s satellites were increasingly used for mass distribution of video programming: the initial control of the satellite transponder was offered on a common-carrier basis, but once control passed to transmitters of video programming, the satellite's use was transformed into an orbiting broadcasting station (with that capacity ultimately used neither for common carriage nor for point-to-point transmission).[78]

Ongoing and potential changes in the uses of the wireline telecommunications network also reflect this functional integration. In the 1980s certain services increasingly relied on the telecommunications network for mass distribution of information. For example, systematic telephone solicitation transformed the use of the network, and toll-free inbound, or "800-number," services served much the same function of widely distributing information.[79] Services offering "gateway" access to databases and other voice and text information services also increasingly allowed the telecommunications network to be employed for mass communications.[80] Microsoft Corporation's on-line network, MSN, is perhaps the most ambitious of these services, and the Internet and the strategic alliance announced between Microsoft and NBC to distribute information products suggest how extensively the new networked telecommunications services might displace traditional media.[81]

Competitive developments in local telephony will hasten this functional integration. Already, alternative delivery systems are beginning to compete with traditional local telephone service providers in particular submarkets (especially for large business customers in the states where competitive entry is under way), and the initial stages of the breakup of the local telephone monopoly for core services may be imminent.[82] The extent of interconnection, resale cost structures, and unbundling of service elements will, of course, determine the pace and scope of local telephony competition. At a minimum, these competitive developments will likely increase the importance of two delivery systems: wireless systems and cable television systems. Wireless systems, now principally cellular service but soon to be augmented by PCS (personal communications services) capabilities, will deliver a broad range of voice, data, and message services. They will separately form a partially overlapping local network and provide one means for cable television systems to become integrated into the telecommunications network, as companies explore using cable systems as the landline "backbone" or infrastructure necessary to link wireless delivery facilities. Developments that would increase competition in local access services (the initiation and completion of long-distance services), much less traditional local exchange services, might also give cable systems the ability and opportunity to provide a greater range of services.

The ability of telephone companies to transmit video images will also accelerate this functional alignment. For example, video conferencing services allow subscribers to construct large, customized networks for widespread distribution of information. Video dialtone services will allow telephone companies to provide programming, with some facilities offered to unaffiliated parties through contract (as cable facilities are) and on a generally available, tariffed basis (as common-carriage voice communications capabilities are).[83] Telephone company facilities will also allow subscribers widespread and simultaneous access to computer databases containing information products, including video programming.[84] This point-to-point access to centralized information could allow the telephone company's facilities to function much like a cable system (both widely distributing information), with the additional offerings of interactive services (through a subscriber's directions to the database, which in turn would respond with a tailored product) and services that allow subscribers to decide when to receive programming of their choice. In addition, the facilities would continue to provide the full range of telecommunications services (augmented by video telephony), presumably on a common-carrier basis. The result could be much like the "full-service network" built through upgrades to a cable system—except that these facilities will be created by adding broadband and additional computing capacity to the switched telecommunications network.

Financial Integration

Functional integration has coincided with increased common ownership of both delivery systems and the information products those systems deliver. This integration has occurred across a variety of formerly distinct industries, and occurs through both direct common ownership and a variety of contractual arrangements and joint ventures. For example, distributors have increasingly acquired interests in video programming, including that produced by Hollywood studios. The FCC has dramatically reduced the limitations on the networks' production of programming and on the financial interests in programming that can be acquired by broadcast networks (which also control important broadcast television stations in several large metropolitan markets).[85] The remaining limitations soon will be eliminated entirely.[86] Similarly, the principal owners of several cable television systems have extensive interests in cable programming networks. In June 1994 cable system operators owned or had equity interest in 56 percent of the 101 national cable networks.[87] They have interests in the preponderance of the most popular cable networks (see table 3-2).[88] The Telecommunications Act of 1996 increased the ability of a single corporation to hold multiple broadcast licenses and removed important restrictions on the integration of cable television systems with broadcast services and networks.[89]

The deregulatory trend for telephone companies' expansion into information services is similar. FCC regulations governing provision of "enhanced services" restrict the form of telephone companies' offerings of computer-based services associated with telecommunications services—including many information products that offer voice, text, and even video services. The services themselves were almost entirely deregulated in the early 1980s, but restrictions remained on how and whether the larger telecommunications carriers could provide them.[90] Initially, those carriers could offer the services only through a separate subsidiary, with extensive safeguards designed to prevent cross-subsidies and discriminatory access that put competing enhanced service providers at a disadvantage.[91] Since the late 1980s, those restrictions have been considerably relaxed, but more recent judicial decisions have reversed important elements of FCC policies that allow joint provision of regulated and unregulated services free from extensive structural safeguards.[92] In addition, the consent decree that restricted the services of the principal local exchange carriers was modified to permit them to provide "information services."[93] Information services overlap considerably with enhanced services and extend to most of the text, video, and programming products that are vested with First Amendment protection.

Local telephone companies' provision of broadband services will only accelerate this trend. The telephone companies' applications to provide video services include provisions that will reserve considerable capacity either for preferred video programmers or for preferred enhanced service providers, and operators will have considerable discretion to use and control the use of capacity on their "open video systems."[94] Those enhanced services include the "gateway" services that will provide subscribers with access to the next generation of information services, including advanced database services and interactive shopping and entertainment services.[95]

Table 3-2. *The Vertical Connection between Major Programming Services and Cable System Operators*

Programming network[a]	Subscribers[b]	MSO with ownership in network[c]	Launch date
ESPN	61.8	None	9/79
CNN	61.6	Time Warner, 19.5; TCI, 23.3; and Times Mirror, Cablevision, Comcast, Continental, Jones, Lenfest, Sammons, TKR, Telecable, and Scripps Howard less than 5 each, totaling 32.8	6/80
USA Network	61.2	Viacom, 50	4/80
Nikelodeon/Nick at Nite	60.9	Viacom, 100	4/79
Discovery	60.5	TCI, 49; Cox, 24; Newhouse, 24	6/85
TBS	60.5	Time Warner, 19.5; TCI, 23.3; Times Mirror, Cablevision, Comcast, Continental, Jones, Lenfest, Sammons, TKR, Telecable, and Scripps Howard less than 5 each, totaling 32.8	12/76
TNT	60	Time Warner, 19.5; TCI, 23.3; Times Mirror, Cablevision, Comcast, Continental, Jones, Lenfest, Sammons, TKR, Telecable, and Scripps Howard less than 5 each, totaling 32.8	10/88
C-Span 1	59.8		3/79
MTV	59.5	Viacom, 100	8/81
Lifetime	58.6	None	2/84
TNN (The Nashville Network)	58.1	Gaylord Broadcasting Co., 100	3/83
Family	57.9	Liberty Media/TCI, 18.1	4/77
Arts & Entertainment Network	57.1	None	2/84
The Weather Channel	55.4	None	5/82
Headline News	53.2	Time Warner, 19.5; TCI, 23.3; Times Mirror, Cablevision, Comcast, Continental, Jones, Lenfest, Sammons, TKR, Telecable, and Scripps Howard less than 5 each, totaling 32.8	1/82
CNBC	50.6	None	4/89
VH-1	49.6	Viacom, 100	1/85
QVC	46.3	Liberty Media/TCI, 28.2; Comcast, 16.4; Time Warner, 10.7; Cablevision, Colony, Continental, Newhouse, Sammons, and Times Mirror, less than 5 each, totaling 42[e]	11/86
AMC (American Movie Classics)	44.5	Cablevision, 75	10/84

Table 3-2. *(continued)*

Programming network[a]	Subscribers[b]	MSO with ownership in network[c]	Launch date
BET	39.6	TCI, 21.4; Time Warner, 17.7	1/80
WGN	35.1	None	11/78
Prevue Channel	32.3	None	1/88
EWTN	32	None	8/81
Comedy Central	30.3	Time Warner, 50; Viacom, 50	4/91
C-Span 2	29.7		6/86

Source: Reprinted from *Implementation of Section 19 of the Cable Television Consumer Protection and Competition Act of 1992, Annual Assessment of the Status of Competition in the Market for Delivery of Video Programming, First Report*, table 7, 9 FCC Rcd. 7442, 9599 (1994).
   a. Top 25.
   b. Millions.
   c. Percent ownership.

Increasingly, and especially for emerging information products, telephone and cable companies will deliver traditional telecommunications, their own or affiliated information products for mass and personal use, and their competitors' products as well.

The most obvious sign of this financial integration, as well as of the broader competitive developments, is the corporate restructuring taking place throughout the new information industry. In the mid- to late 1980s, emerging forms of competition prompted manufacturers of consumer electronics to take interests in programming producers. Matsushita Electronics purchased MCA in 1990 (for $6.1 billion); Sony purchased Columbia and CBS Records in 1989 and 1987, respectively (for $3.4 billion and $2.0 billion); and GE purchased RCA (including NBC) in 1985 (for $6.3 billion).[96] This strategy did not consolidate delivery and transmission systems, integrate them with related information or programming services, or establish a "branded" retail relationship with ultimate consumers in the provision of increasingly consolidated information services—all of which have been the focus of more recent restructuring. For example, some industries have become significantly realigned as companies seek to provide wireless retail services, often in conjunction with traditional wire-based long-distance service and, potentially, cable service.[97] Some companies have sought to increase programming interests or combine them with delivery facilities, in anticipation of increased delivery capacity. All of the regional Bell companies have now secured significant interests in or entered into ventures with Hollywood studios. The combination of Time Inc. and Warner Communications in 1990 ($14.1 billion) and of Viacom in 1994 with both Blockbuster Entertainment ($7.6 billion) and Paramount ($9.7 billion) in part reflect this trend.[98] There are ongoing efforts to combine the switching expertise, transmission capacities, and retail relationships of local telephone companies with the programming interests, transport facilities, and retail relationships of cable television systems.[99] Various firms in the new information industry are seeking alignment with and financial support from foreign communications companies.[100] Still other ventures are designed to gain advantages—through standard-setting or integration with delivery facilities—by developing the software and equipment that will allow consumers to gain access to an increasing range of information services.

The total value of merger and acquisition activity in these subsegments of the information industry also reflect the restructuring prompted by technological and market changes. After several years of declining cable system transactions, the number and value of transactions increased sharply in early 1995, to $13.5 billion (in sixty-three transactions affecting 7.3 million subscribers).[101] In 1994, in the telecommunications sector, 110 merger and acquisition deals, reflecting $40.07 billion in value, led all other sectors in merger activity (followed by the drug industry).[102] In the same year, 108 transactions affecting entities holding radio and TV stations were valued at $11.8 billion.[103] Perhaps more important than the activity within particular sectors, many of the most significant deals in the information industry during 1994–96 involved combinations of entities engaged in different core activities or reflected efforts to enter new markets. Illustrative significant transactions are listed in table 3-3.

Scope of Product Integration

Developments in the information industries have also undermined a final distinction that is essential to current regulation and interpretation of the First Amendment: that between electronically delivered information products and packaged products delivered by other means. As noted, this distinction roughly divided broadcast video programming from printed materials distributed through retail outlets and personal delivery systems (public or private). Motion pictures and music products for home use were exceptions, but as a general matter separate industries—broadcast and print—fell under separate legal regimes, for purposes of regulation and First Amendment protections.

Increasingly, print and other packaged products cannot usefully be distinguished from electronically delivered products, and the integration of

Table 3-3. *Illustrative Telecommunications Acquisitions and Mergers, 1994–96*

$ billions

Entities	Year	Services	Approximate value
SBC Comm./Pacific Telesis	1996	Telecommunications	16.7
NYNEX/Bell Atlantic	1996	Telecommunications	23
MFS Comm./UUNET Tech.	1996	Internet/Telecomm.	2
Time Warner/Turner Broadcasting	1995	Programming/cable	7.5
Walt Disney Co./Capital Cities-ABC	1995	Programming/broadcast	19
Westinghouse/CBS	1995	Broadcasting	5.4
AT&T Trivestiture	1995	Computing/manufacturing/carriage	
AT&T/LIN Broadcasting	1995	Telecomm/cellular	3.26
Ameritech/BellSouth/SBC Comm./Disney	1995	Video programming	.5[a]
Bell Atlantic/ NYNEX/Pacific Telesis/ Creative Artists	1994	Video programming	.3[a]
News Corp./MCI	1995	Broadcasting/telecommunications	2.0
Gannett/Multimedia	1995	Broadcasting/newspapers	2.4
TCI/Viacom	1995	Cable	2.25
NYNEX/Bell Atlantic	1994	Cellular	13
Time Warner/ Cablevision	1995	Cable	2.4
MCI/British Telecom	1994	Telecommunications	4.3
AT&T/McCaw Communications	1994	Telecommunication/cellular	16.5[b]

Sources: *Communications Daily*, September 25, 1995, p. 1; August 1, 1995, p. 1; August 2, 1995, p. 1; September 21, 1995, p. 1; April 10, 1995, p. 3; April 19, 1995, p. 1; November 1, 1994, p. 1; May 11, 1995, p. 1; July 25, 1995, p. 1; July 26, 1995, p. 2; February 8, 1995, p. 1. *Telecommunications Reports*, July 4, 1994, p. 9; September 26, 1994, p. 13–14; October 3, 1994, p. 23. *Wall Street Journal*, April 10, 1995, p. A4; May 2, 1996, p. A3; May 3, 1996, p. A3. *Chicago Tribune*, May 6, 1996, p. 1.

a. Spending commitment.
b. Including debt.

delivery systems with "content" will increasingly extend to include electronic variations and replications of nonelectronically distributed information products. Two related developments allow the electronic distribution of a vast array of print products. First, computers are increasingly integrated into the telecommunications network, particularly through servers that allow hundreds or thousands of subscribers simultaneous access to and choices among enormous databases of information products.[104] These services provide text, pictures, sound, and video programming, in a preestablished format or in a form requested by a customer. Servers may be located in the community served or linked electronically in a hierarchy according to the frequency of use (with distant servers allowing vast areas access to seldom-used materials). Second, the ability to convert print and video products into digital form allows those products to be provided through servers, other databases, and other electronic means. In combination, these developments theoretically allow cable systems, telephone companies, and other information service providers to use electronic means to provide subscribers with access to nearly all print products and (taped) performances that were traditionally provided through personal interactions or nonelectronic delivery.

This migration of print products to this emerging information network has been reflected in a series of joint ventures between formerly distinct industries. Publishers, especially news publishers, are making their products available through electronic means and tailoring them for presentation in unique electronic forms. For example, since the *Chicago Tribune* initiated the first electronic newspaper available on-line nationwide, others have followed: in late 1994, 28 newspapers offered or were planning to offer services through the five principal national on-line services, and 60 dailies offered or were poised to offer electronic services.[105] Since then, eight of the nation's principal newspaper owners have joined in a venture to provide on-line services using their newspapers' information and features, and the Internet is a recent focus of media interest.[106] Media will also shift from traditional to emerging networks, as foreshadowed by the alliance between Microsoft and NBC to develop on-line information services (to be distributed through Microsoft's network), CD-ROMs, and interactive television services.[107] The performing arts have for decades also taped and broadcast performances that were originally presented live, and libraries and museums are increasingly providing their holdings in electronic form. This integration operates in the other direction as well. Electronic transmission may make available a far broader array of packaged music products, and both video programming and interactive products are also widely available in packaged form for home use (in the form of videocassette recordings of motion pictures and other programming, and CD-ROMs and other retail products designed for use with personal computers).

CHAPTER FOUR

Structural Reform of Regulation

TECHNOLOGICAL and service developments in the delivery of video, data, and voice communications pose tremendous challenges for current regulatory policies. Chapter 3 and the introduction described the transformations in information services and delivery that are creating a new information industry, one increasingly marked by overlapping systems of delivering voice and video information, by facilities that offer combinations of diverse services, by services that combine delivery technologies, and by service offerings that replicate many information services not traditionally available through electronic means. Chapter 2 described the origin and evolution of separate regulatory regimes. Each regime addresses only certain service providers and certain delivery technologies that constitute this new information industry. None responds comprehensively or directly to problems presented by these emerging networks and services, and each arose in response to competitive conditions that have long since disappeared. The 1930s through the 1970s might be thought of as the Bronze Age of information services, and our regulatory structures and public policy strategies must be pulled from that Bronze Age into this information moment. This chapter examines the problems of regulatory structure and policy created by this divergence between distinct and relatively rigid sets of regulations and the cross-cutting and rapidly changing developments that affect them all.

The following discussion of these emerging challenges proceeds in three steps. An initial section analyzes the market and regulatory developments surveyed in previous chapters and outlines the general disjunctions between current regulation and emerging information delivery services. The principal issues concern the uneasy relation between an increasingly integrated and quickly evolving set of services and a segmented and relatively ponderous regulatory system designed to address an increasingly superseded set of competitive circumstances.

A second section outlines several general, strategic challenges that these new information services pose for regulators. These include assessing the continuing need for administrative regulation to address threats to competition in these industries, the continued relevance of traditional justifications for regulation of these industries apart from protecting competition, and various modifications of the traditional administrative model that might reduce the social and economic costs of regulating these industries.

The third section explores more particular challenges to each of the principal regulatory regimes presented by the emerging information networks and services. The provision of multiple services through new facilities and overlapping systems of transmission challenge the structure of regulation. That is, certain divisions between regulatory regimes or among regulators may become outdated or harmful as information networks increasingly overlap and perform varied functions. In other respects, the challenges may be to the competitive assumptions underlying substantive policies within each of the regulatory regimes. Many of the substantive policies embedded within each regulatory regime arose because distinct networks provided services in a manner that is quickly disappearing, and the new information services present each set of regulations with novel issues and competitive challenges. In accord with the more general strategic concerns outlined above, one response to continuing technological and market changes is the development of a tightly constrained, generally applicable regulatory regime, based on certain of the regulations developed since the early 1980s as part of Title II's common-carrier regulation and designed to identify and redress, through rules, the anticompetitive threat posed by sources of clearly established and persistent market power.

A theme throughout is that the transformations shaping the new information industry likely justify far broader, structural revisions to regulatory mechanisms and requirements than Congress, the FCC, or other regulatory bodies are contemplating. The Telecommunications Act of 1996 is certainly of great commercial importance and will facilitate the industry restructuring that is already under way. Those revisions are, however, essentially marginal changes to the structure and intensity of regulation. They ameliorate the effect of particular restrictions (as with the broadcast ownership limitations) or streamline or refocus existing regulatory structures (as with potentially accelerating local telephone company provision of long-distance service or removing the vestige of the barrier to those companies' provision of video services).

Instead, the technological and service developments since 1990 call into question the core of several if not all the principal regulatory regimes. They suggest that it is now time to leave the regulatory responses of the past to the past, acknowledge the amazing and unpredictable nature of current competitive developments, and address new competitive failures directly with tools suited to that purpose as those failures are clearly demonstrated.

The Disparity between Emerging Information Networks and Traditional Regulatory Regimes

Two salient types of disjunction exist between the emerging information networks and the separate regulatory regimes addressing distinct communications networks and functions. The first is structural: the emerging networks in many senses overlap and merge, and they no longer correspond to the separate networks and distinct modes of communicating that produced the regulatory regimes designed to govern isolated sets of communications facilities and services. The second concerns the pace of and potential for change in the means and forms of electronic communications. Current regulation was designed to govern defined networks subject to marginal change. Now, however, the greatest possibilities of increased competition and improved services arise from efforts to reconfigure and dramatically modify the capabilities and uses of existing networks.

Structural Disjunction

Recent technological and market changes challenge and contradict the essential regulatory structure outlined in chapter 2. That structure reflected the assumed and actual division between point-to-multipoint broadcasting of an editorial product, point-to-point carriage of others' communications, and presentation of information through nonelectronic means, including print. Broadcasting and then cable television regulation address the first form of information transmission. Common-carrier regulation and the statutory provisions that supersede the Modification of Final Judgment (MFJ) address the second. The provisions for telephone company distribution of video programming police the boundaries between the first and second. The third, consisting of packaged products, remains largely beyond the scope of specialized regulators, although certain regulations and new statutory provisions seek to quarantine packaged products from electronic distribution and differentially treat that information once it is communicated electronically.[1] Regulators have adapted each of the resulting separate regulatory regimes to competitive and technological changes, but that process has largely occurred independently within each of the regimes.[2]

Even the more recently developed regulatory regimes have continued to reflect this segmentation and this essential tripartite treatment of communicated information. Cable television regulation arose as part of the regulation of broadcasting but presented different issues principally as a result of the different transmission medium—wire rather than wireless. Even so, the regulation of this new medium generally continued to assume and address point-to-multipoint distribution of programming selected and packaged by the system operator. The new regulation of telephone companies' entry into video services reflects this continuation in a different way: telephone companies are put to a choice between operating cable television systems (that is, becoming broadcasters) or, under a separate regulatory regime, being treated as "carriers" that distribute their own and others' programming. Both the MFJ and the statutory scheme that supersedes it also developed within the basic tripartite structure. That regulation of former Bell system entities arose and once again focuses on competitive difficulties that arise in the core markets for point-to-point voice carriage services.

Indeed, the Telecommunications Act of 1996 failed significantly to restructure this segmented regulatory system and in important respects augmented the problems that segmentation creates. The form and content of the broadcasting and cable television system regulatory regimes were left largely untouched, although important cross-ownership restrictions were removed. Traditional common-carrier regulation continues, with the principal addition of exceptionally complicated additional regulations placed on local exchange carriers and designed to increase local service competition.[3] The act replaced the consent decree's requirements with a distinct statutory and administrative scheme that continues those requirements in modified form.[4] Many of the restrictions on "incidental" services were removed, but elaborate restrictions now govern the threshold for entry into new lines of business and especially the local carriers' ability to provide "content" or "electronic publishing" services in conjunction with carriage services.[5] Together with the new regulation of local telephony services, this regime potentially increases the importance of state regulators' actions—including actions directly addressing the same matters subject to federal regulation.

And the new provisions for telephone company entry into video markets create an absurd degree of disjointed regulation: in providing nearly identical distribution of video signals, telephone companies may be subject to Title III regulation (if they use wireless technology), Title II's common-carrier regulation (if they make general carriage offerings), cable television regulation (if they wish to select most video programming offerings), or an entirely new set of yet to be developed "open video system" regulations (if they submit to a lighter version of common-carrier regulation).[6]

The recent developments in information transmission cut across these disparate regulatory regimes and more fundamentally challenge those regimes because they depart dramatically from the assumed division between broadcasting, carriage, and packaged information products. Three defining characteristics of the emerging networks present particularly important aspects of this challenge to current regulatory structures. Together, they require a considerably more comprehensive rather than segmented regulatory approach and require that regulators for many purposes abandon the divergent approaches currently tailored to broadcasters, carriers, and providers of packaged information products.

First, a single set of facilities may be employed to provide a range of formerly distinct services, including carriage and origination of mass-media products. For video services especially, all networks perform a function that can be isolated and deemed to be carriage, but all increasingly distribute comprehensive editorial products as well. This is now true of wireless systems (single and multichannel), cable television systems, and telephone companies' video transmission systems.[7] All seek to deliver video products to consumers, and several may provide traditional voice communication services as well. Network operators can no longer readily be designated carriers, broadcasters, or content providers.

Traditionally, the telecommunications network provided point-to-point voice messages through facilities separate from those used to deliver video programming, and both types were largely distinct from centers of computing activity. Local telephone companies' provision of video services over broadband facilities provides the clearest case of the transformation. Those upgraded facilities will provide traditional telephone service, but they will also be designed to deliver video programming and advanced interactive services. Cable television systems' facilities may be upgraded to provide similar services and in the near term will likely provide at least voice telephony (especially in conjunction with wireless services). Satellites will have an expanded role in voice and data telephony communicated directly from end users and will continue to provide point-to-multipoint video transmission (for video conferencing and for video programming delivered to cable television systems, consumers, and local telephone companies). Broadcasters, too, are seeking to integrate limited interactive and other tailored or narrowcast communication functions into their services.

The introduction, at the respective ends of the telecommunications network, of personal computers (and facsimile machines) and computers used by information service providers has similarly transformed even the traditional telecommunications network: it now makes information available on a mass basis, and these widely available and person-to-person communications include entertainment, retail, data, text, and bulletin board services. The development of resold telecommunications services and limited-access networks—from the Internet to information distribution systems developed by Microsoft and IBM—especially render obsolete the distinctions between carriage and content and between broadcast information and personal communications. The next generation of wireless telephone services will allow the telecommunications network, in combination with cable television facilities, to provide a similarly complex range of services.

Second, information may reach consumers through an increasingly diverse range of mechanisms—including combinations of facilities that allow information to be transmitted through overlapping and multiple routes. Different types of delivery systems (such as satellite and cable delivery of video programming) may overlap, or new technologies may permit profitable construction of multiple systems of the same type (such as the overlapping long-distance fiber telephony networks). In several markets, such overlapping facilities create actual competition. Just as important, it also often creates the potential for facilities-based competition, depending on the pace and nature of an upgrade to a network serving a distinct market. Regulation tied to a particular established network or even to a particular distribution technology may have increasing difficulty promoting or responding to these sources of actual or potential competition produced by formerly distinct distribution networks.

Until relatively recently, a single, principally wire-based telecommunications system transmitted voice messages, and a set of local broadcasting stations (later largely supplanted by cable television systems) transmitted video programming. Video delivery best illustrates the increasing availability of multiple delivery systems. As described in the previous chapter, for example, consumers can increasingly secure video programming directly from satellites, from cable television companies, through over-the-air broadcasting, from emerging competitors to cable television systems (employing "wireless" cable technologies or wire-based distribution systems), and soon from local telephone companies. (And of course they can visit their local videocassette store or movie theater.)[8] Even for video programming, this phenomenon may be transitory, as certain technologies fall victim to limits of cost or function or to anticompetitive actions by entrenched facilities operators.

Other services promise differing degrees of this multiplicity of delivery routes. For interactive text and video services, the need for broadband connections to large-scale computing facilities, and perhaps more generally to the switched telecommunications network, likely requires that these services be transmitted through facilities of local telephone companies and perhaps upgraded cable television systems. Telephony may evolve more akin to video programming. Already, in the few areas where states have permitted widespread local telephone competition, businesses with large calling volumes are allowed some choice of telephone carriers. Eventually, cable television systems, wire-based local access (and perhaps local exchange) entrants, and wireless and satellite service providers may create overlapping transmission paths for even the most entrenched traditional telecommunications services.[9] Even where single delivery systems exist or are necessary to support alternative delivery systems, regulations and market forces may ensure that multiple service providers in fact provide service through those facilities.

New uses of facilities often have an effect similar to the development of overlapping delivery facilities. For example, a service provider that acquires and resells the transmission capacity of a facilities owner acquires the ability to operate a network that in many respects competes with the network controlled by the owner. This is especially true if the service provider using the owners' facilities establishes a direct commercial relationship with the ultimate consumer. The Internet and Microsoft's network often bypass facilities owners in this manner and may for this reason become a potent competitive force.

Third, the information available electronically is increasingly diverse and includes a broad range of products equivalent to those formerly available only as "packaged" information products. With the exception of the peculiar content regulations developed for over-the-air broadcasters, regulation of electronic distribution systems generally developed separately from the limited independent regulation of motion pictures, print, games, software, and information services. As the newly developing distribution networks make those products available electronically, maintaining this separation will be more difficult. The distribution of computing applications follows a similar pattern, with similar consequences.

Electronic communication used to encompass principally person-to-person voice communication and exceptionally limited broadcast video programming—supplemented more recently by more extensive selections of video programming transmitted over cable television system facilities. As discussed in chapter 3, the range of transmitted video programming is growing rapidly. Facsimile machines and personal computers have expanded the range of even person-to-person communications to include text, pictures, and data. Databases and 800 services have further expanded the range of information available over the traditional telecommunications network, and those services may in many respects replicate the information available through libraries, magazines, and retail publishing outlets. The advent and growth of interactive and bulletin board services will further add to the forms and content of information made available electronically. For text and data services, Internet and on-line computer services already provide vast ranges of information and computer applications, and interactive video and data services will multiply the utility of these services by providing even more information in forms responsive to individuals' own expressions of interest or to the needs of particular companies or even industry segments.

Each of these three characteristics of the emerging information networks makes it more difficult for regulators to respond to competitive and market developments through the traditional regulatory structures. As described in chapter 2, each of the five regulatory regimes arose and evolved in response to the competitive conditions in particular industries, each employing a specific network for a specific type of communication service. Now, the cross-cutting changes are not only eliminating the separateness of networks and industries but replacing the original competitive problems with issues peculiar to the new networks. Like the blind men of parable fame, regulators applying each of the separate regulatory schemes can describe and address only a portion of the elephant.

This regulatory mismatch of objective to object is reflected in the principal regulatory regimes' underinclusiveness and overinclusiveness. They fail to regulate important new providers of services at the core of their regulations, and they sweep beyond the industry and facilities for which their particular regulations were designed. Thus broadcasting regulation now addresses only one of many sources of video programming, and one of decreasing importance.[10] Correspondingly, radio communications requiring licenses pursuant to Title III of the Communications Act now are important elements not only of broadcasting but also of direct-to-home satellite-delivered video programming, satellite delivery of video programming to cable television systems, satellite-based telephony (used both directly and as a link within the terrestrial system), ground-based wireless telephony (both cellular service and personal communications services), microwave transmissions used in portions of the traditional telecommunications network, and wireless systems that compete with cable television systems.[11] Cable television regulation does not generally govern the competing services provided by local telephone companies.[12] Even so, the cable television systems subject to that particular regulatory regime are poised to provide common-carrier services, for both video delivery and traditional telephony. The tariff filing, pricing and service review, and reasonable practice requirements contained in common-carrier regulation do not apply to the core video telecommunications functions of cable television systems and other carriers (including broadcasters) that contract to carry particular messages or otherwise limit their offerings.[13] At the same time, that common-carrier regulation applies indirectly to certain carriers' unregulated services, to carriers in competitive telecommunications markets, and to all carriers in markets that had not yet been found to be competitive.[14]

More fundamentally, and as set forth in greater detail below, the new information industry challenges the rationales that generated and justified several of the principal regulatory structures. Common-carrier regulation embodied a "public utility" model of managing the competitive difficulties presented by control over essential, monopoly facilities. Yet now many important submarkets of common-carrier telecommunications have become or are becoming competitive, and broad classes of carriers do not even arguably possess market power. Broadcasting regulation essentially represented a "public interest bargain" between regulators who provided incentives to certain private parties to construct video transmission infrastructure (including through financial windfalls in the license allocation process) and in return sought to manage the competitive conditions and content of the then uniquely powerful communications medium. Now, many parties other than broadcasters distribute video programming, and the "public interest" obligation has become largely devoid of content, amounting to a general power reserved to the regulator. The government has in any event, at least prospectively, largely stopped distributing new licenses without compensation. The various regulatory systems that now apply to

telephone company entry into video services are defined by no clear rationale and, in conjunction with the practical advantages that cable television
regulation provides to the incumbent operator, will until elaborated continue to impede development of video service competition. And cable
television regulations have reregulated an industry, in order to limit its
monopoly power, on the eve of the onset of significant competition in the
delivery of video programming.[15]

This regulatory patchwork resting on outdated rationales presents particular difficulties for many of the most important areas of potentially increasing competition and service development. Developing competition in local
telephony is a paramount challenge, but current regulation focuses on
switched, wire-based facilities and divides regulation among state regulators, the FCC's regulation of traditional telephone carriers, and administration of provisions derived from the Bell System consent decree. And those
sources and forms of regulation, in turn, are often only tangentially related
to many of the principal potential sources of increased competition: development of new wireless technologies, upgrading of cable television facilities, increasing out-of-region competition among local telephone companies, increased satellite carriage of voice communications, and entry by
nontraditional service providers into local markets. Similar divisions apply
to developing competition in one-way, wide distribution of video programming and related services: nearly every source of that competition outlined
in chapter 3 (including broadcasters, local telephone companies, local wireless distributors, satellite distributors, and cable television operators) is
subject to a separate set of regulatory requirements. Disparate regulatory
schemes also pose a considerable danger to developing advanced video
services, including interactive services. Only cable television systems and
local telephone companies are likely soon to be able to provide the facilities
necessary for these advanced services. If cable television systems are to
upgrade their systems and compete with telephone companies, they will
likely have to raise capital through entry into telecommunications and offer
customers a combination of telephone and video services. Yet state and local
regulation of telecommunications and cable television will continue to impede
new and joint offerings. Telephone company provision of advanced video
services also confronts extensive regulatory barriers that spring from within the
common-carrier regime, as well as new regulation of video services and
electronic publishing. At the same time, continued regulation of traditional
broadcasting limits the ways in which cable television and telephone companies may compete in video services.

Regulating a Dynamic Network

Apart from the structure of the new information services, the pace and scope of changes in communications technology and services pose an equally basic challenge to the traditional regulatory structure. As described in chapter 2, each regulatory regime arose to govern a distinct and fairly stable network and type of communication service and evolved in response to marginal changes largely affecting only that particular network.

Recently, of course, the pace of change and degree of uncertainty regarding future networks and services has increased considerably. The challenge is not only how to structure the existing regulatory regimes but also how the government is to regulate effectively amidst such quickly and profoundly changing conditions. Regulatory proceedings addressing basic issues can linger for years, whether the issues arise within or across regulatory regimes. For example, the FCC has attempted since 1986 to determine how local carriers can better integrate advanced information services with more traditional carriage services, but important aspects of that issue are unresolved.[16] The FCC's consideration of broadcasters' provision of advanced services and high-definition television has been particularly drawn out.[17] The FCC similarly took years to address the most basic questions surrounding telephone company competition with cable television operators, and the Telecommunications Act of 1996 presents a new set of issues.[18] Fault for these delays lies more often in changing circumstances than with the FCC. And because every regulatory change threatens the core interests of an established industry and presents opportunities for new entrants, private industry often seeks protection from competition through perpetuation of regulation. Even so, the resulting uncertainty creates tremendous difficulties for corporate planning and—because many innovations in the core regulated industries are subject to regulatory challenge or require regulatory approval—considerably delays initiation of new services and the advent of increased competition. This is in marked contrast to developments in the far less regulated computer software, networking, equipment, and information service industry segments.

This delay, uncertainty, and potential for competitors to manipulate regulatory processes especially affects competitive developments that combine elements of various networks or depart from established uses of existing networks. These types of developments have already proved extremely important to emerging competition and will likely only increase in importance. Even for the most basic and imminent industry developments, multiple and extensive regulatory proceedings must often precede competitive changes; such proceedings present unusual opportunities for competitors to gain regulatory windfalls. Telephone companies' attempts to compete with cable television operators present an ongoing and unresolved regulatory saga involving multiple regulatory regimes and regulators. The merger between TCI and Bell Atlantic held out the potential for immense competitive benefits in both local telephony competition and video programming services but encountered all of these regulatory barriers as well as traditional antitrust review. AT&T's merger with McCaw required separate approval from state telephone regulators, the FCC (for transfer of control of broadcast licenses), the Justice Department (in its MFJ role and antitrust enforcement role), and Judge Greene in two separate proceedings and capacities (to consider a waiver of the MFJ and to review the Antitrust Division's entry into a consent decree). Realignment of television networks presents a separate cluster of regulatory issues.[19]

The potential for the transformation and emergence of new networks and of new uses of old networks, rather than marginal development of established networks, particularly challenges the traditional process of regulatory decisionmaking. In these circumstances, the traditional regulatory categories have most clearly broken down, and regulators' responses are at their least assured. For example, this is occurring as telephone companies seek to deliver their own video programming. The FCC initially sought comment regarding which portion of the Communications Act—Title II or Title VI—applies to these services, and Congress "clarified" the issue by creating a new regulatory regime ("open video systems") that will likely mix and match existing regulatory requirements.[20] Scraping off the accreted layers of broadcasting regulation has also proved painfully slow, even as the video delivery industry changes with amazing speed.[21] Regulation in the absence of clear statutory direction or competitive theory may also be seen as regulators seek to address satellite provision of voice telecommunication, satellite provision of video programming, the effect of state regulation on local telephony competition, and broadcasters' efforts to expand their uses of emerging technologies.

The nature of recent technological and market developments for information networks poses a related, broader issue of the government's competence to manage and predict change. The FCC has traditionally proceeded by seeking comments regarding the effects of likely changes on whatever industry practice is being challenged or considered, predicting the most likely course of developments, and, based on its predictions, weighing the costs and benefits of the proposals before it. The case for applying administrative expertise to industry developments is strongest when marginal changes in a stable industry are at issue, and in fact the FCC's determinations during most of its history occurred in this manner. Now, much of the turmoil in these industries exists because a plausible case can be made that the networks and services will develop in various and conflicting ways, and companies are increasingly investing billions of dollars on the basis of different assessments of likely outcomes for particular competitive developments. When industry experts differ fundamentally on the most basic of these developments, it is difficult to justify regulators' attempts to direct the industry's development based on their predictions regarding competition.

Strategic Responses to the Mismatch of Regulatory Structure and Market and Technological Developments

The emergence and rapid evolution of overlapping information distribution systems with new capabilities presents specific and general challenges to the traditional regulation of information delivery. A later section addresses the specific challenges to the divisions between regulatory regimes and the assumptions regarding competition and services embedded within each regime. This subsection describes some of the more general challenges to assumptions about government efforts to manage competitive developments in this industry through administrative action.

As regulators and others grapple with the implications of continuing technological and service developments, they will confront at least three types of issues. The first concerns the need for any administrative control of these industries and services. General antitrust law serves as the principal regulatory mechanism and competitive standard for most industries, and conceivably it could suffice for the new information industry as well. A second set of issues concerns which requirements might justify more formal administrative regulation. Concerns about the provision of basic information services have long supported traditional regulation, and recent competitive developments place differing degrees of stress on these rationales. Third, to the extent that regulation is conducted through administrative action, issues will persist regarding the continued efficacy of the current administrative model, which relies on an agency that retains broad and open-ended powers, is relatively independent of executive control, and is relatively free of judicial oversight.

The Sufficiency of General Competition Laws

Applying Ockham's razor to this patchwork of existing and increasingly outdated regulations and regulatory structures might suggest that they should all be dramatically reduced and largely eliminated, with competitive forces allowed to develop the information networks and services. Generally applicable antitrust laws would remain available to remedy competitive abuses.[22] The telecommunications and communications industries would, in this view, simply be treated like any other set of industries.

There is a surprising amount to be said in support of this position. The costs of complying with reporting, accounting, and other regulatory requirements are enormous. Even larger efficiency and opportunity costs stem from consciously or unintentionally distorted pricing, and especially from regulatory barriers to entry and limitations on service offerings. Unintended consequences and reduced services and efficiencies are inevitable whenever regulators intervene broadly in dynamic markets marked by both large investment and great uncertainty. Compounding these difficulties, rent-seeking through the political process is pervasive in these industries. Established industries that are among the most threatened by emerging competition are precisely the ones that can most readily pressure regulators and legislators: newspaper and magazine publishers, owners of television broadcast networks and stations, and local telephone companies that have developed symbiotic relationships with state regulators. There is, in addition, a more general cost of regulation to the values that underlie our libertarian tradition and are reflected most prominently in the First Amendment: as these industries shift to the selection and production of information in a manner that brings them within the First Amendment's scope, continued regulation increases the threat of direct or indirect government limitations on certain speakers designed to shape the content of their speech or overall public debate.[23]

These costs associated with continued regulation are likely to increase considerably. Overbroad regulation has severe social consequences as regulated entities increasingly engage in the production and dissemination of speech protected by the First Amendment and as other industry sectors are influenced by the pricing and capabilities of electronic communication services. In addition, technological and market changes are accelerating— as marked by the realignment of industry participants, increased competition among formerly distinct service providers, and the introduction of new information products and services. With those changes comes greater potential for the unintended consequences of government regulations, as well as the increased opportunity cost of protecting established communications services and providers. This is particularly so when large segments of these industries are vulnerable to the increased competition that outdated regulation precludes.

The most significant objection to wholesale deregulation is that the current electronic transmission systems and those likely to be employed in the foreseeable future are marked by significant concentrations of market power. This is especially so for facilities required by providers of competitive services—in antitrust terms these are ''essential facilities'' to the extent they are not profitably replicable.[24] Cable system operators in most geographic areas are likely to continue to possess market power over video programming delivery,[25] although the pace of emerging competition is sharply debated. Similarly, local telephone carriers retain market power over important elements of local exchange and access services,[26] and more competitive services such as cellular and long-distance services rely on access to those local facilities. Cellular services themselves are provided through local duopolies established by regulation.[27] International services, especially transmissions that require completion by foreign state monopolies, present additional market power issues. In addition, it is a matter of considerable debate whether pockets of market power remain in software development, television and radio broadcasting, satellite services, and even video programming production.[28]

Although some of the technological and market developments described above will result in the erosion of entrenched monopolies (for example, delivery of traditional video programming), many pose the danger of increased monopoly power, particularly for advanced services. This is perhaps most true for interactive video services, especially those offered through improvements to existing cable television systems. These services require sophisticated two-way signaling between consumers and large computer databases, which are functions that in the near future only local telephone companies and cable systems will likely be able to provide.[29] In addition, these systems may well become the conduit through which more traditional telephony and information services must pass. In other words, these advanced facilities could become the ultimate ''essential facility,'' allowing whichever entity that controls them or some vital element of them to exercise market power in pricing access, and to exercise enormous social and market influence by excluding or discriminating against important providers of information.

But these pockets of market power, even in significant concentrations, may not justify continued administrative regulation of these industries. Newspaper markets, for example, often reflect greater degrees of market power. The issue is largely whether the application of antitrust laws through the judicial process or through specific administrative rules best ameliorates anticompetitive conduct in light of regulatory costs. Even the most conservative antitrust analysis (in the sense of reflecting Chicago School influence) would object to operator control of facilities that enabled local carriers to use market power to increase horizontal concentration significantly and, especially because local rate and other regulation could not be wished away immediately, even to gain vertical advantages. Less conservative antitrust analysis—and that likely to find favor in many courts and in the current Department of Justice—would find competitive threats in a much wider range of cases. Thus, even if current regulatory schemes were eliminated, many regulatory constraints would simply reappear through corporations' assessment of antitrust liability or through antitrust proceedings. This would be particularly true for cable television and local telephone services. In addition, the application of general antitrust laws in courts and by the Department of Justice would generate rules, often cast in categorical terms. After all, the MFJ, that source of broad rules specifically limiting the activities of most local telephone carriers, was a judicial decree entered to settle an antitrust suit (a suit and decree endorsed and concluded by the Reagan administration).

Effectively crafted administrative rules potentially have advantages over regulation through antitrust law. Regulatory certainty is perhaps a preeminent virtue in a setting where markets and technology are changing rapidly. The regulatory process is hardly without its delays, but administrative rulemakings may be far more rapid and comprehensive, less expensive, and more responsive to industry's concerns than the judicial process. Antitrust standards are notoriously vague, malleable, and open to manipulation by private plaintiffs. They may be readily misapplied by judges or "creatively" applied by enforcement divisions of state and federal executive departments. The uncertainties inherent in the judicial process regarding the degree of liability and the process that determines it compound these difficulties created by uncertain standards. These antitrust uncertainties have particularly affected the mergers and acquisitions endemic to the new information industry and have hovered over several important software developments. In addition, parties from affected industries and companies participate in administrative rulemakings, which thus can produce more informed and comprehensive rules than might judicial proceedings, which are generally conducted between at most a few private parties (or the government and one or more private parties). Because administrators are familiar with the relevant technologies and market conditions, as well as more likely steeped in basic economic and regulatory theory, they generally possess considerably more expertise than do judges.

At the same time, the administrative process has characteristics that are less advantageous than the judicial process. Many of these are outlined above. The regulatory process is particularly prone to political manipulation and rent-seeking, and it is more likely to result in inefficient price regulation. Persistent regulatory oversight may pose greater dangers to First Amendment values. Poorly designed regulations, with vague standards or lengthy complaint processes, can replicate many of the disadvantages of the judicial process. Even so, measures designed to control the powers of administrators can reduce many of these costs, and administrative reforms that may reduce these dangers are outlined below.

More fundamental is the divergence between current regulation and that which could be justified based on general competition law principles. This is true whether those principles are implemented through agency rules or antitrust enforcement. (Indeed, intelligent regulation of competition generally combines both elements: rules can increase the predictability of antitrust enforcement, as the merger guidelines of the early 1980s did, and administrative agencies can use enforcement proceedings to buttress their more ponderous processes.) Relatively few of the regulatory concerns surveyed in chapter 2 and reflected in the principal regulatory regimes would be embodied in a regime designed to advance the general principles of competition law. Certain cable television and recent common carrier regulation would likely be approximated, but the separate regulatory regimes, open-ended regulatory risk, continuing oversight, and many of the accretions of specific restrictions would likely fall away.

Regulatory Rationales apart from Increasing Competition

Regulators and others often advance various rationales for extensive administrative regulation of information industries that are not directly related to constraining market power. These include the need for government support for infrastructure that requires large capital investments or has particular strategic importance; the need to regulate basic or "universal" services that for reasons of social policy must have a wider distribution than a competitive market might produce; and the need for a central source of coordination among disparate private actors. The technological and market developments outlined above and in previous chapters present differing types of difficulties for these traditional rationales for regulating information transmission. The overlapping and multifold characteristics of the new networks, the pace of the networks' transformation, the private capital attracted to these new services, and the range and variety of the new services in several respects undermine the force of these traditional justifications, but in limited respects they support administrative action resting on these rationales.

A PUBLIC WORKS MODEL.   An extreme response to the emerging information networks and related technological change is to suggest that the government assume a considerably broader role in directing the construction and operation of the emerging networks. A traditional administrative response would be to vest more power in regulators and direct that power to shape and control the new forces that have undermined existing regulations. The federal role might extend, for example, to constructing and operating communications facilities, to coordinating private investment and research, and to directing the terms and scope of offerings of advanced services (including price). The model for this type of intervention might be government backing or operation of local public utilities, or construction and maintenance of federal highways. If these possibilities seem far-fetched, consider both the speculation that greeted Vice President Gore's initial campaign discussions of the ''information superhighway'' and the scope of the Clinton administration's health care proposals. Indeed, the information superhighway trope has embedded within it an analogy to ground transport and to the federal role in constructing the interstate highway system.

The scale of the emerging information networks and the enormous uncertainty surrounding them and their associated services suggest that government direction of the networks is unnecessary or would have tremendous costs. First, there is no indication that government action is required to compensate for a lack of industry ability to develop the required facilities. Because the new networks are essential to various industries' ability to maintain current revenues and to enter potentially enormous emerging markets, private industry appears to have both the incentive and the ability to construct and operate them. Second, there are large costs associated with directing any particular outcome for evolving technologies and markets.

There would likely be vast unintended consequences of such regulation, enormous opportunity costs of forgone offerings and novel means of providing them, efficiency losses from any pricing and service regulation, enormous opportunities for government capture, and tremendously increased threats to First Amendment values. Public investment of this magnitude would create tremendous pressures on regulators to foreclose competitive developments inconsistent with the market structures that would support return on and operation of those public projects. Third, no group of experts, and certainly none in government, has any clear notion of what services can be profitably provided ten years in the future, much less of the combinations of technologies that will most efficiently provide them. In the absence of even an abstract consensus, command-and-control regulation would seem particularly futile and the risk to public investment difficult to justify. In contrast, corporations are willing to risk billions of their dollars on differing and likely incompatible visions of the future. Finally, politicians probably lack the stomach and political support for intervention. Government expenditures would likely have to be tremendous. There is no specific class of beneficiaries, and more general political benefits are difficult to define or predict. As the health care debate in 1992–93 showed, public confidence in comprehensive government intervention is in short supply.

UNIVERSAL SERVICE.   A common justification for regulation of emerging information services is that government must ensure that carriers provide universal service. The term is slippery but generally rests on the notion that many advanced services will be vital to individuals' economic and social well-being and that government must thus ensure that carriers make at least "basic" or "vital" services affordable and widely available. The concept is a long-standing one for provision of basic telephone service but has also led to many of the most wrenching and anticompetitive telephony pricing distortions.[30] Universal service has been a centerpiece of recent legislative proposals, but the Telecommunications Act of 1996 principally leaves the terms and related regulatory requirements undefined and awaiting further definition.[31]

Initially and quite apart from the merits of these objectives, universal service hardly supports administrative regulation of emerging information services and networks. In contrast to local telephony services, where administrative rules are deeply implicated as a result of decades of state command-and-control regulation to achieve universal service goals, considerably more flexibility exists to advance any universal service objectives for more advanced information services. For those services, universal service goals could be advanced, with minimal distortion, through direct outlays or means other than administrative direction of services. For example, there might be subsidies to low-income consumers (or other purchasers, such as libraries) to reduce the effective price of certain services or even subsidies to companies to engage in activities they would otherwise find unprofitable.[32] Even for traditional telephone service, such direct subsidies (often funded through levies on telecommunications companies and services) are becoming more common.

A potential objection to direct outlays—that political difficulties could readily bar the availability of government funds for these purposes—suggests that some skepticism might be warranted regarding the merits of the universal service objectives. Intrusive government regulation of the information industries often has the effect of, and may indirectly be touted as, crafting rules with broad distorting effects to achieve relatively confined distributional goals that would be defeated if subjected to the political process. There would likely be less political support for the necessary taxation and outlays than for the government's policies of granting broadcast licenses free of charge, or subsidizing local telephone subscribers in the postwar era through inflated long-distance prices, or shifting costs by requiring cable television stations to carry particular broadcasting signals without charge. Extending universal service obligations to advanced information services, to the extent that they require regulation of carrier services rather than subsidies, holds this same danger of capturing the regulatory process and subverting the political process. Regulatory requirements designed to benefit small groups of consumers or information suppliers could also raise prices for other services and limit their development and availability.[33]

Uncertainties surrounding the development of emerging information services and networks, as well as the nature of many of the most likely services, also suggest that the universal service rationale for regulation applies with considerably less force in this context than for traditional voice communication services. First, these networks and services are at an early stage of development. Advanced networks are exceptionally costly and risky. No one knows with certainty what advanced services will be offered, what demand will exist, and what resulting return might be available. To the extent that universal service obligations extend to these barely developed services and impose costs on service providers or otherwise require deviations from the offerings that purely commercial determinations would produce (the intended effect of such regulation), that risk and cost increase. In this way, premature universal service requirements—like other indirect taxes imposed on service providers—may stunt development and provision of advanced services and networks, or even frustrate their development altogether.

Second, many of the advanced information services that will initially be available are hardly the "basic" or "essential" services that many believe justify universal service requirements. In the near term, the most likely services include additional video programming (including motion pictures), variations of gambling services, shopping services, video games, and perhaps video "adult entertainment." For any "vital" educational and information services that are eventually widely provided, policies designed to make them available in schools, libraries, hospitals, and other central locations—rather than in each home—may achieve the goals that underlie universal service proposals. In the end, debates over universal service requirements for advanced information services may simply replicate debates over more general inequalities of material resources. For a broad range of economic, political, and moral reasons, we tolerate unequal access to nearly all social goods, including many of the most important. Those social goods are now increasingly able to be provided over the electronic network. This migration of services to electronic form allows those who desire a different distribution of goods another occasion to press their case, which may prove successful, but it is hardly clear why that migration to the network should itself yield a different outcome.

COORDINATION. A different, more limited type of government action—as a coordinator—provides a perhaps clearer case for limited regulation distinctly addressed to the information industries. As discussed in greater detail below, there may be extensive efficiency gains associated with government oversight of the creation and allocation of rights in the electromagnetic spectrum. Regulators may also serve as a clearinghouse or locus of coordination for industry participants and others who seek to set technological standards for aspects of the network such as interfaces, elements of the set top unit or other consumer equipment, and aspects of interconnection. The government has also traditionally served a role of coordinating connections among various carriers' networks (for railroad and energy transport networks as well as information networks), and this function may be discharged either as an aspect of limiting the potential anticompetitive consequences of facilities that yield market power or to further a more general interest in developing a uniform network.[34] Even these coordinating functions, if accepted as legitimate, support only a limited regulatory strategy and government role. They may justify vesting regulators with certain additional, ancillary powers and responsibilities, but they rarely support extensive regulation of the pricing, terms, and nature of services deployed in constructing and operating the emerging information network.

Limiting the Costs of Administrative Action

As the merits and form of regulation of the emerging information industry are debated, another set of issues will focus on reducing the costs of administrative policymaking for these services. If administrators continue to formulate rules governing information services—especially to check abuses of market power—then a number of measures might reduce the social and economic costs of this type of administrative action. The traditional model of administrative action, refined in the New Deal and underlying the structure and powers of the current FCC, grants expert administrators broad discretion to formulate policy in the public interest. It assumes that those regulators, shielded from all but the most limited political and judicial oversight, will apply their expertise to satisfy vague statutory commands by identifying both the relevant problems and the policy solutions to them.[35] In practice, the model can increase the costs outlined above and in chapter 5: contradictory and overlapping policies created by ideologies and policy objectives that shift with new sets of regulators, unjustifiably broad regulation, rent-seeking and political capture, intrusions on First Amendment interests, pricing distortions, unjustified limitations on service offerings, and other ''hidden tax'' or unexpressed redistributional policies. Limiting administrative discretion, clarifying and specifying regulatory objectives, and increasing administrative accountability might reduce many of these costs.[36]

LIMITED REGULATORY OBJECTIVES AND POWERS. Administrative powers could with relative ease be confined to the regulatory objectives that justify specific oversight of the information industries. For example, if checking abuses of market power justifies FCC intervention, then the FCC's jurisdiction and remedial powers could be limited to identifying and crafting rules to redress harms caused by control of essential facilities and other sources of market power. Carriers without market power or carrier activities in competitive markets would escape FCC oversight. To the extent that regulation might preclude emerging competition and unjustifiably protect established competitors, the FCC's powers could be additionally limited by requiring the commission to meet particular evidentiary showings before it could act. Thus, it could be required to identify the particular source of carrier market power, demonstrate that the threat of anticompetitive conduct will likely persist for a substantial period, and justify those conclusions with detailed evidentiary findings. Similarly, the FCC's remedial powers could be limited to imposing antitrust and, perhaps, common-carrier remedies that traditionally have been applied in judicial and regulatory proceedings to redress control of essential facilities and other sources of carriers' ability and incentive to harm competition. The FCC could be required as well to justify its remedial choices as directly tailored to the competitive failure it has identified, and even to overcome a presumption in favor of an unregulated market.

In fact, as part of its common-carrier regulation developed during the 1980s, the FCC itself developed the essential tools and framework for this limited type of regulation. In one of its most important proceedings, it essentially deregulated certain carrier activities that posed no anticompetitive potential, and it declined to regulate broad submarkets of the communications industry that were effectively competitive. For carriers that controlled essential facilities, the FCC developed remedial tools that closely mirrored antitrust remedies and other measures that directly addressed the potential for abuses of market power. It imposed equal access and unbundling requirements, developed measures for detecting and preventing cross-subsidies between regulated and unregulated activities, conditioned entry by monopolists into relatively competitive markets on creation of subsidiaries and related structural separation requirements, limited certain entry that would increase horizontal concentration, and developed incentive-based price regulation. As developed below, more focused versions of these regulations designed to redress abuses of market power (and to deregulate where no market power exists) can form the core of a comprehensive regulatory structure applicable to the entire information network—and can increasingly displace other regulatory measures designed for distinct delivery technologies. Combined with a higher threshold for regulation, they would also nearly exhaust the scope of industry-specific regulation.

EXECUTIVE BRANCH COORDINATION. The FCC is an ''independent'' administrative agency, but incorporating its functions more squarely within the executive branch may reduce the possibilities of regulatory failures identified above. The traditional administrative model underlying the FCC's creation and powers sought to insulate expert regulators from political pressures by placing them within the "headless" fourth branch—with commissioners appointed to fixed terms and not subject to removal at the discretion of the president. For communications policy and more generally, this strategy frustrates coordination among executive branch agencies (the NTIA within the Department of Commerce and the Antitrust Division of the Department of Justice, among others) that conduct important elements of communications policy. It also has the paradoxical effect of depriving administrators of presidential authority and protection and thus making them more sensitive to the political pressures of the "iron triangle"—either from the House and Senate members and staff on committees that oversee the agencies or from the industries traditionally subject to regulation.[37] Integrating the FCC's administrative functions within the executive branch, if only by making the commissioners and top staff positions subject to dismissal as political appointees, could somewhat reduce these handicaps.

JUDICIAL OVERSIGHT. Under the Administrative Procedure Act and most other statutory provisions for judicial review of agency determinations, the extent of judicial scrutiny is minimal and accords with the traditional model of administrative decisionmaking developed during the New Deal. Because Congress has often set forth only vague statutory commands and delegated most substantive decisions to administrators, courts will generally set aside administrative determinations only if they are grossly strained constructions of the governing statute or are "arbitrary and capricious"—a standard that requires little more than that regulators explain the rationale for their course in light of the evidence and principal arguments presented to them.[38]

Increased judicial scrutiny of FCC determinations would buttress efforts to confine administrators in their regulation of the new information industry to pursuing particular objectives through application of limited remedial powers. This process would not be a matter of substituting judicial for administrative expertise but would seek to employ the judicial process to ensure that agency rules conformed to the limited circumstances justifying regulation. For example, to enforce a presumption favoring competition and limiting the FCC to remedying abuses of persistent market power, judicial review could help ensure that the FCC had identified a clear source of market power, had adopted remedies narrowly tailored to the problem identified, and had chosen the most efficient means of achieving that objective among the principal alternatives presented to it. A similarly less deferential standard of judicial review could be instituted to evaluate claims that the FCC had harmed First Amendment interests. This process of judicial review would come at the cost of increased delay and the oft-proven danger of judicial overreaching in policy determinations, but it would at the same time provide an important incentive for the FCC to conform to any limitations on its mandate and remedies.

Challenges to Disparate Regulatory Regimes Posed by an Emerging Information Industry

In addition to the general difficulties presented for administrative regulation by recent developments, as outlined above, the nature of the emerging information networks poses more particular challenges for each of the principal existing regulatory regimes. The increasing competition among entities subject to separate regulatory regimes, the combinations of delivery systems, the provision of differently regulated services over common facilities, and the increasing range of information provided through the varied services challenges central underlying assumptions of each existing regulatory system. These challenges may be to the structure of regulation, in the sense that divisions between regulatory regimes or among regulators may become outdated or harmful as information networks increasingly overlap and diversify. Or the challenges may be to the competitive assumptions underlying substantive policies in each of the regulatory regimes. For each set of regulations, the changing nature of information services and networks calls into question existing policies and presents regulators with novel issues and competitive challenges.

Common-Carrier Regulation

As noted above, the switched telecommunications network provides a potentially comprehensive delivery system capable of distributing an increasing number of services. A network designed for traditional voice telephony directly provides a vast range of data, text, and other information services and, principally through upgraded capacity and integration of computing facilities, will likely be capable of providing a full range of traditional video programming and most advanced interactive and other video services. Wireless telephony and many satellite services are already largely integrated into this network, which could encompass any type of transmission technology. Cable television systems and certain broadcast services will either integrate directly into the switched network or can be viewed as providing functionally equivalent services.

Title II and related regulations already provide the care of a common regulatory system for this broad portion of the information network. In accord with the general strategy outlined above, this regulatory scheme provides many of the tools and mechanisms necessary to identify and redress the traditional anticompetitive dangers that are most likely to justify regulation of the information industry.[39] It is also the source of regulations governing interconnection between and among separately operated networks, including the technical and competitive issues that arise in that context. There are, however, three important elements of Title II regulation that are increasingly difficult to justify in light of recent changes in the information technologies, markets, and services discussed above.

First, regulation of the telecommunications network is divided between interstate functions subject to Title II and certain intrastate functions subject to state regulation—even though an integrated and comprehensive network delivers telecommunications and other information services. This division of regulatory responsibilities is not purely geographic (most local facilities complete or initiate interstate transmissions), but state regulators nonetheless have enormous control over the conditions of entry into services provided locally and the terms, if any, on which those services may be offered.[40] Although the Telecommunications Act of 1996 limits state regulators' ability to preclude entry into local services, those regulators retain broad powers that may significantly influence the scope and form of competitive opportunities.[41] Indeed, the act's new provisions for regulating local telephony considerably expand state regulators' role and particularly their ability to administer federal regulatory requirements.[42] However readily local services may have been separated for regulatory purposes from interstate services in 1934, there is no ready division of the current information network that provides voice, data, and video signals without regard to whether the entities that communicate are within a particular state. The assumption that local markets are readily severable is also incompatible with the various markets for which information services are provided on a national, metropolitan, or even regional basis.

In addition, this dual system of state and federal regulation creates tremendous impediments to the development of new services and facilities (including activities that pose little or no threat of anticompetitive abuses).[43] In contrast to an industry divided between local telephone service providers and interstate carriers, most carriers and service providers now seek to have comprehensive and coordinated offerings that do not conform to state boundaries. In this way multiple regulators and regulations may impede broad and uniform service offerings. Other information service providers not subject to Title II similarly seek to develop national products for an increasingly integrated information industry, and none faces such a pervasive and onerous system of dual regulation (even local regulation of cable television systems is limited in comparison). In addition, state regulation may be far more intrusive and less incentive based than federal regulation. Almost all states have severely restricted entry into local telephone service either formally or indirectly, and they continue to wield powers that may practically restrict entry significantly.[44] The resulting continuation of local service market power, in turn, is the overriding source of concern that competition may be harmed in related markets, including the markets for long-distance services, information services, telecommunications equipment manufacturing, and provision of video programming and advanced video services.[45]

Second, common-carrier regulation developed by the FCC is still formally conducted within the statutory framework organized around tariff filing and review requirements.[46] These requirements serve a reporting function and trigger regulatory oversight of new service offerings or new pricing and were particularly designed to buttress nondiscrimination obligations. Such a pervasive regulatory structure, applicable to all common-carrier services, conceivably made sense when nearly all carriers possessed market power. But that condition is now the exception, albeit an important one, rather than the rule. For carriers without control of facilities that create persistent market power and for services in competitive markets, competition can prevent the discriminatory and predatory pricing, and the inefficient allocation of resources, that ostensibly justified administrative review and enforcement of tariffed services.[47] For these carriers and services, tariff filing and review requirements impose needless regulation and allow substantial opportunities for carriers to manipulate the regulatory process to coordinate offerings and price and to impede competing service offerings. Indeed, the tariff regime—which mandates price and term disclosure, requires adherence to those rates, prohibits nonprice benefits that amount to price discounts, and punishes carriers that depart from published rates—is difficult to justify even for established carriers and can be viewed as an unusually efficient mechanism for the formation and policing of cartels.

For particular instances of carriers' market power, the FCC's regulations developed under Title II are available to seek the price and term information necessary to detect anticompetitive practices. A comprehensive tariff regime, indeed any tariff regime, is now unnecessary to prevent those carriers from engaging in anticompetitive activities. And it is not particularly difficult to remove the mandatory filing requirements while leaving in place discriminatory filing or FCC regulations designed to prevent abuses of market power. The Telecommunications Act of 1996 empowers the FCC to "forbear from applying any regulation or any provision of this Act to a telecommunications carrier or telecommunications service" after considering various competitive, public interest, and consumer protection factors.[48] In light of the FCC's prior, unsuccessful efforts to limit the tariff filing and review requirements, these requirements will likely be an initial focus of the FCC's new powers. This new power is breathtakingly broad: it purports to provide an agency with not only discretion to waive its own regulations, but also power to undo or choose to give no effect to statutory requirements (including those designed to constrain the FCC itself). To the extent that this open-ended provision might be defended as necessary to advance competitive goals, its creation illustrates how Congress missed the opportunity for significant regulatory relief: it chose instead to defer deregulatory determinations until subsequent administrative proceedings and to add to rather than eliminate statutory requirements and related regulations that can no longer be justified.

In accord with the general strategy outlined above, two more efficient means exist to retain the FCC's ability to identify and redress abuses of market power while eliminating Title II's tariff scheme. Congress could categorically eliminate from the FCC's jurisdiction any services or markets for which it found that no danger of persistent market power exists.[49] Or, rather than empowering the FCC to exclude carriers and markets from its core regulations based on the lack of market power, it could reverse the presumption. Instead, the FCC would be vested with particular administrative tools designed to redress certain clearly defined anticompetitive activities, but it could apply those powers only in markets and against facilities operators that it concluded (on a sufficient record and subject to stringent review on appeal) actually possessed the ability and incentive to harm competition. This approach would be consistent with a strategy designed to encourage investment and innovation by reducing regulatory uncertainty, favoring market over administrative mechanisms, and conforming regulation of the information industry with the competition law applied to other industries.

Third, Title II regulations apply only to services offered on a common-carrier basis—through a general offering of service to the public for carriage of others' messages. The Telecommunications Act of 1996 contains a new definition of "telecommunications service" that emphasizes this limitation.[50] This limitation developed when the regulated industry provided precisely this type of service for voice telephony, but now some of the thorniest regulatory problems arise when carriers or other service providers offer equivalent service on a non-common-carrier basis. Thus, carriers may structure certain of their carriage services so that they are available only to certain customers on a contractual basis (and thus provide private rather than common carriage), and a company provides the same telecommunications transmission function whether it carries messages it selects or whether it carries the messages of others. Certain regulatory requirements may be justified only when a carrier limits its offerings to the underlying carriage function, but there is no reason categorically to limit properly constrained regulatory power on the basis of whether the carrier conforms to or evades the elements that establish common carriage.

Recent developments in information transmission also challenge the use of the "common-carrier" distinction to focus the FCC's Title II powers on oversight of carriage services that are for competitive or other reasons offered on nondiscriminatory and generally available terms. For many services of "common carriers" in competitive markets, these requirements do no more than limit service offerings, constrain commercial negotiations between carrier and customer, impose administrative burdens, and provide an opening for ungrounded regulation and manipulation by rent-seekers of the administrative process. In these circumstances, the essential consequence of emerging competition among transmitters of information is that, in the absence of anticompetitive potential or actions, the segment of the industry associated with traditional carriage does not require this regulation of pricing and service offerings any more than other information service providers or any other segment does. In circumstances where market power abuse or other competitive failure is clearly established, the tools the FCC has already developed to identify and constrain those abuses apply equally to all information service providers—whether operating as common carriers, private carriers, or other information providers. Indeed, service providers that control essential facilities (such as cable system operators in certain circumstances), that deliver their own advanced services, or that favor particular customers through contract may also or especially possess the market power that calls for application of the equal access, separate subsidiary, interconnection, nondiscrimination, and related requirements developed in the context of Title II.

Cable Television Regulation

The essential difficulty created by the emerging information network for cable television regulation is that the services and transmission capacities of cable systems are becoming more difficult to distinguish from those of the traditional telecommunications network. The telecommunications network is increasingly likely to perform the functions of cable systems. Once telephone companies can transmit video programming, what justification remains for distinct regulations for the traditional cable systems that deliver only video programming? Correspondingly, cable television systems will likely increasingly perform telecommunications functions and become integrated into the telecommunications network. This could happen to the extent that cable systems are linked to the network to enable them to provide local access (and eventually, perhaps local exchange) telephony services, through cable systems' provision of the infrastructure used for cellular or advanced wireless telephony services (such as personal communications services, or PCS), and through their offering of advanced, two-way services through integration of computing capabilities (such as servers) into their systems. It has already happened to the extent that the core business of cable television systems is to provide telecommunications services and even to distribute particular messages to particular recipients. The regulatory difficulty presented is how to separate and whether to separately regulate traditional switched telecommunications services and cable television services.[51]

Formulating a regulatory response to this difficulty turns in part on the relative virtues of cable television networks and traditional switched telecommunications networks as well as the relative capabilities of current cable television regulation and telecommunications regulation. Technological developments themselves favor reliance on the tools developed to regulate telecommunications networks: the capacity of telecommunications networks to provide switched communications, two-way exchanges, and multiple services provides service advantages that will likely be integrated into cable television systems. In addition, there are tremendous social benefits in creating incentives that promote the expansion of telecommunications networks (or transformation of cable networks into fully switched telecommunications networks), rather than the perpetuation or growth of traditional cable television systems (or transformation of telephone companies' facilities into closed, cablelike services). Networks being developed by local telephone companies have considerably more capacity than traditional cable systems, and their uses can be multiplied through introduction of limited, two-way communication capabilities between households and centrally located servers—and, eventually, introduction of true switched services. In combination with traditional access, interconnection, and nondiscrimination requirements, switching allows a nearly unlimited number of programmers and other information service providers to reach customers and allows customers to select among the various information service offerings. When local switching also connects consumers to the national telecommunications network, the potential sources of information and services expands commensurately, as the Internet illustrates for other services. Without switching, limited channel capacity provides the carrier (usually, a traditional cable system operator) with the incentive and ability to select among video programmers and greatly limits the offerings available to consumers.[52] Perhaps more important, integration into the broader network could allow network users to initiate their own communications.

Telecommunications regulation also has advantages over cable television regulation. In regulating telecommunications carriers, the FCC has developed and refined the structural requirements that ensure that the switched network will remain transparent, permeable, or relatively open to consumers and suppliers: these include access, nondiscrimination, interconnection, and unbundling requirements. At the same time, these requirements can be narrowly targeted and implemented in a manner that protects legitimate network investment and operator interests, encourages investment, and preserves integration efficiencies. For these types of systems, networks can develop vigorously and information service providers can more likely offer their services to consumers. Largely because cable television regulation assumes and seeks marginal adjustments to one-way, limited capacity systems, it cannot create commercial incentives to ensure that particular providers of video programming, traditional information services, advanced interactive services, or telephone services can gain access to consumers through cable systems.[53] There are few regulatory incentives for cable system operators to upgrade their systems to allow two-way communication, much less to provide means for consumers to communicate or secure services from providers other than the network operator (indeed, to provide such capabilities would be to provide what has been traditionally understood as traditional telecommunications services rather than cable service). In addition, only common-carrier or telecommunications regulation provides a relatively comprehensive set of regulatory tools applicable to a variety of often overlapping and interconnected networks. Regulations developed pursuant to Title II could be widely applied to services offered over cable systems as well as those offered over the switched telecommunications network, but cable television regulations have been developed in response to the peculiarities of traditional cable services.

The relative advantages of telecommunications networks and regulatory mechanisms suggest that, as the technologies and networks increasingly overlap and regulatory schemes collide, there should be a preference for Title II regulation and other regulatory measures that produce the social advantages of switched telecommunications networks while protecting incentives to invest in advanced networks (which may mandate quite limited regulation). Title II regulation is flexible and comprehensive enough to subsume the competitive and technological difficulties posed by cable television systems. Indeed, regulation of cable television systems could benefit from more formal competitive analysis and from remedies drawn more from traditional antitrust doctrines and those embodied in aspects of common-carrier regulation. It would be necessary to accommodate Title II regulation to the three functions of cable television systems: those performed as cable operators expand their offerings to include traditional voice and other communications services (especially local access services); the transmission of unaffiliated programmers' offerings presented to viewers with limited mediation (public, educational and governmental, and leased-access channels); and the "carriage" of programming selected and presented as part of the system operator's retail offering. Title II currently addresses the first type of service, as the Telecommunications Act of 1996 confirms. It could address the second readily (and with far more success than the current leased-access provisions of the Cable Act), and could be modified to accommodate carriage of the third type. As discussed above, a limited version of Title II regulation would better address the current and developing forms of even traditional transmission services if the regulatory tools developed for Title II services were applied beyond the strict common-carrier context.

In addition, several more limited regulatory measures could usefully constrict or confine the relative scope of cable television regulation as the different technologies and markets shift. The first is to limit carefully the scope of services that trigger cable television regulation. That regulation applies to persons who become "cable operators" by providing "cable service," which comprises "one-way transmission to subscribers" of "video programming" and "other programming service."[54] A reviewing court has upheld the FCC's conclusions that entities (such as local telephone companies) that do not select programming are not "transmitting" such programming and that providers of video programming employing common-carrier facilities do not fall within the definition of cable operators.[55] If this interpretation is adhered to and expanded, it could provide the basis for excluding from cable regulation (and encompassing within common-carrier regulation) nearly all services provided even by cable system operators when they integrate their systems into the telecommunications network. The FCC had also noted that cable service excludes two-way services and has defined "video programming" as the equivalent of television broadcast programming offered in 1984, which had the effect of eliminating from cable service many advanced and interactive video services. The Telecommunications Act of 1996, however, sought to expand the scope of cable regulation to include certain of a cable system operator's "interactive services such as game channels and information services . . . as well as enhanced services."[56] This expansion of cable system regulation encompasses the very services that telephone and other companies will offer under separate regulatory regimes and those that may be most important to the advanced networks. The expansion thus also frustrates the integration of cable and switched telecommunications networks and exacerbates the difficulties created by segmented regulation of an increasingly integrated information industry.

A second measure that would align cable television regulation more closely with emerging information services concerns rate regulation. The 1992 Cable Act and subsequent implementing regulations imposed extensive rate restrictions that employed only limited incentive regulation; required rate levels appeared somewhat arbitrary because the FCC imposed an initial level, only to substitute more stringent standards after politicians claimed that the initial regulations insufficiently lowered rates. The irony of this rate regulation is that it responds to cable operators' market power precisely when the basis for competition in the delivery of video services is becoming apparent. The danger is the common one—and pervasive for the information industries—that regulation will outlive its initial justification, and that revisions to regulation will be blocked by regulatory inertia, political resistance to potentially destabilizing change, and established interests benefited by regulation. The 1992 Cable Act contains measures designed to reduce this threat: the FCC is to undertake annual assessments of competition in the delivery of video programming, and cable systems can escape rate regulation when they show that they are subject to "effective competition."[57] The Telecommunications Act of 1996 reduces the scope of rate regulation and ends rate regulation of certain programming services after March 31, 1999.[58] Even so, and especially as local telephone companies prepare to deliver video programming, continued regulation of basic cable rates poses additional dangers to competition. Such regulation might not only distort cable television pricing and potentially inhibit new cable offerings, but might also make competitive entry by other providers *more* difficult, because artificially lowered rates for basic cable services also constrain the pricing and thus profitability for potential substitute services or alternative delivery systems.

Another method of limiting cable television regulation and accelerating the process of merging cable television systems into the switched telecommunications network and telecommunications regulatory regime is to reduce the role of local franchising authorities. Municipal authorities retain broad control over the franchising of cable systems, the fees imposed on them, and the rates and terms of their service offerings. That role has steadily been reduced—for example, by somewhat narrowing local authorities' control over cable programming (in 1984) and restricting local authorities' ability to grant exclusive cable franchises (in 1992)[59]—and the Telecommunications Act of 1996 limits local authorities' power over cable systems' telephony and noncable service offerings.[60] The political calculation that has generated these local powers is clear: the franchising arrangement provides local governments with large fees, additional powers, the ability to require community access programming that often benefits incumbent officials, and on occasion, personal financial benefits. The justification for those local powers is far less clear. Local franchising and related regulations impose a web of regulatory entry barriers and costs that lack any coherent rationale.[61] Local regulation is predicated on and perpetuates the existence of distinct delivery systems confined to the local community, but market and technological developments increasingly allow those systems to be linked together and linked to the broader telecommunications network. For the reasons discussed above, there are reasons to desire this integration, as well as the entry of telephone competition into services equivalent to cable service. In addition, overlapping local and federal regulation imposes costs and inefficiencies that mirror those imposed by duplicative telecommunications regulation, as discussed above. Finally, certain local powers, such as creation of entry barriers and programming restrictions, are likely to run afoul of the First Amendment.[62]

However Title II and Title VI are eventually reconciled, regulation can provide greater incentives for network development and for competition between cable television companies and local telephone companies—in both industries' current core businesses and in advanced video services.[63] For video programming delivery, increased competition lies in local telephone companies' incentives to build delivery systems that overlap with existing cable television systems. Efficient structuring of the open video system regime may be a principal source of entry, and certain exemptions from regulatory requirements in initial stages of service might also provide incentives for entry (but would have to be balanced against potential, longer-term, anticompetitive effects). Similar incentives could be applied to encourage and enable cable television system operators to develop local telephony capabilities. Those incentives could include relief from rate regulation or from regulation by local governmental authorities, or cable operators could be required to incorporate those telecommunications capacities before providing any services other than traditional cable service. Reducing the costs, uncertainties, and lost efficiencies of the broadest Title II regulation for network operators would also increase those incentives, for both cable and traditional network operators. As with other facilities operators, these incentives to develop services and facilities include recognition of efficiencies (and risk), flexible pricing, clearly defined and focused domains of regulation, increased regulatory certainty, a high threshold for regulatory intervention, differential treatment of established and developing networks, and reliance on market mechanisms.

It is far from clear what incentives, if any, would successfully prompt cable systems eventually to open their systems through switching and interconnection with the telecommunications network for video programming. On the one hand, incorporating switched and two-way capability would have the (intended) effect of reducing the importance of the limited channel capacity that is a principal source of their market power and establishes their retail relationship with consumers—because system operators largely select the programming presented to consumers. On the other hand, cable systems are poised to provide lucrative telecommunications services as local telephone markets become subject to increasing competition, and cable systems will eventually be faced with competition in their core business from local telephone and satellite companies. The desirable outcome for consumers—separate provision of telephony, video programming, and advanced information services by both cable systems and local telephone carriers—would create competition in two enormous current markets served principally by monopolists, as well as in an emerging interactive market of potentially enormous significance.

Restrictions on Telephone Company Delivery of Video Programming

For telephone companies' provision of video programming, technological, market, and now regulatory changes have focused attention on the particular form of delivery rather than on whether delivery is to be permitted. Although Congress has in the Telecommunications Act of 1996 established that telephone company provision of video services is to be encouraged, it has established only the crudest outline of the regulatory regimes that are to govern those services. Nearly all the important regulatory issues are left to be resolved in subsequent FCC proceedings.

The immediately preceding sections address the principal regulatory issue for these services: whether the telephone companies' provision of video programming should be regulated under Title II, Title VI, or some hybrid. Put to this choice, Congress did not choose—or, rather, it chose all the options.[64] If local telephone companies used wireless facilities to distribute video programming, they would be bound by the evolving FCC regulations governing each particular wireless distribution system. If they operated as common carriers, they would be bound by common-carrier regulations to be developed by the FCC. (Congress at the same time eliminated the video dialtone regulations, which attempted to apply common-carrier concepts to video services.) If telephone companies operated relatively closed cable systems, Title VI would apply. If they wished to have some of the benefits of cable systems without some of the associated regulatory burdens, they could operate "open video systems." Here, too, the relevant regulatory regime was to be defined almost entirely by FCC regulations implementing only the broadest statutory commands.[65]

As the FCC creates and elaborates these new common-carrier and "open video system" regulations, it has the opportunity to return to first principles. It could dispense with many of the regulatory detours and accretions of the past decades and instead rely directly on antitrust principles in constructing and implementing the new regimes. As described above, these principles already provide the means to balance the access to be afforded to certain classes of facilities in order to increase consumer welfare and the protections to be afforded to network operators to encourage network investment and preserve efficiencies of scale and scope. And those rules could even serve as the eventual basis for regulating cable system operators as well, thus encouraging the integration of those facilities into the broader telecommunications network, opening those networks for use by additional service providers, and eliminating one of the principal sources of differential regulation of directly competing services.

Whatever general model the FCC adopts, it will have to address various subsidiary issues in constructing and construing the common-carrier and "open video system" rules for telephone companies' provision of video services. Certain issues turn on the competitive costs and benefits of particular forms of entry. Enormous competitive benefits potentially accompany entry through construction of facilities that overlap with existing cable television systems. This type of entry would bring consumers a far greater choice of programming and other video services, reduce prices (both to consumers and to upstream service providers) by reducing cable systems' market power, and increase the incentives for cable system operators to improve their services and facilities—both for their core services and to enter the local telephony market. Local telephone companies might also benefit significantly by acquiring cable television systems that serve areas beyond the telephone carrier's local service area. The telephone company's financial backing and telecommunications expertise make it more likely that the cable system would be upgraded to improve traditional services and to increase local telephony competition between telephone companies, based on use of cable system facilities. In contrast, the form of entry that poses the greatest competitive threat is a local telephone company's acquisition of a cable television system within its service area, at least where a geographic area is capable of supporting dual systems.[66] Not only would the cable system's market power be preserved for video services, but the telephone company would eliminate a principal potential competitor for local telephony in that geographic area.

Other subsidiary issues concern the relation between a telephone company's provision of video services and its provision of local telephone services. Cable system operators in particular have used these issues to resist telephone companies' construction and operation of competing video systems. Even so, the underlying regulatory problem and potential response are hardly new: problems of cross-subsidy and anticompetitive potential presented by joint provision of carriage and other information services have been at the forefront of regulators' concerns at least since computer services could be offered profitably and widely over the telephone network, and extensive regulations have developed that seek to shield competitive markets from abuses of market power over local telephone service.[67]

Despite this history, it is often contended that local telephone companies have a special interest in the relation between video services and local telephony because cable systems are potential telephony competitors. Defense of core telephony revenue is doubtless essential to the business cases underlying video services, but that incentive and response is not, in itself, anticompetitive. A danger exists of cross-subsidy from heavily price-regulated telephony services to video dialtone, but the characterization of the danger is important. That danger is *not* that telephone customers will support development of video facilities; they surely will, because telephone companies will entirely properly secure profits from their local telephone services that they will use to fund entry into video and other new services. The anticompetitive danger arises instead, where telephone prices are heavily regulated, from insufficient checks on local telephony pricing or the possibility that expenses of constructing video facilities and providing video services will be misallocated to local telephony costs (which through affecting regulators' actions may directly or indirectly increase telephone rates). The first of these dangers points to potential flaws in the elaborate price regulations and is independent of difficulties presented by video services (for all services, telephone companies have a general incentive to increase profits). The second danger presents complex difficulties, but the concern about misallocated costs resulting in cross-subsidy is long-standing, applies to accounting for various services, and has generated an elaborate regulatory and accounting regime in response.[68]

More generally, skepticism may be warranted regarding the need to regulate to meet this danger. The threat to competition usually raised is predatory pricing—that is, that telephone companies will provide consumers and upstream customers with prices that are too low, in order to secure a long-term monopoly. Intervention that will at least in the short term increase prices requires a particularly strong justification. This is particularly so for a dynamic market marked by technological change and many potential entrants, where little assurance exists that a long-term monopoly position could be secured or maintained. The developments surveyed in chapter 3 suggest that the video distribution market, and to a lesser extent core telephony markets, may be or may soon become particularly dynamic in this sense.

The persistence of telephone companies' market power over local telephony services could be relevant in other respects. Opponents of telephone companies' provision of video services have likened the telephone companies' threat to that posed to the long-distance market or equipment manufacturing. The concern raised by local telephone company entry into those latter markets, which depend directly on access to local telephone facilities, is that those relatively competitive markets would provide local carriers with the ability and incentive to act anticompetitively by manipulating their local facilities (through rates, configuration, and interconnection).[69] Here, in contrast, local telephone carriers would be constructing an additional, separate delivery system that would compete with an incumbent cable television system. They would be providing an additional outlet or means of delivering programming. Cable television system operators, which seek to prevent the entry at issue, possess their own delivery facilities and do not depend on local telephone facilities to delivery video programming.

Some, however, would use the telephone companies' desire to enter video markets as an additional incentive to create local telephony competition. Although increasing local competition is a laudable goal, the relation between the goal and the requirement is not entirely clear because cable operators' services and telephone operators' provision of video programming are not yet directly linked through common networks. However, the networks may well be interrelated in a relevant sense for provision of telephony services. That is, local telephone companies' provision of video services before the development of local telephony competition would considerably increase video competition, as long as the absence of local telephony competition did not unduly restrict cable operators' ability to provide a full range of services (in part through entering the local telephone service market). In the absence of that showing, which may yet be made, comparable incentives created through other means would achieve the same general goal without impeding competition in video services.

Regulation of the Former Bell System Entities

The consent decree that governed certain activities of AT&T and the regional Bell companies, and the administrative regime that supersedes it, raise many of the issues touched on above regarding the proper regulatory strategy for redressing anticompetitive activities in the communications industries. As noted above, an aggressive strategy for deregulating the information industries would repeal nearly all regulations crafted especially for those industries and instead leave regulation of anticompetitive activities to the operation of generally applicable antitrust laws. The MFJ is the result of precisely that process, and it raises the issue of the relative competence of administrators and the judiciary to redress competitive problems posed by the new information industry. Because the FCC is now implementing restrictions drawn from the MFJ, the new administrative regime tests the general strategic choice between enforcement by the judiciary and enforcement by administrators. That test will have broader implications, too, because issues surrounding the MFJ's restrictions and administration will likely reemerge in the course of additional private antitrust actions.

In certain respects, the MFJ illustrated many of the strengths of narrowly targeted regulation identified above. The MFJ's restrictions responded directly to a carefully identified and persistent competitive threat. Rules governed industry conduct, and they were relatively few and clear. They both reflected and were administered on the basis of generally applicable, widely understood antitrust principles—although intervention by an appellate court was required to reduce initial reliance on relatively open-ended "public interest" principles.[70] The opportunities for powerful interests to benefit directly from political advantages were limited, especially through efforts to influence the judicial process itself. The MFJ contained different internal mechanisms that permitted adjustments to, and even elimination of, the restrictions once the burdened carriers made a traditional antitrust showing—generally that the proposed relief posed no substantial possibility of anticompetitive harm.[71] Indeed, all the parties to the decree sought and secured alterations in its operation.[72]

Correspondingly, many of the difficulties in the MFJ's administration reflected weaknesses in regulating competition in these industries through the judicial process. The predilections of a very few generalist jurists, and particularly of a single federal district judge (Judge Harold Greene), shaped the decree's administration and thus the development of the telecommunications industry. The parties had to absorb the costs of extensive litigation, and delay was an inevitable aspect of a decree addressing vast enterprises and administered by a single judge (even with the Department of Justice serving a screening function for requests to waive or modify the decree). The possibilities of delayed or premature relief increased as the affected or potentially affected parties used the judicial process, including the waiver proceedings, for competitive ends. As with most judicial decrees, the MFJ achieved its relative clarity and simplicity through broad rules and did not regulate through detailed or quickly evolving requirements crafted to particular industry conditions or practices. At the same time, the decree's waiver provisions were administered in a manner that allowed ongoing alterations of and attacks on the decree's restrictions—which increased responsiveness at some cost to certainty.

The efficacy of administrative action is likely to be vigorously tested as the FCC administers the restrictions. Not only does administration shift to the FCC, but the general antitrust standard governing entry into currently prohibited markets has been replaced with more specific determinations[73]—changes that could increase certainty and administrative burden but that also might, depending on the sophistication of the provisions' implementation, come at some expense to the underlying objective of advancing competition. At the same time, certain administrative powers are not particularly tightly constrained and introduce a "public interest" determination.[74] As addressed above, this result holds out the possibility of increasing uncertainty, opening the administrative process to political pressures or inertia, and increasing the potential for arbitrary agency action—where regulation would be forgone or perpetuated for reasons other than application of an accepted or defined competitive standard.

Three issues will be particularly important in assessing the efficacy of the new administrative regime. The first is how and whether the FCC's administration of the continued restrictions reflects an underlying competitive theory and purpose. The MFJ rested on established antitrust principles. The new regime implements similar restrictions, designed for identical threats to competition presented by the local exchange carriers, but does not expressly direct the FCC to rely on antitrust standards.[75] Even so, determinations regarding the regional companies' entry into new markets will continue to depend on more far-ranging analysis of local competition. On the one hand, nontraditional competitors—for example, cable system operators and PCS providers—will likely increasingly enter core telephony services and reduce the regional companies' market power in local telephony. When that occurs, continued restrictions cannot be justified by the decree's original theory or other antitrust analysis, and judging when market power has been reduced sufficiently will require increasingly sophisticated determinations. On the other hand, the growing potential for competition in this vital market, and the incentive for regional companies to protect their core revenues, would make relief before the establishment of local competition particularly unfortunate.

This balance must be struck whether the determination at issue is the antitrust standard that evaluates competitive effects, more specific standards regarding whether the conditions for local competition have been satisfied, or more open public interest standards.

Second, the new regime's success will depend in part on the efficiency of administrative action. For determinations regarding whether relief is appropriate from statutory restrictions on the local carriers' activities, the Telecommunications Act of 1996 constructs an elaborate Rube Goldberg mechanism involving negotiations between service providers, state commission oversight, FCC proceedings, consultation with the Department of Justice and other administrators, and judicial review.[76] Wholly apart from whether the output of this process increases competitive benefits, the uncertainties and delay incurred in reaching any determination may prove significant.

Finally, the new regime clearly tests the extent to which the administrative process is subject to political capture. In one sense, the entire mechanism reflects the predominance of political power, to the extent that the local exchange carriers pressed for and achieved legislative relief once they became dissatisfied with the results of the judicial process. More narrowly, the implementation of the new statutory provisions may also come to reflect a balance of political interests. Already, the act reflects special solicitude for the powerful newspaper and print interests that were virtually irrelevant to the administration of the consent decree.[77] The state commissions also have a potentially expanded role.[78] The statutory standards to be administered and their underlying purposes (other than those embodied in antitrust principles) are not particularly clear, and there are opportunities for ongoing influence by members of Congress. Implementation of the new provisions will test its ability to separate political considerations from accepted administrative bases of agency action.

Regulation of Broadcasting

Of the different regulatory regimes, regulation of radio and television broadcasting rests on assumptions that are most at odds with the emerging information industry. Broadcasting regulation has been designed as though it controlled a comprehensive and unique system of delivering video programming, with licenses allocated and competition limited as part of a broad government effort to ensure that this unique service would operate in the public interest. Now, for most households with television and for a rapidly increasing percentage of them, over-the-air broadcasting is one of many sources of video programming. Those competing sources will soon multiply. The FCC has increasingly concluded that far from posing a threat to other markets, or controlling programming distribution to consumers, broadcasters now are vulnerable to the actions and competition of other industries. In addition, the government now treats most new classes of licenses as factors of production for which it collects a fee and parts with most attributes of control; television broadcast licenses, in contrast, were practically given away subject to continued government oversight. As becomes more apparent each year, no clear purpose or rationale guides that oversight or defines the content of the "public interest" element of it. These changes raise the question, what role, if any, remains for traditional regulation of broadcasting?

As noted above, there is likely a continuing need for government to serve as a coordinator among entities that seek to transmit signals through the electromagnetic spectrum. Even so, a variety of mechanisms exist to discharge this role, short of the traditional focus on allocating licenses according to the fitness of applicants to provide a unique broadcasting service. At least since Coase's writings in the late 1950s, it has been noted that government could conceivably discharge this role simply by creating a clear set of property rights.[79] A minimal government role would include delineating property-like rights defined by electromagnetic frequency, geographic scope, and time. These rights could be registered and allocated much as rights in land are registered, with coordination of services and difficulties of interference between spectrum users settled through contracting and tort claims. A slightly more extensive coordinating function would use not the model of a common-law land registry, but that of a zoning commission. In this model, the government would respond to the transaction costs of bargaining and litigation by designating portions of the spectrum for noninterfering uses. Thus certain portions of the spectrum would be set aside for satellite broadcasting, television services, wireless telephony, and so on. Under either system, the government would be paid for rights in the spectrum and would have little role in controlling what messages were transmitted or who may provide services.[80] And in fact the FCC's policies for new classes of licenses have largely fit this latter, zoning-commission model. The commission "zones" a portion of spectrum for a particular service, auctions it, and leaves development and use of the resulting communications system almost entirely to private parties.

The existence of so many sources of video programming especially challenges government efforts to manage the scope and content of public debate. As noted, many of the FCC's structural regulations seek to increase the "diversity" of broadcast information, and other regulation more directly shapes broadcasters' choice of programming. As discussed in greater detail in chapter 5, there is considerable basis to believe that the FCC's regulation of content has been largely ineffective or counterproductive and that—in light of recent changes in technologies, markets, and legal doctrines—nearly all such regulation designed to alter the balance or content of messages conveyed violates the First Amendment.

Even if government regulation designed to shape broadcast content were both effective and constitutional, the emergence of substantial competition in video programming delivery further undermines the basis for regulating broadcasters' practices to ensure either diversity or high quality of programming.[81] Broadcast programming was perhaps once a uniquely important source of information, arguably to an extent that justified government oversight of its content, but over-the-air delivery of broadcast programming is now a decreasingly important source among many for even electronically delivered information. This is so even if the domain of relevant information could logically be limited to video rather than also including printed information and personal communications. When a viewer can choose among varied types of video and text information that appear on a television or personal computer screen—which may have been delivered by cable, over-the-air broadcast, telephone line, or satellite—the case for shaping the information originating from over-the-air stations becomes considerably weaker. That particular subset of messages—and especially the much smaller subset broadcast by any single station—is becoming considerably less important as a source of information to citizens. Advocates of regulation have tremendous difficulty pointing to any specific deficiency in the information available to consumers that justifies intervention (even if there were a generally accepted standard to allow that judgment) or to any specific function uniquely served by broadcasting that justifies government oversight of its messages in particular.[82]

This disappearing rationale for content regulation of broadcasting is part of a more general unraveling of the "compact" or bargain that was initially invoked to justify most regulation of the broadcasting industry: as part of entrusting electronic mass media communications to a small number of broadcast licensees (and providing them with a tremendous financial windfall), the government would both protect that broadcasting system as a crucial means of informing the public and regulate it closely to ensure that it operated in accord with the "public interest." Most elements of broadcast regulation were and continue to be justified as necessary to create the principal system for delivering video programming and for shaping the content of that programming. Policies based on "spectrum scarcity," encouragement of investment in programming and delivery facilities, and the need for diverse programming simply reflect the fact that broadcast regulation once shaped the nearly exclusive source of electronic delivery of video products and the products they delivered. Distribution of free spectrum licenses, severe limitations on the number of licenses in particular geographic areas, and limitations on ownership of multiple licenses constituted a relatively primitive infrastructure development program. Certain carriage obligations, the licensee's "public interest" obligations, network exclusivity and retransmission rules, syndication regulations, and "fairness doctrine" and political broadcasting regulations all sought to alter the nature or quality of the service provided over this government-supported communications system.

As described at length in chapter 3, broadcasters are no longer a comprehensive or unique source of electronically delivered information. Over-the-air broadcasting has decreased tremendously in importance as both a delivery system and a source of programming. Whatever the relevance of the financial windfall secured by the original broadcast licensees (and any corresponding regulatory obligations that rested on it), that windfall does not exist in the usual case where a third party has directly or indirectly purchased the license. And no pretense is made for new classes of licenses that some special duties inherently or necessarily attach to the function of using the spectrum. Now, a nearly comprehensive, multilayered infrastructure for delivering video programming exists and is growing rapidly—apart from that supported by licenses and related government subsidies. Particular licensees in any event neither produce nor control most information available through those delivery systems.

Recognition of the end of the public interest bargain would have three broad implications for broadcast regulation. One is that the continuing process of deregulating broadcasting would accelerate. As noted, content regulation in particular lacks any competitive or other justification. Similarly, the measures designed to manage competition within the broadcasting industry, to protect other industries from broadcasters' influence over programming, and to diffuse concentration of license ownership would require further reexamination. Under traditional antitrust principles, few restrictions would likely remain, and the "diversity" rationale of limiting competition to ensure an optimal number of broadcast licensees in an area would meet increasing resistance—especially as applied to geographic areas where broadcasters face effective competition. This deregulatory process is already under way.

A second implication concerns license policies. As noted, treatment of new classes of licenses has shifted almost altogether toward treating licenses as a factor of production that the government auctions to the highest bidder—for reasons of equity, allocative efficiency, and government finances. Like concerns and reasoning may apply as well to *existing* uses of the broadcast spectrum. Debates surrounding the spectrum licensing provisions of the Telecommunications Act of 1996 were the first in what will likely be a series of prominent conflicts over this issue.[83] The value of the electronic spectrum, especially for video delivery, is enormous.[84] The logic of the auction process and the management of the spectrum as a public resource subject to market principles is not inherently limited to new uses or licenses; the nature of a license is, after all, that ultimate ownership inheres in the licensor and reverts to it on the expiration of the license term. It is entirely plausible that current allocation presents the most efficient use of that spectrum, especially given enormous reliance interests and the potential for alteration of existing licensing to disrupt a valuable industry. The purchase price for broadcast licenses, too, reflects how current licensees are generally not the beneficiaries of the financial windfalls resulting from the original license allocation, and purchasers have in important respects paid dearly for a continuing property interest. These arguments, in addition to broadcasters' political clout, could lead instead to a solidification of license ownership, as the Telecommunications Act of 1996 began to accomplish (thus in effect treating the license more as a property interest fully vested in current licensees).[85] Separate and more difficult issues surround the current allocation of public television licenses, where private investment and market pressures for efficient use of the spectrum resource are much reduced.

A third implication of the unraveling of the "public interest" bargain is that regulation can increasingly integrate broadcast services with related networks and services. If broadcasting is viewed as part of a network providing various information services rather than as an isolated system for delivering a unique service, then broadcasters' functions can change. This change has for some time been reflected in measures that address retransmission of broadcast signals but will also increasingly affect the scope of services that broadcasters can provide. Broadcasters will seek to use their facilities and spectrum rights to provide emerging video services as well as services that would traditionally be classified as carriage or communications, and the traditional broadcasting regulatory regime is particularly at odds with the new information industry to the extent that it frustrates this integration.

These issues that arise within each regulatory regime point to and might be addressed through a more general regulatory strategy, as outlined in previous sections: a narrowly focused and clearly delimited administrative regime addressed to network coordination issues and implementation of rules clearly required by general competition law principles. Antitrust law enforcement, preferably itself foreshadowed through clear guidelines fashioned to reflect the great degree of commercial uncertainity, could buttress this relatively minimalist regime. This approach could consistently regulate what are now overlapping networks and services provided by various industry segments, reduce divergence between regulation applied to the information industry and the general competition law applicable to other industries, and use the general competition principles peculiarly apt for circumstances of commercial uncertainty, enormous investment, and continuing technological innovation. It would free an increasingly integrated and competitive industry from the patchwork of conflicting and highly intrusive regulatory regimes that are based on conflicting competitive and technological premises, operated without clear regard for consumer welfare, and still haunted by the political fears and imagined commercial dangers of other eras.

CHAPTER FIVE

Extending First Amendment Protections

JUST AS RECENT changes in communications technologies, services, and market structure justify broad challenges to the continued operation of traditional regulatory regimes, so do they require a wide-ranging reconsideration of the First Amendment's application to electronic communications. Electronic communications and their delivery have traditionally rested at the periphery of First Amendment doctrines and have received inconsistent and often quite reduced protection from government intervention. Now, of course, those communications are hardly peripheral to the public discourse the First Amendment is designed to protect. Nor are the commercial activities of the highly regulated information distribution businesses. The changes since the late 1980s that are producing the new information industry, along with the principles underlying the First Amendment itself, provide the basis for extending to the less traditional but crucially important forms of electronic communication the traditional protections afforded to speech.

First Amendment protections for the selection and transmission of electronically delivered information have developed in a manner similar to that of regulatory regimes governing communications. Like the regulatory schemes described in chapter 2, First Amendment doctrine and protection have varied in accord with rough divisions among information technologies. Both those regulatory regimes and First Amendment doctrine continue to reflect the postwar technologies that deliver information in three principal forms: (1) through wireless, point-to-multipoint voice and video broadcasting, which constituted most electronically delivered mass information products; (2) through wire-based communications systems, operated principally by common carriers, designed to transmit others' point-to-point communications; and (3) through "packaged," or nonelectronically delivered, information products (including print), which until this century constituted most of the sources of information available to individuals.

As with divisions among regulatory regimes, different First Amendment doctrines, offering different degrees of protection, developed for each of these three forms of delivered information. Broadcasting regulation governed this first form of information, wireless broadcast transmission. Correspondingly, the Supreme Court developed a First Amendment jurisprudence that applied particularly to the wireless mass media and that recognized broadcasters' exercise of editorial control and personal expression yet afforded less than the traditional level of First Amendment protection.[1] The elaborate and open-ended common-carrier regulations governed the second form of communication, wire-based telecommunications, which generally received the least degree of First Amendment protection. This type of carriage service presented few litigated First Amendment issues, in large part because telecommunications carriers themselves provided few widely distributed information products (apart from directory services). The greatest degree of First Amendment protection and least burdensome regulatory requirements applied to the third form of communication, packaged information products, especially in print form.[2] As a general matter, the lack of the print media's control or use of electronic facilities, the long tradition of relatively limited regulation of print products, and the First Amendment protections that applied to them precluded application of more extensive regulations.

As described in previous chapters, this division of information technologies is now collapsing. The emerging information network has undermined the technological, social, and legal bases for the traditional tripartite division of First Amendment doctrine, just as it has for the varying and distinct regulatory regimes. Mass distribution of voice and particularly video information products is hardly confined to licensed broadcasting stations and will soon be even less so. Wireline and other information delivery systems are performing varied and overlapping functions, including providing information that the First Amendment protects. Information products themselves are increasingly delivered in any number of forms: a "packaged" product, print or otherwise, might often be provided in electronic form or over an electronic network, and networks can replicate many of the functions once peculiar to packaged products and other forms of nonelectronic communication.

These technological and market changes pose two crucial and related First Amendment issues. First, what type of First Amendment protection will be extended to the entities that assemble and deliver information electronically? Traditionally, broadcasters receive lesser First Amendment protection than producers of print products, and that lesser protection is generally traced to how broadcasters distribute their products. Carriers often receive even less protection. Other electronic distributors could be treated similarly to broadcasters or be subject to separate, newly developed First Amendment standards. Second, how can the First Amendment be reconciled with common-carrier, antitrust, and other competitive regulations, when applied to entities that produce and distribute information products? Various pricing, entry, and term-of-service requirements apply to carriers and other entities that are now producing, assembling, and disseminating information products. For print, the First Amendment protects those information products and the editorial choices often associated with their formulation and dissemination, and dramatically limits the regulations that apply to them. Long-standing regulations and the First Amendment are now potentially colliding.

Principles underlying traditional First Amendment doctrines provide the beginning to answers to both of these questions. Those principles establish, above all, that the government may not seek to alter the content of messages conveyed in private parties' communications. An exception to this command has existed for broadcasting, but recent technological and market developments have confirmed that no basis remains for allowing content-based regulation of broadcasters or any other entity that distributes information electronically. Traditional First Amendment principles also allow the government considerable latitude in designing regulations that are unrelated to the content of messages conveyed, even when those regulations incidentally affect speech. This principle extends to rules directed against particular sectors of the information industries and provides the basis for reconciling the First Amendment and regulations designed to affect competition.

Extending First Amendment Protections to All Electronic Media

The First Amendment prevents the government from seeking to regulate the content of communications, at least for print and other nonelectronically delivered media. An exception to this rule has existed for broadcast communications, and some would apply that exception to other electronic delivery systems. This distinction has long been attacked but has persisted because there existed a widespread social understanding that broadcast stations perform a unique role in distributing a powerful form of information; that government's licensing of those stations reflects a vesting of fiduciary duties that accompanies the temporary relinquishment of control over government resources; and that broadcasters serve a unique role in assembling and distributing information. Whatever their original validity, these ideas cannot survive the recent and continuing transformation of the delivery and production of information. Their collapse will eliminate the ideological and practical bases for differentiating between print and electronic media for purposes of the First Amendment. Instead, recent developments underscore how adherence to First Amendment principles should bar the government from seeking to regulate the content of communications, however delivered.

The Libertarian Model and the Broadcasting Exception

The basic elements of traditional First Amendment doctrine are well established and may be understood as representing a "libertarian" model of restraint on government action that affects speech. In this model, only in exceptional circumstances may the government undertake measures designed to affect the messages communicated in public debate when doing so limits a person's expressive activities, even those conducted through the corporate form.

Each element of this summary statement is important. First, even though an elaborate set of judicial decisions sets forth the boundaries of what types of expressions the First Amendment protects, the information, political expression, and artistry communicated through the print and video media and developing information products rest at the core of protected expression.[3] In addition, even the editorial arrangement and presentation of others' information products receive extensive First Amendment protection.[4] This is so for traditional print media, broadcast programming, cable programming, and the various interactive products that are only now being offered. This First Amendment interest does not disappear simply because information is communicated via electronic media,[5] and, as protections afforded newspapers demonstrate, it does not evaporate when individuals own the means of producing information through a corporation.[6]

Second, First Amendment doctrine distinguishes between government measures that seek to manipulate or balance the messages communicated and measures that clearly are designed for other, non-content-related purposes but that incidentally affect private parties' communications.[7] "Content-based regulations are presumptively invalid."[8] If government action of this type limits a private party's communications, it is subject to the most stringent judicial review and is rarely upheld: the government must show that its interest is "compelling" and that it has chosen "the least restrictive means to further the articulated interest."[9] In contrast, government action that is not content-based is subject to a lesser standard that allows a range of regulations, even if they incidentally restrict speech.[10] For example, time, place, and manner laws that govern parades or noise are upheld if they meet limited safeguards and do not unduly limit speech opportunities.[11]

Third, the government may assert only limited justifications, reflecting "a state interest of the highest order," for measures that burden some persons' speech and that are designed to alter the messages that others receive.[12] The government cannot seek to restrict speech on the basis of its disagreement with or disapproval of the message communicated, and it may seek to limit advocacy only when speech is "directed to inciting or producing imminent lawless action and is likely to incite or produce such action."[13] The government is also barred from limiting speech to affect the overall tone or balance of messages communicated. Thus the government cannot "dictat[e] the subjects about which persons may speak [or] the speakers who may address a public issue."[14] Similarly, "the concept that government may restrict the speech of some elements of society in order to enhance the relative voice of others is wholly foreign to the First Amendment."[15] That restriction may not occur directly or through requirements that seek to bolster a particular party's message by having others distribute it in lieu of their own.[16]

This model may be termed "libertarian" on the basis of related assumptions that support its underlying distinction between private and public action: leaving the dissemination of ideas largely to market forces and the efforts of groups and individuals, the model assumes the general benefits of private communications and values self-expression as both an end and a means; and the model reflects a robust appreciation of the unintended consequences of coordinated government action as well as the potential for government failure and capture by established interests.[17] Private rather than public restrictions on speech are believed to leave sufficient latitude for self-expression, the maintenance and construction of community, and the distribution of information necessary for deliberation. For these reasons, "the First Amendment mandates that we presume that speakers, not the government, know best both what they want to say and how to say it."[18] The press, broadly viewed as the full array of industries engaged in producing information products, is believed capable of "informing and educating the public, offering criticism, and providing a forum for discussion and debate."[19] Correspondingly, government efforts designed to alter private speech activities contradict both the principle that personal expression is an end in itself and the pragmatic conclusion that efforts to shape the private "marketplace of ideas" will ultimately prove more harmful than beneficial.[20]

This set of principles underlies nearly all First Amendment determinations. It applies not only to the activities of traditional media but also to individuals' artistic and expressive activities and to a vast array of political activity. Certain exceptional treatment applies according to subject matter (for example, for speech deemed obscene or libelous) and context (for example, for government employment).[21] As noted above, the model allows for the government to pursue a range of carefully limited measures that are not designed to affect speech and not justified on that basis, and to limit speech to respond to certain exigencies.[22]

For purposes of the transformation of information delivery and the emergence of a new information industry, one departure from the libertarian model has general significance: the lesser protection afforded to government-licensed television and radio broadcasters. In contrast to the fundamental prohibition on content-based regulation of other speakers, courts have permitted the government to undertake a variety of measures designed to shape the content of programming presented by broadcasters. Current doctrine often permits the government to restrict broadcasters' choice of programming or to impose requirements designed to improve broadcasters' information products—with standards of quality determined and applied by government officials.[23] Unlike in any other setting or for any other class of speaker, the government may justify restrictions on broadcasters' speech and expressive activities by asserting that it seeks to alter the messages and information presented.

The asserted basis for the regulations of content applied to broadcasting, which have been extended to other forms of electronic communication, originated in cases addressing the Fairness Doctrine. That doctrine, which had its heyday in the 1960s and 1970s but was abandoned by the FCC in 1987 as counterproductive and inconsistent with the First Amendment, imposed two general requirements on broadcasters: their coverage had to address controversial issues of public importance, and they had to "fairly" present or allow presentation of different sides of those issues.[24] Aspects of the doctrine required broadcasters to give persons attacked in their programming or who were subject to adverse political editorializing by the station the opportunity to respond.[25] Both the general and specific rules focused on the content of the broadcaster's programming and imposed sanctions if that content was found to be unbalanced or otherwise unfair.

In *Red Lion Broadcasting Co. v. FCC*, the Supreme Court upheld and set forth the rationale for this unique government power. The case involved a challenge to agency rules embodying the personal attack and political editorializing response requirements, as well as to an application of the personal attack doctrine in favor of an author who sought to reply to unfavorable remarks about his book.[26] The Court's reasoning proceeded in three steps. First, the Court concluded that the electromagnetic spectrum is a uniquely limited or scarce resource, which in turn creates a unique medium of communication.[27] Second, the potential for signal interference between competing broadcasters establishes a legitimate government role in defining noninterfering broadcast areas and in allocating licenses to broadcast in those areas among particular speakers.[28] Third, licensees have no greater speech interests than those denied or otherwise without licenses, and thus, "Because of the scarcity of radio frequencies, the Government is permitted to put restraints on licenses in favor of others whose views should be expressed on this unique medium."[29] In particular, a political endorsement or "personal attack" simply "triggers . . . time sharing" with a nonlicensee.[30] In sum, "nothing in the First Amendment . . . prevents the Government from requiring a licensee to share his frequency with others and to conduct himself as a proxy or fiduciary with obligations to present those views and voices which are representative of his community and which would otherwise, by necessity, be barred from the airwaves."[31]

This "spectrum scarcity" rationale has attracted extensive criticism. Critics have repeatedly pointed out that, in economic terms, any scarcity associated with the electromagnetic spectrum is indistinguishable from the scarcity of other goods. As one court noted, "All economic goods are scarce, not least the newsprint, ink, delivery trucks, computers and other resources that go into the . . . dissemination of print journalism. . . . Since scarcity is a universal fact, it can hardly explain regulation in one context and not another."[32] Other commenters have also noted that the spectrum could be regulated in much the same way as any other property regime.[33]

Red Lion and subsequent decisions themselves noted that a different outcome might be required upon a showing that the Fairness Doctrine in fact stifled expression of controversial views or if technological and other developments eliminated spectrum scarcity.[34] The FCC in fact abolished the doctrine in 1987 on both these grounds, after concluding that broadcast journalists and programmers avoided controversy to avoid regulatory disputes and sanctions and that ample alternative means existed for the public to receive an array of competing views.[35]

Despite the FCC's abandonment of the Fairness Doctrine, which it or Congress could readily reverse, the authorization for government regulation of broadcast content for the moment remains good law, and content-based measures continue to underlie much of broadcast regulation. For example, broadcasters remain subject to various programming restrictions as well as other duties the FCC finds to serve "the public interest, convenience, and necessity."[36] They can at least theoretically have their exceptionally valuable licenses revoked if the government concludes that they have not complied with those duties. The FCC continues to oversee broadcasters' programming and to require reports about programming content.[37] Statutes or regulations govern children's programming and advertising,[38] sponsorship identification (especially for political matters),[39] lottery information,[40] and "indecent" and "offensive" programming.[41] Networks are limited in the sources and financial interests in their programming, and affiliated stations are required to secure certain prime-time programming from sources other than network programming (these restrictions are being phased out).[42] By statute and regulation, broadcasters must allow reasonable access by candidates to their stations, and broadcasters that allow "use" of their station by a political candidate—including advertising and some instances of coverage—must include programming provided by competing candidates (and must generally do so on favorable terms).[43] The government has allocated television and radio licenses through criteria designed to influence the ultimate broadcast message.[44] The government invokes this goal to justify policies that disbursed licenses on the basis of residence and activity in the local community, race, gender, and absence of other broadcasting interests (use of race as a criterion is suspended and being reconsidered).[45] In addition, FCC policies favoring localism in broadcast programming and diversity of programming through dispersion of ownership and control also reflect efforts to shape broadcast content.[46]

Without any extended justification, similar and occasionally more extensive content-based restrictions are being applied to electronic media and delivery systems that do not rely on wireless transmission or any associated spectrum licenses. As described in later sections, recent Supreme Court decisions (especially *Turner Broadcasting System* v. *FCC*) provide the basis to prevent the broadcasting exception from being extended to cable television and emerging electronic delivery systems, but lower courts have barely begun to develop the implications of these decisions.[47] Instead, access and lowest-rate regulations benefiting political candidates have been imported directly from broadcasting to cable television.[48] Statutory authorization for local government requirements that cable operators set aside channels for certain public, educational, and especially government uses appears to be designed to augment particular views and types of programming.[49] So too, arguably, do proposals to require video providers to extend special rates to favored classes of programmers.[50] Because the ''spectrum scarcity'' rationale does not apply to wire-based systems such as cable television systems and local telephone networks, or even to information delivered over switched ''wireless'' systems,[51] these and other content regulations applied generally to electronic media and emerging information services would require a dramatic extension of the broadcast exception to established First Amendment principles.

Even so, this extension is taking place precisely when the rationale for *any* different treatment of even over-the-air broadcast programming is disappearing. Changes in electronic delivery of information pose the issue whether any government content regulation is permissible in any delivery medium, including broadcasting—rather than how the broadcasting exception to First Amendment principles might be extended. Indeed, they justify extending the decisions that have declined to expand the scope of *Red Lion* and to create a uniform doctrine applicable to print and electronic forms of communication.

The Identity of Media: The Transformation of the Social Understanding and Treatment of Wireless Video Transmission

The departure from traditional First Amendment principles for broadcast media has reflected perceived peculiarities of wireless, and especially wireless video, transmission. As the arguments of Coase, Bork, and others have repeatedly pointed out, economic theory provides no support for the regulatory distinctions between wireless media and other information providers. Yet the distinction persists and may be traced to the unusual coincidence of the social perception or accepted understanding of three distinguishing characteristics of broadcast media. Even though "scarcity" may be a matter of degree rather than kind, ideological structures based on accepted social facts about power and information led to widespread acceptance of at least limited content regulation of broadcasting.[52]

First, wireless transmission has been perceived as a rare and unusually potent source of information and thus of power, particularly for video transmissions. This perception was well founded, even if government action itself contributed considerably to the rarity of broadcasting outlets and competing video distribution systems.[53] The ability to engage in immediate point-to-multipoint communications did confer power, and video images especially can shape public opinion. Initially, technology restricted alternative means of distributing video products that might supplement motion picture distribution, and regulations later limited those alternatives even as new technologies developed.[54] Second, the manifest and distinct government role in allocating this rare power led the licensing process to be viewed as a transfer or implementation of public trust. Prompted by the social costs of reducing signal interference, the government's allocative role also fostered this social understanding because the divestment of government control and ownership was only partial. Like many other New Deal undertakings, the broadcasting regime was designed to achieve public purposes through organizing and directing private activity. The government was perceived to be vesting power in particular corporations and individuals, and it issued licenses only on terms that ensured those individuals continued to exercise a form of government power.[55] The license transfer was thus understood as one of trusteeship or fiduciary duty, as well as direct control and power. The government was viewed in part as deputizing or venturing with the licensee. Third, and related to both, the public understanding of the broadcaster's role differed from that of other powerful speakers. An editorial role was acknowledged (and indeed protected),[56] but the broadcaster was viewed also as discharging peculiar duties associated with this unique public resource. The government had selected broadcasters as particularly suitable to exercise a powerful public role, whether manifested in broadcasting's functions in times of public emergency or for more general public-service and community-oriented programming duties. In part to avoid having the license perceived as an enormous windfall, broadcasters initially conformed to and indeed trumpeted their obligation to discharge a set of public-interest obligations.

These factors describe the impetus for but do not justify the differential treatment of broadcasting, but they point to many of the justifications that regulators and their defenders later developed. Thus ''spectrum scarcity'' serves as shorthand for the unique and limited opportunities to provide immediate, point-to-multipoint information products, especially video programming. *Red Lion*'s focus on the government's role in allocating licenses and on the broadcaster's ability to exclude others,[57] and resulting authorization ''to treat licensees given the *privilege* of using scarce radio frequencies as proxies for the entire community,''[58] relies on and captures all three elements: only a few outlets for a distinct type of expression exist; the government owns and has authorized temporary control over those outlets; and broadcasters, employing that government-provided resource, may be forced to fulfill the duties accompanying their unique and uniquely public role.

The most recent developments in telecommunications and information services undermine the factual bases that support this ideology that exempts broadcasting and other nontraditional media from traditional First Amendment principles. The conditions that led to a social understanding of the distinctness of broadcasting are eroding. New information services and delivery systems will shortly lead to a different understanding of mass market video products, one at odds with the justifications for differential regulation of broadcasting. Even regulatory practice, which reflects these social understandings, is becoming inconsistent with the old ideology. As described below, video programming is distributed from a variety of sources, whose number is increasing dramatically. The government's own allocation process has shifted from a vesting of the public trust to the provision of a factor of production. Providers of new information products (including broadcasters) increasingly perform the same functions as those served by distributors of products entitled to the greatest First Amendment protection. These developments also confirm the validity of the traditional, economic critiques of differential regulatory treatment of broadcasting. As a matter of economic theory or social understandings of inherent differences, no general distinction can be maintained between traditional print or packaged media and electronically delivered information. And without that distinction, no basis exists to resist uniform application of the First Amendment.

COMPETITION IN VIDEO DISTRIBUTION. As described earlier, substantial competition has developed in the distribution of video programming. Cable television systems, ''wireless'' cable systems, and satellite broadcasters all widely distribute information products that are substitutes for or equivalent to programming distributed through licensed broadcast stations, and that distribution is rapidly increasing. Indeed, those distribution systems not only provide their own programming but often also provide nearly the identical programming that local broadcast stations also distribute or initially distributed.[59] Soon, local telephone companies will likely join those distributors on a massive scale. Packaged information products, especially CD-ROMs and videocassettes, provide additional distribution outlets for video products. The Internet may provide close substitutes.

Two types of competition are particularly relevant to the collapse of the assumptions that support differential regulation of broadcasting. First, a multitude of entities other than broadcast licensees exercise editorial control over the distribution of video products. This type of control may arise from operation of a distribution outlet. These operators may control programming carried over local distribution systems (cable television systems, local telephone company broadband facilities, and alternative cable systems) or national distribution systems (such as satellite delivery systems). In addition, entities that bundle programming and provide it in a uniform format also exercise considerable editorial control over viewers' choices. For example, broadcast television network programmers and cable programming networks develop products that reflect their programming preferences.[60] This control is largely independent of their control, if any, of local or national distribution systems and is implemented through negotiations with those distributors.[61] In selling a single programming product to distributors (such as local television station affiliates or cable systems) they exercise a degree of control over what programming is distributed.[62] Eventually, ''control'' over available programming might largely disappear or be vested principally in consumers rather than producers. With switched or high-capacity systems, combined with two-way capabilities, certain suppliers may be able to control the supply of particularly popular offerings or libraries of offerings, but they will not be able to limit the range of offerings in the manner assumed by the broadcast regulatory model.

Second, competition and the decreasing ability of licensed broadcasters to control programming distribution are reflected in the capacity available for distribution. A television broadcaster controls a single video channel, but the local cable system likely makes available scores of channels, and satellite broadcasters provide more than a hundred channels of programming. Local telephone companies' plans include two types of offerings: hundreds of channels dedicated to particular programming sources, as well as switching functions that have the potential to make available a vastly expanded array of programming. As broadband switching becomes more sophisticated and is integrated into both cable systems and local telephone delivery systems, capacity constraints could diminish dramatically, if not altogether.

These types of existing and emerging competition will further erode the social understanding that a broadcast license confers a unique and unusual source of power over information products. In the initial decades of television licensing, the license reflected one of a very few video distribution outlets and an enormous percentage of the capacity available for transmission to households. That power not only is no longer unique but is also smaller than the power exercised by entities that operate without a spectrum allocation. Indeed, broadcasters must increasingly rely on competing sources, especially cable systems, to deliver their programming. The peculiar power supposedly transferred from the government to licensees charged with exercising that power in the public interest has disappeared. That particular distribution system confers no unique role.

It might be argued that broadcasting is different because network programming is so popular, but network programming's popularity is peculiarly unrelated to the rationales for lesser First Amendment protection. First, most broadcast licensees simply do not have any power that might be associated with network programming. Instead, they operate public television stations, independent television stations, and low-power television stations. Second, whatever control over public discourse might exist through distribution of network programming has diminished dramatically with the relative decline in any particular network's influence. Alternative information sources have multiplied and, even among television viewers, audience shares for individual network programming have plummeted, although there are recent signs of at least a temporary stabilization of combined network shares. Third, provision of popular programming does not amount to control—at least not control in the sense raised in *Red Lion* and traditionally invoked to justify differential regulation of broadcasting.[63] *Red Lion* focused on the licensee's ability to bar others from addressing the public, but no issue of a captive audience exists if viewers may choose other programming from other sources. Fourth, network programming is logically and, increasingly, practically independent from control over broadcast licenses. Networks are limited in the number of stations they may own, and in fact principally operate through contractual affiliation agreements with separately owned stations scattered throughout the country. In theory, any of the "network" operations of the principal television networks could be entirely separated from the ownership and operation of licensed television stations. For example, a "network" need not even own licensed stations, and absent certain regulatory barriers, network programming could be presented directly over cable systems through affiliation agreements between the network and cable systems.[64] Finally, the popularity or influence of network programming cannot form an independent or sufficient basis for differentially regulating broadcast licensees. This is especially so when viewers may choose programming from other sources. Using this rationale to regulate would amount to burdening a party because the government deems its message to be unduly popular (and thus presumably valuable to consumers), which is both unusually hostile to First Amendment values and a perverse basis for *protecting* consumer interests.

TRANSFORMATION OF THE LICENSING PROCESS. The common basis for traditional broadcast regulation rests in part on the understanding that licensing yields temporary control over government resources, which are to be managed in the public interest, but recent developments are undermining this understanding as well. No longer is the licensing process a matter of selecting a trustee over unique public resources. Instead, government allocations of rights of use in the electromagnetic spectrum reflect the "commodification" of licenses. Increasingly, that allocative process is similar to any other government—or private—transfer of a factor of production: like rights in real property, rights in the spectrum simply pass from government ownership and control to private control. They become one element of a private enterprise, and carry with them no basis for continued government oversight of that resource.

This transformation in the social understanding of licenses and their allocation has occurred in three steps. Initially, the government licensed persons it deemed qualified to use them in the public interest. The criteria for license ownership reflected this conception, as did subsequent public-interest restrictions imposed on licensees.[65] In an intermediate step, the government employed a lottery method of distributing licenses—especially licenses to engage in certain forms of wireless common carriage, most prominently cellular telephony.[66] This method, principally in its abandonment of selecting licensees according to their ability to act in the public interest, reflected greater recognition that transmission rights were simply one of the production elements that a carrier needed to secure to provide service. In this sense, the rights embodied in the license were little different from the switches or management and billing services that any carrier—wireline or wireless—had to obtain before providing service. Even so, the lottery method retained an element of the "public-interest" grant to the extent that the government received no fees for its license allocation. Third, the auction system of license allocation has recently moved far closer to treating the license as a factor of production.[67] Initial license allocations for new services are generally determined at auction by the highest bid, thus removing the "public-interest" determination inherent in distributing a resource at cost to the government—indeed without charge. In addition, the auction system applies both to common-carrier licenses (most prominently, for personal communications services) and for licenses associated with control over information products (such as interactive television services).[68] Although broadcast licenses are not generally subject to payment of fees or auctioning, the Telecommunications Act of 1996 establishes that payment will be required for spectrum used for certain services that are ancillary to advanced television services.[69]

These changes in the allocation of licenses remove a principal basis for the differential regulation of broadcast licensees. When the government did not purport to part with the spectrum but in effect deputized an agent to oversee its resources in the public interest, regulating the licensee's conduct might have seemed plausible or justified. But the fiction of government proprietorship can no longer be maintained. Spectrum licenses have in practice become, even in the government's own treatment, no different from other factors of production that pass from government to private control entirely by sale or lease. The social understanding of the sale of any ordinary government resource—mineral rights, land, forfeited real estate, or surplus vehicles—does not ordinarily justify the continued government regulation of the resource. This is all the more so in the context of speech rights. If a newspaper publisher acquires real estate through purchase from the government—or even benefits from public goods such as highways or police protection—that transaction provides no basis for a peculiar or additional government role in the production or shaping of the information product. The same is true, increasingly, with broadcast licenses. The once apparent nexus between license grant and content-based regulation is now disappearing.

IDENTITY OF EDITORIAL FUNCTIONS.   Even decisions affording broadcasters lesser First Amendment protections have recognized that broadcasters perform editorial functions that are entitled to First Amendment protection.[70] Even so, the widespread understanding that broadcasters perform a distinct public role as a conduit for information has contributed to the lesser

First Amendment protections afforded them. The structure and operation of emerging media and distribution systems, and the form of many of the new information products, have undermined this understanding as well. Instead, they show the essential identity of functions performed by entities receiving traditional First Amendment protections (such as newspaper publishers) and those performed by distributors of established and emerging electronic information products (including broadcasters). As these functions of various media become indistinguishable, yet another element supporting the differential regulation of electronic media disappears.

Editorial choice over the content of an information product is a hallmark of entitlement to First Amendment protection,[71] and various emerging media and novel information products throw into relief the similarity of this choice across media and products. The archetypical protected speaker, the newspaper or magazine publisher, produces a product comprising three types of information: information directly produced by employees—(for example, staff-written news articles); information secured for a fee or in a barter arrangement from an independent source, often a syndicator (for example, editorial cartoons, weekly features by brand-name columnists, and many news stories); and information that a third party directly or indirectly pays the publisher to disseminate (most commonly advertising, including political advertising). The most esteemed newspapers secure their reputations in large part through the first of these categories of information, but many smaller newspapers and magazines rely overwhelmingly on syndicated material without any reduction in their First Amendment protections.

Entities that produce and distribute electronic information products exercise the same judgment and undertake much the same enterprise. For example, a cable system operator might directly or indirectly produce its own cable programming for a portion of the product it sells to subscribers. Or it might, through barter or purchase (or sale, if the programming is insufficiently valuable to subscribers), secure programming produced by independent parties. Finally, it might sell portions of its distribution capabilities to advertisers or other program producers. As with print media, the distinction here often fades between "advertising," for which distribution is valued primarily by the programmer, and "copy," whose appeal to the subscriber is paramount. Motion picture listings or classified advertising in print products and home-shopping channels for cable systems illustrate the mixed roles. This same process of constructing an information product extends to other media and distribution facilities. The producer of an interactive product can draw on all three sources of information, whether that product is distributed electronically or in CD-ROM form. Broadcasters similarly draw on internal production, purchases of independently produced materials, and sales (or the equivalent) of advertising and related programming. A television affiliate, for example, commonly produces the local news, secures early evening material from an independent syndicator through barter or agreement and later evening material from the broadcast network, and constructs much of its remaining product with advertising (or advertising procured by others that have provided programming).

Recent developments in information technologies have underscored two additional types of identity shared by traditional and electronic information products. First, both forms are increasingly capable of communicating identical information—and, for purposes of the First Amendment, identically valuable information. A newspaper's text and photographs (and even editorial placement) can be communicated over electronic facilities. This identity runs in the other direction as well. The ability to peruse a newspaper or magazine at will, skipping among stories and switching between sections, is one of a print product's great attractions. Interactive information products, whether delivered in CD-ROM form or over electronic transmission facilities, provide a tremendous advance over traditional video programming to the extent that they allow the viewer to approximate this type of control and to exercise it for vastly greater amounts of information. The newspaper is, in this sense, a superb interactive product as well as a forerunner of the next generation of information products.

The final identity is one of transmission technology. At one time, video products (apart from motion pictures) were equated with over-the-air broadcast transmission. No more. Identical video and text information can be distributed through a broadcast station's wireless transmission or through the fiber and coaxial cables of a telephone company or the coaxial cables of a cable television system. The identity can be extended to media in tangible form (taped or printed) with the addition, at the conclusion of the cable system of a telephone company's line or broadcast or satellite receiver, of a facsimile machine, a printer, or a videocassette recorder. Indeed, transmission facilities are increasingly mixed. This is true of cable systems (which generally receive a satellite-delivered transmission at the cable head-end, which initiates a wire-based communication), broadcast stations (where over-the-air transmission is completed by wire, either over a cable system or from antennae to television or VCR), and even nationally distributed newspapers (whose content may be distributed by satellite, or eventually by broadband wire, to multiple printing plants and then further in broadsheet form).

All of these identities suggest that the common understanding of a distinct role for broadcasters in collecting and distributing information is collapsing. A common editorial role and role in distributing information exist for print information products and electronic information products. No sharp distinction can be drawn between broadcasting (and other electronic media) and print on the basis of the nature or distribution path of the communicated information. That form and distribution once seemed distinct and thus seemed to justify a distinct First Amendment standard, but the developments reflected in the communications revolution have eroded this apparent basis for affording lesser First Amendment protections to broadcasters and other users of electronic communications.

Offensive Speech

Many proponents of regulating broadcast licensees defend current broadcast regulation by pointing to a perceived need to prohibit the broadcast of offensive language and images. The FCC has recently focused on regulation in this respect, as has Congress in the Telecommunications Act of 1996.[72] Although this issue will likely continue to arise concerning many media, including print, the most striking feature of this regulatory rationale—even if accepted as legitimate—is how little of the current regulation it justifies and how tenuous is the link between the rationale and the range of regulation associated with licensed broadcasting.

For all media, a broad class of offensive speech and images already falls beyond the First Amendment's protection. The government has broad latitude in regulating the production, dissemination, and, occasionally, possession of material that fits the definition of obscenity.[73] This regulatory power applies to printed material as well as to electronic communications, whether those communications are produced by a licensed broadcaster or by others. Speech that many would find offensive but that would not be deemed obscene for this purpose (for example, because it is part of socially valuable communication or is not contrary to local community standards) is often referred to as "indecent" speech. A considerable element of the difficulty in attempts to regulate this speech is that there is wide disagreement regarding what constitutes indecency, in this context as in others.

The Supreme Court and lower courts have at times departed from their traditional hostility to government regulation of speech when addressing "indecent" speech made available through electronic means, and the Court has announced that it will in mid-1996 begin to revisit this issue.[74] They have at times been particularly forgiving of content regulation defended by the government as required to protect children from gaining access to indecent or offensive materials. In one case involving George Carlin's use of the now infamous "seven dirty words," a plurality of the Supreme Court justified regulation of indecent (as opposed to obscene) broadcast programming on the ground, in part, that such speech was peculiarly available in the home, particularly to minors.[75] Lower court cases have indicated that attempts to regulate indecent speech are permissible as long as they are narrowly directed to the asserted purpose and do not unduly restrict speech opportunities (for example, measures that restrict broadcast materials that may be unsuitable for young children to later hours). Other recent cases, including a Supreme Court case addressing pornographic messages available by telephone, suggest that extensive limits exist on regulation of nonobscene electronic communications.[76]

Several provisions of the Telecommunications Act of 1996 will test these issues and government interests. As an example of a particularly broad and vague provision, the act imposes criminal penalties for anyone who in interstate communications "by means of a telecommunications device . . . makes . . . and initiates the transmission of . . . any comment . . . or other communication which is obscene, lewd, lascivious, filthy, or indecent, with intent to annoy, abuse, threaten, or harass another person."[77] Separate liability arises for communications to minors.[78] Cable operators are required to scramble certain "sexually oriented programming" to nonsubscribers, and the leased access and "public, educational, and governmental" access rights over cable systems are reduced for programming that "contains obscenity, indecency, or nudity."[79] In certain circumstances, the act proscribes using "any interactive computer service to display in a manner available" to minors "patently offensive" descriptions of "sexual or excretory activities."[80] An operator of those facilities may avoid liability by taking sufficient actions to prevent access by minors, and the FCC is provided with the unusual role of describing what restrictive measures may suffice. The FCC's role also extends to developing a "television rating code" for video programming that contains "sexual, violent, or other indecent material" if the industry fails to develop an adequate code and broadcast the resulting ratings.[81]

These provisions not only create considerable tension with traditional libertarian principles but also depart considerably even from the circumstances in which regulation of broadcast "indecency" has been permitted. The scope of material potentially leading to criminal liability and other sanctions is greater, and liability may arise even when minors' interests are not implicated. More dramatically, liability extends to various communicative uses of computers, as well as to networked computing and interactive services, and may in certain circumstances be imposed on the operators of those facilities. The FCC's power to classify and regulate information and communications is novel and, if in fact exercised, particularly suspect. In light of the unsettled legality of these and other provisions, the act contains an expedited judicial review mechanism for certain broad challenges,[82] but most constitutional issues will likely have to await the application of the new provisions in particular cases.

Whatever regulatory latitude the Supreme Court finally permits, solutions other than broad government intervention may best protect legitimate interests, including advancing the principles underlying the First Amendment. In many instances, limited regulation could directly address the availability to minors of certain violent or "indecent" electronic communications to the home. Parents might be provided with greater control over that material through measures that assigned controversial material to particular channels or later hours or through technological measures that take advantage of communication capabilities, and the Telecommunications Act of 1996 seeks to foster the development of reception equipment that would allow parents to block undesired programming.[83] A more extensive conception of First Amendment protections, however, would rely almost entirely on private determinations, robustly shaped by extensive community pressure on the corporations and other purveyors of violent and sexually explicit material.

This new focus on regulating violent and sexually explicit material may not generally support or result in greater administrative regulation of information providers, but it potentially endangers the development of advanced information services. Broad and uncertain liability for operators of networks and facilities provides a disincentive for developing those services and increases their costs, and unclear liability that may arise from using those facilities similarly decreases demand for them. This focus also poses risks to First Amendment principles and to the benefits accompanying open communication. The interest in protecting children could be invoked to mask broader measures designed to limit unpopular speech, and regulation designed initially to protect children from materials broadcast to the home could slip those moorings and extend to all materials that children could conceivably reach from the home (through telephone communications and including the Internet). The developments outlined above, especially the increasing importance of electronic communications and the migration of traditionally printed products to electronic networks, underscores some of these fears. Allowing government to regulate electronic communications is no longer an exception to the general First Amendment limitations; rather, electronic communications increasingly constitute the speech and debate that the First Amendment is designed to preserve. At least in the absence of clear limits to regulation and protection for valued expression, the risk increases that our principal sources of information could be limited to material palatable to the majority and justified as suitable for children.

However the interest in protecting children from indecent communications is implemented and resolved, that interest is largely tangential to the broader regulatory and First Amendment issues surrounding the new information industries. As a result of the development of electronic networks, even this limited concern with indecent speech applies to the different forms of electronic communication (and, indeed, applies to print as well) and hardly supports categorically different or greater regulation of broadcast licensees. More important, nearly all of the current broadcast regulation of content outlined above and that which threatens to extend to other forms of electronic communication is unrelated to the issues surrounding the small class of indecent speech. Rather, the elaborate structural regulations of license allocation and ownership limitations, and the varied broadcast and cable television regulations designed to ensure the proper balance of classes of speakers or types of messages, amount to the type of content regulation that the First Amendment most clearly prohibits.

Reaffirming Traditional First Amendment Principles

Establishing that no special characteristic of broadcast licensees or broadcasting justifies content regulation of broadcast communications and that print and electronically delivered products are alike for nearly every First Amendment purpose might be thought sufficient to establish that the government cannot regulate the content of any information product. After all, the ''libertarian'' prohibition on content regulation is the established First Amendment tradition; a limited exception emerged for broadcasting, linked to specific characteristics of that form of delivery; and the basis for that exception no longer exists. Even so, some prominent observers have accepted several of the premises of this argument but have reached a contrary conclusion. Professor Cass Sunstein, for example, accepts that broadcasters and print publishers engage in similar activities and that no relevant distinction can be drawn between them, but concludes that government should generally be permitted to ensure the adequacy and balance of information presented to the public—for newspapers as well as broadcasting.[84]

This argument for comprehensive regulation of content (but not necessarily, directly, of viewpoint) is an argument beyond legal sources, at least as they are traditionally understood. Sunstein and others proffer an interpretation of the First Amendment in light of its general "purposes," but not one that seeks to accommodate or apply First Amendment doctrine as developed in judicial opinions (beyond noting that regulation of broadcasting has been upheld).[85] Those doctrines, however, bar the inference, drawn from the equivalence of print and electronic products, that the First Amendment permits such widespread content regulation. Instead, under established doctrine, such regulation is presumed to be unconstitutional unless some rare justification is demonstrated.[86]

Even if government oversight of the content of communications were only an issue of policy and not law, the libertarian model should not so quickly be abandoned. A defense of the First Amendment tradition is beyond the scope of this discussion, but a few general points apply. The conservative virtues might be invoked: the model—and its related assumptions about the value of personal autonomy reflected in personal choice, the potential harm of government action designed to improve speech, and the benefits of private choices and offerings for self- and community fulfillment—underlie much of our structuring of government powers and private affairs, especially in political activity and the print mass media. We depart from it at our peril. In addition, even if the issue could be resolved empirically, the model finds considerable support. Examples abound of the unintended consequences of government regulation as well as conscious abuses of that power, especially over a set of industries so vital to the electoral process and to limiting the harmful actions of bureaucracies. The Fairness Doctrine provides a test case that supports many of the assumptions underlying the libertarian model. Considerable evidence supports the conclusions that the Fairness Doctrine invited abuses of political power, fostered manipulation of administrative and judicial processes by elites, and most important, reduced rather than increased speakers' editorializing and presentation of information about controversial issues.[87]

The benefits of content regulation are particularly uncertain in light of the alternative means available, even to the government, for giving citizens access to information. The government could readily create many more broadcasting outlets, or opportunities to broadcast using existing allocations, or it could otherwise increase the opportunities to speak and the availability of information, through electronic or traditional means. As more information is available electronically (through databases, bulletin boards, and private products), without necessarily being produced or controlled by powerful private parties, creating these opportunities should become far less burdensome. What the libertarian model especially requires is that the government not create these opportunities by limiting others' communications.

The merits of the libertarian model are likely not subject to empirical proof, and adherence to the model rests in part on acceptance of the values underlying it. Perhaps a more interesting question is why pressure for greater government control over particular speakers' messages, particularly from progressives, is increasing precisely when unprecedented diversity of sources and types of information is emerging. One answer lies in the enormous democratic potential of the new media. Individuals will soon likely have enormously expanded opportunities both to secure information and entertainment they want, when and in the form they want it, and to produce information for distribution to others. Elites, particularly liberal elites, have had tremendous influence over many of the electronic media, whether through administrative actions, the legal process, or direct influence over broadcast television programming.[88] Increased government regulation of content would buttress that waning influence. The possibilities of competing sources of information also pose difficulty to progressives who, like Sunstein, believe that they—and by extension the government—can distinguish good information from bad, and that citizens left to their own devices will remain insufficiently exposed to "high-quality broadcasting" and "better choices."[89] Regulations such as the Fairness Doctrine, advocated as imposing a "better speech" obligation on every source of information, or at least every popular source, respond to these opportunities for flight from improvement.

Perhaps the strongest argument in favor of regulations such as the Fairness Doctrine is that they are necessary to prevent a few large corporations from assuming precisely the role of censor that the libertarian model bars to the government. Leave aside for the moment the efficacy of these measures. Whatever the validity of this concern when three television networks, confronted with limited competition and targeting the same viewers, dominated the electronic mass media, it must be far less now that information sources available to individuals are growing dramatically. And the concern should diminish even more as individuals gain access to large databases and can initiate mass communications, as the Internet foreshadows. Advocates of regulation might reply that this period of relative information anarchy, if it comes, will be brief and passing, threatened by a few large information providers wielding market power. If so, regulatory tools far short of content regulations are available to limit that power, and the following section addresses those government measures.

The First Amendment and the Regulation of Competition in the New Information Industry

The shift from a telecommunications network to an information network comprising overlapping systems that deliver mass-media products, traditional personal communications, and new information products has an additional consequence for traditional regulation and First Amendment doctrine. The transformation requires not only, as just discussed, that the government conform its regulation of electronic communication to the First Amendment's generally applicable libertarian constraints against content-based regulation. The transformation also requires reconciliation between, first, the First Amendment interests threatened by regulation directed at producers and distributors of information and, second, the extensive regulation of communications carriers that perform editorial and related functions protected by the First Amendment. That is, more and more, the First Amendment potentially conflicts with antitrust enforcement and common-carrier regulations. Again, a return to traditional First Amendment principles, applied to reflect peculiarities of the new information industry, largely provides the basis for addressing this apparent conflict.

The Increasing Potential Conflict between First Amendment Principles and Antitrust and Common-Carrier Regulations

Until recently, the panoply of regulations that affect a traditional carriage industry such as telecommunications presented relatively few First Amendment issues. Traditionally, editorial functions have been largely distinct from carriage functions. Telecommunications firms provided few services entitled to First Amendment protection and were instead common carriers, largely confined to transmitting messages formulated by third parties to destinations of those parties' choosing. Indeed, the definition of common carriage for telecommunications embodies this limitation.[90] Telecommunications carriers often provide carriage through essential facilities or bottleneck monopolies, and more often exercise market power, and thus have been subject to extensive regulation modeled on antitrust principles[91] as well as the full common-carrier regulatory regime derived directly from railroad regulation.[92]

In contrast, providers of mass-media and related information products traditionally have distributed their products in ways that did not subject them to antitrust or common-carriage regulation. Thus they might employ third parties' delivery facilities—for example, by distributing their products through the mails, over telephone facilities, or in theaters or bookstores. Or, they might employ nonelectronic distribution channels (such as newspaper delivery) which could be replicated fairly readily. These forms of information distribution generally did not involve control over monopoly or common-carriage facilities, and antitrust suits addressed exceptions to this rule.[93] Until the widespread development of cable television, broadcast television and radio were the principal exceptions to this division between information carriage and information production. As long as technology remained relatively stagnant, this exception could be treated as such, and no general conflict of principle arose. The Court's peculiar First Amendment jurisprudence in this area matched Congress's peculiar regulation of broadcasters, and both avoided any general conflict between First Amendment principles and traditional antitrust and common-carrier regulation.[94]

But technology has hardly remained stagnant, and it threatens to produce precisely that conflict of general principle. Technological and market changes have collapsed the distinction between information carriage and production of mass-media products, creating potential conflict between First Amendment principles and antitrust and common-carrier regulation. Cable television system operators as well as satellite broadcasters and wireless cable systems combine selection or origination of programming with control over delivery facilities. Those facilities may increasingly also carry traditional person-to-person communications. Traditional common carriers, particularly local telephone companies, increasingly seek to produce and deliver information products that they own or select, and they can deliver mass-media products as well as person-to-person communications. Correspondingly, traditional information producers such as publishers of books, magazines, and newspapers increasingly seek to own or employ electronic carriage facilities. And radio and television broadcasting, which had always combined these carriage and editorial functions, present this conflict particularly directly and should soon no longer be subject to the unique First Amendment treatment that avoided the need to resolve that conflict.

This integration of information production and transmission capabilities raises broad First Amendment issues because the economic regulation traditionally applied to transmission services and facilities is difficult to distinguish from that which triggers First Amendment concerns when directed against information producers. In many circumstances, restricting the carriage of information can be recast as limiting speech. Thus antitrust restrictions imposed on a carrier's monopoly distribution facilities might considerably affect any information products also offered by the monopolist—both by restricting offerings directly and by requiring transmission of competing information products.[95] Similarly, the traditional antitrust safeguard of a cross-ownership restriction, which bars entities under common control from participating in related lines of business, might operate as a significant and discriminatory restriction on speech—and might even be designed and intended as such a restriction—when one of those related businesses has control over content. Or, the various interconnection, nondiscrimination, and access requirements traditionally imposed on common carriers might limit the financial return on and nature of the transporter's own information services when applied to an integrated delivery facility.

For telecommunications regulation in particular, all of these difficulties are augmented because both Congress and the FCC have generally regulated through broad rules directed at specific segments of the industry rather than through generally applicable antitrust or other laws applied in judicial proceedings to individual parties. This type of targeted regulation of information producers raises its own set of First Amendment concerns, based on the fear that the government is engaging in de facto content regulation.[96] In addition, these regulations preclude reliance on a plausible way of reconciling antitrust and First Amendment principles: by sanctioning only the judicial application of general laws, such as the Sherman Act, which set forth general competitive standards without attempting specifically to shape competition in markets for delivery or production of information.

Reconciling First Amendment Principles and Regulation Ostensibly Designed to Enhance Competition

The same First Amendment principles that support extending traditional First Amendment protections to all electronic media also point to the reconciliation of antitrust and First Amendment interests. In both settings, the paramount First Amendment concern is preventing the government from seeking to shape public debate or otherwise become the "guardian of the public mind."[97] First Amendment doctrine accomplishes this by focusing on whether a challenged measure is designed to affect the content of communications, but it allows relatively broad latitude for government measures designed to achieve substantial goals unrelated to content but that incidentally affect speakers' ability to distribute their messages. This essential distinction applies throughout First Amendment law and can be extended to rules purporting to shape competition in the information industries. If those rules are content-based, or designed to change public debate, they should be prohibited in nearly all cases in which they limit a private party's speech. Correspondingly, rules that seek to achieve important objectives unrelated to the content of speech should be subject to less scrutiny and upheld if sufficiently justified in light of those objectives and if other safeguards designed to protect opportunities to speak are satisfied. This distinction, which might be called the "antitrust principle," raises a host of problems and presents considerable administrative difficulties. But the principle seeks to protect two vital traditions: preserving speech rights and preserving the government's ability to check exercises of market power (a function that itself may also indirectly preserve speech rights).

ANTITRUST AND THE FIRST AMENDMENT.   Even before the Court's decision in *Turner Broadcasting*, the validity of applying antitrust principles to speakers was well established, at least when general antitrust statutes were applied in legitimate judicial proceedings. This was so even when the suits curtailed protected speech. Quite simply, such antitrust and other commercial regulation statutes were subject to the same rationality review applied to any other exercise of Congress's Commerce Clause powers.[98] No special First Amendment defense was available, and no heightened judicial scrutiny was appropriate, when those general rules applied to producers of information or others engaged in First Amendment activities.[99] Indeed, removing anticompetitive conduct within information production industries was held to advance First Amendment values:

> [The First] Amendment rests on the assumption that the widest possible dissemination of information from diverse and antagonistic sources is essential to the welfare of the public, that a free press is a condition of a free society. Surely a command that the government itself shall not impede the free flow of ideas does not afford non-government combinations a refuge if they impose restraints upon

that constitutionally guaranteed freedom. . . . The First Amendment affords not
the slightest support for the contention that a combination to restrain trade in
news and views has any constitutional immunity.[100]

In particular cases the Court elaborated on this principle to uphold many
of the types of competitive restrictions that limit entry into and production
of information services—and that are often applied to telecommunications
carriers. For example, a prominent antitrust doctrine requires that operators
of essential facilities—that is, facilities necessary to compete in a related
market yet that cannot necessarily be replicated—allow competitors reasonable access to those facilities.[101] Not only have variations of this doctrine
proved important in telecommunications regulation,[102] but the doctrine has
also applied to core First Amendment activity. Thus, in *Lorain Journal Co.
v. United States*, a newspaper was found to be an essential facility, and its
market power over distribution of information required that it sacrifice its
editorial control to provide access to a competitor's advertising.[103] Newspapers' market power gained through control over production or distribution facilities has led to broad divestiture decrees[104] and to limitations on
choices regarding distribution of information products.[105] In all these cases,
application of antitrust principles to information producers protected by the
First Amendment justified no unusual or protective treatment, much less
strict judicial scrutiny.

A more difficult question was whether Congress or the FCC could
embody antitrust concerns in rules directed specifically to practices and
conditions in the information production or distribution industries, rather
than relying only on good faith enforcement leading to judicial application
of general antitrust statutes. A series of cases expressed hostility to ostensibly general taxation and other laws that could mask actions undertaken
against particular classes of speakers,[106] and the central doctrine expressed
hostility to laws expressly directed to activities protected by the First
Amendment.[107] Even so, the Court had also and more specifically suggested
that genuine antitrust concerns could be effectuated through rules crafted by
administrative agencies as well as rules produced by the judicial process. In
FCC v. National Citizens Committee for Broadcasting, the Court rejected a
First Amendment challenge to the FCC's rule that limited the ability of
newspaper publishers to operate broadcast stations.[108] The Court noted:
"The regulations are in form quite similar to the prohibitions imposed by
the antitrust laws. This court has held that application of the antitrust laws
to newspapers is not only consistent with, but is actually supportive of the

values underlying, the First Amendment.'' Even so, the Court ultimately rested its decision on the nature of the broadcast licensing process rather than on this ground because the FCC's decision had ''relied primarily on First Amendment rather than antitrust considerations.''[109]

REFINEMENT OF THE ANTITRUST PRINCIPLE.   In *Turner Broadcasting System, Inc.* v. *FCC*, the Court resolved two central aspects of this general problem of the scope of permissible regulation of information production and distribution industries.[110] The Court considered First Amendment challenges brought by cable television system operators and cable programmers to the ''must-carry'' provisions of the 1992 Cable Act.[111] Those provisions require cable system operators to devote a portion of their channels to transmitting the signals of local commercial and public broadcast television stations.[112] The cable operators principally asserted that the act constrained their editorial discretion over their program offerings, and programmers asserted that the act impermissibly favored over-the-air broadcasters over them. The cable interests asserted that the must-carry provisions were content-based regulations triggering the most stringent, ''strict'' judicial scrutiny, and that the statute was invalid as overbroad and unjustified under any level of heightened scrutiny.[113] The Court concluded that cable operators and programmers engaged in activity fully protected by the First Amendment, that the must-carry provisions were content-neutral and thus subject only to mid-level judicial scrutiny, and that further fact-finding was required before it could be determined whether the challenged provisions directly advanced important government interests.[114]

For present purposes, two of the Court's holdings are particularly important and constitute *Turner*'s refinement of the antitrust principle. First, the Court held that the government may use rules specifically to regulate even information industries without triggering strict scrutiny, as long as those rules are justified on grounds unrelated to the content of expression.[115] On this vigorously contested threshold issue, all justices shared this conclusion.[116] An important aspect of this conclusion is that rules designed to check market power over distribution facilities, even by requiring access to those facilities by competing information providers, are content-neutral and subject only to intermediate scrutiny.[117] Second, the Court concluded that because such rules nonetheless incidentally burden First Amendment interests, they must satisfy the intermediate level of scrutiny, which requires sufficient matching of chosen means to asserted state interests.[118] It concluded that ''because the must-carry provisions impose special obligations on cable operators and special burdens on cable programmers, some measure of heightened First Amendment scrutiny is demanded.''[119] Thus, rules that specifically regulate entities engaged in editorial and speech functions must be justified by a heightened showing that the purported regulatory interest exists and that the regulation directly addresses that content-neutral objective.[120] Together, these conclusions address the central issue posed by the application of antitrust principles specifically to information industries: the government may craft general rules directed to particular industry conditions or participants if it designs those rules to advance purposes unrelated to the messages conveyed, but courts will scrutinize even such measures to determine that they directly advance a genuine content-neutral objective.

The significance and strengths of *Turner*'s resolution of the collision of antitrust interests and the First Amendment emerge when compared with four alternatives presented to the Court. At one extreme, cable operators and cable programmers argued that the First Amendment requires strict scrutiny of any regulations specifically directed toward, and distinguishing among, particular entities engaged in protected speech activities.[121] In this view, antitrust concerns must be advanced through generally applicable laws that apply specifically to First Amendment speakers only when enforced through judicial proceedings.[122] At the other extreme, certain interest groups claiming to represent consumers argued that the relevant First Amendment right inhered in television viewers, and that the First Amendment thus supported government intervention to ensure that a full range of information was presented to subscribers.[123] In contrast, the government relied on cases developed to support restrictions on broadcasters' editorial discretion and argued that each medium should be differentially regulated according to its particular competitive failings.[124] For cable television, the solicitor general principally argued, the government could engage in content regulation designed to benefit particular classes of speakers as long as it did not favor particular viewpoints.[125] Finally, broadcasters defending the statute suggested that the regulatory nature of the must-carry provisions justified only rationality review.[126]

In rejecting each of these proffered alternatives, the *Turner* decision upholds traditional First Amendment interests of speakers, the related interests in preventing market power abuses from limiting speaking opportunities, and government interests in traditional economic regulation. The cable system operators and cable programmers sought a rule that would have exempted them (and other entities that deliver and produce information) from regulations directed at them and designed to further procompetitive objectives unrelated to speech or the messages communicated. Both statutes and FCC regulations rely extensively on measures intended to address market power and justified on that basis; but they identify that power as held by industry participants that increasingly engage in protected editorial activities and related speech. It would unjustifiably extend First Amendment protections, and hamstring government regulation of an increasingly important sector of the economy, to limit government regulation of information industries to specific applications of general laws. Indeed, even if the choice between particular enforcement actions and industry-specific rules were judged according to the effect on speech interests alone, the choice is hardly clear: allowing executive officers to apply or threaten to apply general rules against specific media entities, rather than having that discretion confined by rules produced through a legislative process and subject to judicial review, hardly affords greater First Amendment protection. The doctrines barring unnecessary vagueness in laws applied against speakers, as well as requirements that licensing and related regulatory schemes be precise and contain procedural safeguards, favor rules over enforcement discretion to protect First Amendment interests.[127]

The Court also appropriately rejected the interest groups' theory that the relevant First Amendment rights inhered in television viewers rather than cable operators and programmers. For the reasons set forth earlier in this chapter, cable operators and programmers do in fact perform essential "speech" and "editorial" functions traditionally protected by the First Amendment. Defining the First Amendment interest as principally a right to receive information would dramatically transform the role and function of the First Amendment. Rather than enforcing the command that "Congress shall make no law ... abridging the freedom of speech," the First Amendment under this interpretation would become a license for the government to ensure that citizens receive a properly balanced or correct mix of views from appropriately divergent sources.[128] The government, reflecting the preferences of the politically ascendant groups of the moment, would also determine the propriety of the transmitted views and information sources. This government power, previously suggested only for the regulation of broadcasters, would extend to all electronically delivered information products. Indeed, the principle would extend to like government efforts to benefit the interests of consumers of traditional media as well, with no logical reason why newspapers and political campaigns—or even particularly persuasive or otherwise powerful individuals—could not equally be subjected to oversight to ensure that their views were fair, balanced, and otherwise sufficiently informative. Not surprisingly, this position also suffered from a considerable number of contrary decisions and gained support only from a scattered few cases peculiar to broadcasting.[129]

The government's position, too, represented an unjustified departure from established First Amendment doctrine. Although the solicitor general emphasized the legitimacy of regulating to achieve traditional antitrust objectives, the government also sought to preserve its role of balancing views issuing from particular sources—the role authorized by *Red Lion*. Thus, the government awkwardly straddled the issues by arguing that peculiarities of the cable industry justified content regulation designed to amplify valuable but excluded speakers (because their additional views were valuable) but not content regulation designed to foster particular viewpoints.[130] This was an unprincipled muddle. No cogent explanation was provided, or perhaps could be provided, for why standards developed to discern when market power existed also established any peculiar deficit in the nature or variety of information available to citizens—or why government powers to shape information delivery followed from the power to correct market failure.[131] In the government's view, the Court would have to develop a First Amendment jurisprudence unique to each emerging medium. No general principles were to be identified and applied, but rather the resulting rules would resemble the political balancing that apparently led to the government's position. More ominously, *Red Lion* would take on new life, providing the government with broad regulatory powers over who may speak and the sufficiency of the information distributed whenever a competitive failure might be identified. Government's power to coerce those who failed to balance their speech or to speak in a responsible manner, as determined by government officials, would extend beyond broadcasting to all electronically delivered media (and potentially to traditional media whenever a "competitive" failure was alleged).

The Court's rule is also superior to the position that rationality review is appropriate for all traditional government efforts to limit market power or provide access to bottleneck facilities, even when directed against information industries. If the inquiry into purpose or design were simple or direct, this position might have considerable logical force; it is, after all, a corollary to the conclusions that rules designed to advance commercial regulatory goals (also reflected in generally applicable antitrust laws) can be crafted for particular contexts, including the information industries, and that the First Amendment provides no particular exemption for those industries from such non-content-based regulation. But the inquiry into purpose is hardly simple. Because the government may readily assert neutral reasons to mask efforts to shape speech, either by favoring particular views or by altering the mix of views, heightened scrutiny is necessary to distinguish legitimate from pretextual or mixed-motive regulation.[132] This function is performed by a requirement that the challenged means directly advance the government's asserted, content-neutral objective.[133] Similarly, requiring that ample alternative means of expression remain and that the challenged measure does not unduly restrict speech also ensures that the government is not in fact seeking to suppress particular views or the speech of particular classes of affected speakers.[134]

Apart from the relative strengths of the Court's analysis revealed through these comparisons, a basic value of the antitrust principle enunciated in *Turner* is the application of general principles governing both traditional First Amendment doctrine and traditional oversight of economic regulation. The essential distinction in *Turner*, between government measures designed to regulate the content of speech (which are almost always prohibited) and measures undertaken for unrelated reasons but that incidentally affect speech products (which are permitted if narrowly crafted), pervades First Amendment doctrine. Originally designed for communications achieved through regulated conduct,[135] that distinction and related tests have been applied more generally to a broad range of measures that ostensibly regulate the time, place, and manner of speech.[136] For example, essentially the same test applied in *Turner* had previously been applied to First Amendment challenges to regulations limiting destruction of draft cards (and thus affected political protests that included burning the cards),[137] regulations limiting camping in national parks (thus limiting the duration and nature of protests designed to change homelessness policies),[138] and regulations limiting disturbances in public parks (thus affecting the volume of musical performances).[139] Similarly, the focus in *Turner* on the design or "justification" of the statute, to determine whether it is content-based, accords with the tests developed by the Court to discern when regulations that affect particular media in fact are designed to limit particular messages.[140] For example, the Court has scrutinized tax and related burdens imposed on certain media participants to ensure that neutral purposes are being pursued, but it has indicated that "differential taxation of speakers, even members of the press, does not implicate the First Amendment unless the tax is directed at, or presents the danger of suppressing, particular ideas."[141]

All of these doctrines, now including the principle set forth in *Turner*, accomplish the libertarian objectives of the First Amendment by prohibiting measures designed to influence the substance and balance of public debate. In addition to securing the traditional benefits of the First Amendment, the integration of doctrine governing the electronic media (or at a minimum, cable television) into broader First Amendment jurisprudence avoids the corresponding danger of disparate rules: the impulse to allow greater regulation of the electronic media, precisely because their messages carry such great social influence. *Turner* represents an initial and important barrier against encroaching government regulation of the content of speech based on its manner of delivery and provides the basis in turn to subject broadcasting regulation to standard First Amendment principles.[142]

At the same time, the solution adopted in *Turner* accommodates traditional government regulatory objectives that do not pose the dangers of content regulation. The government may pursue a range of economic and related regulation as long as two conditions are established: (1) that after scrutiny, it is apparent that the measure is not a subterfuge designed to shape the form of public debate, and (2) that pursuit of even the content-neutral objective does not in practice unduly constrain public debate, particularly by limiting the speech opportunities of individual burdened parties. Under this test, traditional economic regulation, especially that designed to check abuses of market power, may continue even as applied to producers and distributors of information and even through rules, as long as regulation does not unduly restrict the underlying information products.

UNRESOLVED TENSION BETWEEN THE FIRST AMENDMENT AND REGULATION OF INFORMATION INDUSTRIES. Even admitting these general strengths of the Court's resolution of the basic conflict between regulation of competition and the First Amendment, the decision is hardly without difficulties, and the resolution is only partial: it raises issues that will continue to bedevil efforts to reconcile the First Amendment with regulation in these industries.

First, the Court enunciated its principle in a particularly difficult and close case. A not insignificant amount of evidence supported the conclusion that Congress designed the act to benefit broadcasters because their information products are particularly valued—and thus that the act was in this respect content-based.[143] Section 5 of the act, for example, requires cable television systems to carry the signals of public television stations.[144] Public television stations do not compete with cable systems for advertising revenue (thus lessening the incentive for, if not ability of, cable systems to act anticompetitively toward them), and section 5 could be interpreted as an aspect of the established government scheme designed to foster the supposedly valuable and supplemental programming presented over public television stations.[145]

Second, the Court's analysis could have better linked its inquiry into whether the must-carry provisions are content-based with its invocation and application of heightened scrutiny. As noted above, the "tailoring" requirement, that the government's means should sufficiently advance its substantial, asserted ends and not sweep too broadly, should be an integral part of determining whether the government in fact has designed the challenged measure to pursue a legitimate, content-neutral goal or has instead pursued invidious objectives. Instead, the Court first examined whether the "must-carry" provisions were content-neutral (and concluded they were) and then separately considered (but did not resolve) whether Congress had directly advanced legitimate objectives.[146]

Third, the decision's evidentiary requirements create difficulties of administration and depart from the Court's traditional judicial consideration of facial challenges to rules, particularly acts of Congress. In remanding the case for further proceedings, the decision directed that a more sweeping record be compiled to determine whether the cable industry in fact posed the competitive and other threats that Congress asserted and to assess the efficacy of the must-carry provisions. Apparently, the record to be developed would include evidence based on events *following* the act's passage.[147] In other contexts, the Court generally assesses the "fit" or "tailoring" of a statute by comparing the asserted interest and the statute's scope as revealed by its terms, and shows considerable deference to Congress's express or implied statements of the necessity for regulation—especially when Congress sets forth factual findings and when presented with a facial challenge to a statute.[148] For cable television regulation (and likely for regulations addressing related information industries), the Court has now created a much more burdensome and less deferential process. For these industries, nearly any stated legislative goal may be subjected to extensive evidentiary challenge, even based on events or evidence adduced after the legislation's or regulation's passage. The judiciary will inevitably be drawn into extensive oversight of the regulation of these industries, because what had previously been matters of law have been transformed into complicated factual disputes.

Fourth, and perhaps most troubling, the decision's treatment of what state interests are content-neutral will at least create ongoing confusion and may pose significant danger to First Amendment interests. A plurality of the Court identified three government interests that underlie the must-carry provisions and held all of them to be unrelated to content: (1) preserving the benefits of free, over-the-air local broadcast television, (2) promoting the widespread dissemination of information from a multiplicity of sources, and (3) promoting fair competition in the market for television programming.[149]

This final interest represents the application of traditional antitrust principles to a particular industry and has been the focus of this discussion. As noted, this represents the quintessential interest that is unrelated to content and which the government should be able to pursue, even by crafting rules directed to specific submarkets of the information industries.

The additional two interests identified by the plurality pose separate and considerable difficulties. If interest 1 is understood as recognizing the importance and legitimacy of fostering broadcasters' speech in particular, and if interest 2 is understood as recognizing the legitimacy of ensuring a rich or balanced set of messages, they are apparently related to the content of speech and illegitimate under traditional First Amendment doctrine.[150] In defense of the plurality's conclusion, these additional interests might be explained as not truly independent, and as simply buttressing or reflecting the interest in promoting fair competition. As the Court has repeatedly stated, applying antitrust principles to information providers advances the First Amendment because anticompetitive conduct in these areas reduces the availability of information and undermines the "marketplace of ideas."[151] Observing that preventing cable systems' abuse of market power results in additional sources of information (interest number 2) and preserves broadcasting (interest number 1) simply elucidates social benefits of a measure designed to achieve content-neutral antitrust objectives. The same could be said of a particular application of the Sherman Act, and the Court has done just that in applying antitrust laws to the press.[152] Focusing on the social value provided by particular beneficiaries of regulation that enhances competition does not necessarily alter the underlying antitrust purpose of the must-carry provisions, any more than noting the social benefits of a fully competitive shipping industry as a result of comparable rail or trucking regulations would transform the antitrust nature of those measures.

If interests 1 and 2 are, instead, truly independent bases of state action rather than expressions of the ancillary benefits of applying antitrust measures in this context, then they would appear to be impermissibly content-based. Under traditional First Amendment principles, the government may not burden one group's conceded First Amendment rights simply by claiming an interest in advancing the views or information product of a separate group.[153] (It may, of course, pursue other, content-neutral objectives that have a similar incidental effect.)[154] However, the Court would be allowing just that result if it concludes that preserving widespread dissemination of broadcasters' speech is an independent and legitimate rationale for state action. Similarly, the interest in ensuring dissemination of information from multiple sources assumes the peculiar value of the additional messages, and the content-based nature of that interest is underscored when certain speakers are identified as uniquely qualified to provide that additional information. In addressing these two state interests, the plurality discussed only the importance of these interests rather than the basis (apart from competitive concerns) for concluding that the interests are content-neutral.[155] That importance may provide a justification for subsidizing the identified speech or distribution outlets that the government wishes to favor, or for inferring an agency's regulatory power, and the precedents the *Turner* decision relies on arose in just these contexts.[156] The crucial First Amendment concern arises in a separate context, when the government not only endorses a message but also burdens particular speakers or speech interests, and only a justification unrelated to the messages communicated will allow the government to take that second, additional step of impairing speech.[157] Later cases, including a subsequent Supreme Court case, have failed to resolve this underlying issue and present similar difficulties.[158]

A final unresolved difficulty is what additional limits, if any, exist on the types of content-neutral government interests that may justify regulations crafted specifically for the information industries. This problem is raised, for example, by measures that are designed to foster competition but that rest on theories or adopt standards that differ from those applied through generally applicable antitrust laws. That is, Congress or the FCC may implement measures that prohibit, as anticompetitive, actions that do not violate the antitrust laws.[159] Using one approach, no special difficulty exists: as long as the measure's purpose or design is unrelated to the regulation of the content of communications and otherwise meets the standard "tailoring" test, the First Amendment is satisfied.[160] *Turner* does not address the issue directly but appears to countenance a variety of government interests.[161] Using another approach, however, measures that apply different standards of competition for the information industries might warrant additional scrutiny.[162] The danger to First Amendment values is that the legislature's or agency's conception of "competition" has been shaped by a perceived danger to the balance or source of information, or that it reflects its perception of the importance of particular speakers or information products. Such asserted state interests invoked only in the context of the information industries might be subjected to an increased evidentiary showing, or it might be prohibited altogether as a prophylactic measure.

Despite these difficulties, *Turner* represents an important refinement of principles reconciling antitrust and First Amendment objectives. These difficulties do not undermine the most far-reaching aspect of the decision, its determination that antitrust measures are content-neutral even when directed to information industries (and thus did not trigger strict scrutiny), but they do implicate First Amendment concerns sufficiently to justify heightened scrutiny. These difficulties are also distinct from the principles underlying this determination—that First Amendment challenges for emerging media are to be evaluated in accord with traditional First Amendment principles, including the focus on whether a challenged regulation is designed or justified to influence the messages communicated. The decision's holdings regarding the underlying purpose of the must-carry provisions at issue, the link of judicial scrutiny to legislative purpose, and the requisite evidentiary showing all present separate issues. The decision's treatment of the antitrust rationale may be disentangled even from issues presented by the additional, arguably content-related purposes. Subsequent cases will resolve whether the interests in preserving specific industry subsegments or ensuring multiple sources of information can themselves justify restrictions on speech. It will also be left to other cases to resolve the more difficult question: whether the government may pursue "procompetitive" objectives for information industry regulation that differ from the antitrust standards applied to nonspeech industries.

Application of the Antitrust Principle

The core principle confirmed in *Turner*, that traditional antitrust standards may be applied through rules addressing information industries only as long as they directly advance that content-neutral purpose, is crucially important to regulations that permeate these services. An especially important benefit of this antitrust principle, and perhaps its most significant aspect, is the latitude it allows for applying and developing traditional regulatory measures to the information industries, while ensuring that the government cannot design regulations to affect information products or public debate or regulate in a manner that has an undue incidental effect on speech.

Under these principles, the government is not necessarily precluded from imposing requirements developed for common carriers (including interconnection, access, unbundling, and nondiscrimination requirements), certain cross-ownership restrictions, and rate regulations. These measures will likely be the essential tools available to regulators to curb market abuses in the provision of emerging information services, and to ensure full access by individuals both to speak and to receive speech over the developing information networks. An interpretation of the First Amendment that opposes rules crafted specifically for the information industries whenever they incidentally affect speech would have effectively barred application of nearly all of these measures. In contrast, the antitrust principle as developed in *Turner* presents no categorical bar to these measures when they are shown to be (as they often are) designed to prevent anticompetitive conduct or to advance other competitive objectives developed for noninformation industries. At the same time, these regulations when applied to the information industries continue to present significant dangers to First Amendment interests, and the heightened scrutiny and tailoring requirements also embodied in the antitrust principle provide a ready basis to check abuses of regulatory powers.

INTERCONNECTION, UNBUNDLING, ACCESS, AND NONDISCRIMINATION OBLI-GATIONS.   A significant aspect of the focus on content-neutrality, and of the principles set forth in *Turner*, is that they permit the continuation and development of the range of common-carrier regulations—even as carriers of information also increasingly become the purveyors and producers of information products. Common-carrier regulation developed first for railroads and then was extended to telecommunications. Those regulations include duties to provide interconnection (connection among carrier facilities or networks, or between networks and telecommunications equipment), unbundled offerings (separate provision of elements of carriage services including those necessary for interconnection), access (provision of carriage facilities necessary for services to be provided to ultimate consumers), and nondiscriminatory service (offering of like service on equal terms to similarly situated customers, including carriers). These or similar regulatory requirements will likely be vital to constructing the emerging ''network of networks'' and to limiting exercises of market power in the provision of developing information services. Because these measures were largely developed beyond a First Amendment context and were designed to limit market power and achieve other competitive goals, they pose relatively limited dangers to core speech interests and should generally be found to be content-neutral. Although these regulations as applied to information producers and carriers will generate a range of ongoing First Amendment issues, the framework set forth in *Turner*—and the decision's holding addressing what is essentially an "access" requirement—establish the government's ability to employ these regulatory strategies in a broad range of settings.

For telecommunications regulation, as with similar regulation for railroads and energy carriers and producers, regulators have grappled with two central problems. The first is market power accompanying control over the relatively little-used facilities that connect end users to more centralized facilities used in common by multiple consumers and suppliers. For telecommunications, local exchange carriers control the "last mile" of telephone plant that allows residences and small businesses to connect to switches and other more heavily used facilities, as well as to the services of other carriers, including long-distance carriers.[163] Whether controlled by a local telephone company or a cable television operator, the broadband connections between home and central facilities serve a similar function for video services.[164] For either type of local facility, potential providers of local services, long-distance carriers, information service providers, video programmers, and others must either secure access to the local facilities (through purchase or otherwise) or construct and operate overlapping facilities. Correspondingly, local facilities may limit consumers' or end users' ability to originate or receive messages and information products. The second problem arises through the incentives created by joint provision of delivery or carriage services as well as provision of the carried product. For telecommunications, this bundling issue often involves whether programming and broadband delivery facilities are jointly owned or offered, or whether local exchange telephone services may be combined either with other carriage services or especially with information services offered over those local facilities. Integrated carriers and producers, it is often asserted, have incentives in many settings (and especially when subject to regulation) to restrict their competing producers' offerings through discriminatory services, cross-subsidies, or otherwise.[165]

Interconnection, unbundling, access, and nondiscrimination requirements together constitute important elements of common-carrier and related regulation that address these perceived competitive dangers. The requirement that carriers interconnect their networks on agency direction is derived directly from statutes governing regulation of railroads and was contained in the original Communications Act.[166] The duty is analogous to that imposed under the essential facility doctrine in antitrust law.[167] Interconnection duties form an increasingly important element of efforts to check telecommunications market power, and particularly to erode the local bottleneck monopoly.[168] Interconnection requirements are also an important element of the FCC's attempts to create competition in the provision of switched and special access services (which carry telecommunications between long-distance carriers and end users).[169] The Telecommunications Act of 1996 also relies heavily on this type of requirement in an effort to increase local service competition.[170]

Unbundling requires in part that local monopolist carriers offer their services on a piece-part basis, so that customers and potential competitors may secure only the services they require (usually on a cost-based basis), rather than having to purchase the full array of services that the monopolist chooses to offer. Here, the analogy to tying doctrines in antitrust law is clear.[171] Unbundling is an important element of the plans developed to increase local exchange service competition as well as competition in the provision of local access services. Unbundling (in combination with interconnection requirements) also serves as a predicate and protective measure for competition in related, competitive markets. For example, one set of unbundling requirements have been efforts to ensure that local carriers' entry into enhanced and other information services does not limit competitors' service offerings or connections to end users.[172]

Access requirements impose on a carrier, often a bottleneck monopolist, the obligation to connect ultimate subscribers to competing carriers or producers (by allowing subscribers "access" to carriers, or carriers or producers access to end users). When the party seeking access to end users is another carrier, access essentially amounts to a particular type of interconnection. Access can also require carriage of information produced by others, and in this sense it extends beyond regulation of dealings between carriers. The first type of duty includes regulations requiring local exchange carriers to provide "equal access" for long-distance carriers to serve local carriers' subscribers. This duty, imposed in slightly different forms by the consent decree governing the divestiture of the Bell System and by FCC regulations and now by legislation, allows consumers their choice of long-distance carrier for the call originated (and completed) by a local exchange carrier.[173] The second type of access exists both as part of common-carrier regulation of telecommunications carriers (no carrier may unreasonably deny service to end users, whether for traditional voice transmissions or more sophisticated information and video products) and for other entities such as cable companies.[174] Indeed, the must-carry regulation addressed in *Turner* is a type of access requirement, because the statute guarantees access—indeed, access without charge—by local television broadcasters to cable system subscribers.[175]

Finally, nondiscrimination requirements routinely apply to telecommunications carriers, independently or in conjunction with the requirements set forth above. Derived directly from railroad regulation, the duty to provide like service on equal terms and conditions to similarly situated customers is an essential part of the common-carrier obligation.[176] For telecommunications, the duty originated in the Communications Act of 1934 and has been refined by the FCC through applications in a variety of contexts.[177] The duty is one to treat all similarly situated customers equally and requires affording customers (including unaffiliated carriers and information providers) terms equal to those attributed to the carrier for its own services.

These interconnection, unbundling, access, and nondiscrimination requirements present three types of First Amendment issues. The first inheres in the traditional common-carrier role itself, when a carrier must hold itself out to carry all customers' messages, in voice or video form. Even here, a carrier might object, on First Amendment grounds, to being forced to carry a message that it would otherwise decline for business or ideological reasons. Second, additional difficulties arise when the carrier provides its own information products as well as services as a common carrier. A carrier may hold itself out as providing carriage services to third parties but also provide video programming or information services such as classified advertising. In that case, additional First Amendment objections might be asserted against requirements that the carrier deliver its competitors' information product: that the competitor's product is objectionably associated with the carrier, or diminishes the communicative value of the carrier's own information offerings, and that, whenever capacity constraints exist, the carriage obligation in fact displaces or limits the carrier's own communications. Third, still more First Amendment difficulties arise when the local carrier does not make a general offering of its services—for example by barring access to end users by particular competing information service providers. In this case, the carrier's entire offering is presented as its own information product (whatever the source), and any access or interconnection obligation alters that product. When this situation is combined with limited capacity, the distortion of the information product (and underlying editorial judgment) greatly increases. In these circumstances, entities that seek to provide information products to the carrier for resale to subscribers, and are prevented from doing so by virtue of the carrier's obligation to carry others' messages, may possess an additional and separate First Amendment claim. This situation is, of course, the one presented by access requirements imposed on traditional cable television systems.[178]

The principles underlying *Turner* provide a framework for analyzing all three of these types of First Amendment claims. The third, and most difficult, is the one that *Turner* itself addressed. As noted, the Court held that the government could impose such access requirements, as long as they were designed to advance content-neutral, procompetitive objectives, shown to be directly related to a genuine competitive threat, and still preserved significant speech opportunities.[179] Similar analysis may establish the validity of measures subject to the other two types of First Amendment claims. For common carriers—whether they provide their own information services or not—interconnection, access, and related regulations often can be justified as designed to prevent abuses of market power, depending on the context. As noted, these requirements may reflect generally applicable tying and essential facilities doctrines drawn from antitrust law. In addition, these requirements could be supported more directly through the argument that common-carrier obligations themselves embody sufficient, content-neutral government objectives. Like antitrust doctrines, common-carrier principles were developed for application to industries unrelated to speech interests or products and provide a ready baseline for evaluating whether a challenged regulation is designed to achieve traditional regulatory objectives or in fact seeks to influence the content of communications.[180]

CROSS-OWNERSHIP RESTRICTIONS. The focus on whether a measure is content-based, as embodied in the antitrust principle, also provides the basis for analyzing the threat to First Amendment interests posed by a range of statutes and regulations that restrict the ability of particular media or communications entities to engage in related lines of business that include production or distribution of information. These restrictions could, and have been, characterized as flat prohibitions on speech. Even so, the focus on whether the measures are designed to influence the messages communicated establishes that the government may in certain circumstances regulate broadly through use of such restrictions. Under *Turner*, these types of restrictions are, however, unusually vulnerable to First Amendment claims based on allegations that the ostensible competitive threat no longer exists. Courts initially applied *Turner* and addressed this issue in response to challenges to the statutory restriction on telephone company provision of video services in their local telephone service areas (a provision that Congress repealed in 1996 and that, if considered apart from related FCC rules, was particularly outdated, categorical, and thinly documented).[181]

Cross-ownership restrictions have arisen in various guises throughout the information industries. For example, cable television operators were until 1996 prohibited from owning an interest in a television broadcast station in the system's service area.[182] Cable television operators could not take significant interests in television networks (and vice versa),[183] and cannot acquire certain alternative delivery systems that operate in the cable system's service area.[184] Newspapers could not generally own television stations in their principal service area.[185] The consent decree that broke up the Bell System rested originally on three specific lines-of-business restrictions, which prohibited the Bell operating companies from engaging directly or indirectly in long-distance service, telecommunications equipment manufacturing, and information services (this last restriction was lifted in 1991).[186]

Less categorical restrictions on entry into activities that may be protected by the First Amendment also are common. For example, separate subsidiary and accounting restrictions are imposed on local telephone company entry into a range of information services (so-called "enhanced services").[187] Cable systems are limited in the percentage of affiliated programming that they can transmit.[188] The number of television and radio stations under common ownership is similarly limited, both nationally and in particular locales.[189]

Before *Turner*, these restrictions were subject to broad First Amendment challenges. The Supreme Court had twice considered and upheld two provisions that raised cross-ownership issues: the "chain broadcasting" restrictions on coordinated control of station programming, and the prohibition on joint ownership of a newspaper and a broadcasting station in the same local market.[190] Both decisions rested, however, principally on the peculiar standards applicable to radio and television licenses and particularly on the government's ability to impose ownership conditions on the licensee.[191] For information production and delivery systems not dependent on radio licenses, however, the cross-ownership restriction could be characterized as a direct prohibition on speech—or even as a prior restraint on speech. For example, before *Turner* local telephone companies had argued that the statutory prohibition on telephone companies' provision of cable programming to subscribers in their local telephone service areas must be subjected to strict judicial scrutiny under the First Amendment.[192] Although no court had accepted the telephone companies' broadest First Amendment claims through 1996, various courts consistently applied a heightened standard of review as indicated in *Turner* and concluded that the restriction could not be enforced because it did not directly advance sufficiently established, neutral interests in preserving competition.[193]

The focus on whether a rule is content-based, set forth in *Turner*, both preserves the government's ability to impose cross-ownership restrictions where truly justified by competitive concerns and allows challenges to such restrictions that in fact seek other objectives, including altering the content of or participants in public debate. In the abstract, a ready content-neutral basis exists that may justify either categorical prohibitions on a monopolist's entry into a related market or entry restrictions that require structural separation of operations. Cross-ownership restrictions are traditional antitrust remedies.[194] Many of the restrictions, especially on a dominant local service provider's entry into potentially competitive technologies in the same service area, simply generalize the conclusion that individual antitrust cases would produce. The content-neutral, competitive basis of a challenged regulation is even clearer when the government prohibits not entry altogether, but simply entry in the absence of traditional safeguards designed to prevent cross-subsidy of products in competitive markets through manipulation of pricing or product offerings in less competitive markets subject to regulation.[195]

At the same time, the antitrust principle provides ample opportunity for challenges alleging that such regulations in fact reflect efforts to manipulate the content of communications or sweep too broadly, in relation to the asserted government interest. If proved in the former case, strict scrutiny would apply, and in the latter even intermediate scrutiny would require that the challenged measure be invalidated. If anything, *Turner's* requirement of evidentiary showings in support of a challenged regulation creates considerable and ongoing uncertainty regarding the validity of various cross-ownership restrictions. This is particularly so for categorical bars on entry into lines of business that reflect speech activities. Not only will entities subject to such restrictions be able to challenge the basis for initially imposing the cross-ownership bar, but they will thereafter likely be able to reassert their claims based on allegations of changed circumstances. Indeed, many of the categorical cross-ownership and related restrictions rest on antiquated market analysis and crude conceptions of the necessity for separation between markets. Unless the courts apply *Turner* by allowing the government to adopt broad prophylactic rules to constrain monopoly power (demonstrated when the rules are enacted), such restrictions will remain extremely vulnerable to First Amendment challenge.

RATE REGULATION.   Rate regulation is a traditional element of oversight of the information industries and poses potential First Amendment dangers as well. Here, too, the antitrust principle establishes the presumptive constitutionality of a broad range of rate regulation while also beginning the process of setting bounds on rate regulation that may harm First Amendment interests.

Rate restrictions by federal and state authorities have been a hallmark of regulation of the carriage industries, including telecommunications. The power of the federal government to regulate rates extends nearly as far as federal jurisdiction over communications services and is always subject to expansion through legislative revision. In practice, federal regulation of telecommunications rates generally has been applied to common-carrier services rather than to telecommunications carriers' provision of information products,[196] but rate regulation of cable television services has recently increased dramatically.[197] For both federal and state rate regulation of telecommunications services, traditional rate-of-return regulation (designed to allow only a reasonable return based on an assessment of prudently incurred costs) has given way to various forms of incentive regulation (especially price cap regulation, which seeks to constrain prices and increase the carrier's incentive to provide services efficiently).[198] Recent rate regulation of cable television services has aspects of price cap regulation in the establishment of the benchmark but for departures relies on measuring costs and directly limiting profits.[199]

Despite its pervasiveness, rate regulation potentially poses severe First Amendment difficulties. When rate-making powers are directed at individual producers of information products or classes of speakers, the government has the opportunity to restrict products or messages its officials find to be disruptive or threatening, or to strike at unpopular views or associations. For entities that produce and deliver information, this danger of overt or subtle coercion exists whether the government regulates rates of carriage services only or directly sets prices for information products. In these ways, the rate-making power presents many of the same dangers inherent in the taxation power. In that setting, courts have applied heightened scrutiny to ensure that the taxation power is exercised through general rules and is not designed to coerce particular media entities or industry subsegments.[200]

Under the framework set forth in *Turner*, the government will generally be able to defend rate regulation as content-neutral. In industries unrelated to the production or dissemination of information, rate regulation is common and generally responds to market power possessed by regulated entities. For information industries, the government can similarly defend rate regulation as directly furthering its interest in checking abuses of market power, and courts have been quite willing to uphold traditional rate regulation where the government can demonstrate that competition is restricted or largely absent.[201]

Even so, rate regulation that departs from these circumstances would likely be subject to both facial and as-applied challenges on First Amendment grounds. Attempts to regulate rates when no market power exists might be challenged as furthering no legitimate, content-neutral purpose. Attempts to formulate or apply rate principles to particular speakers or classes of speakers may be subject to as-applied First Amendment challenges. For these challenges, the government may be able to defend the scope and form of its regulations by demonstrating that they do not differ significantly from regulations adopted in industries that embody no First Amendment interest. Even so, the principles developed in *Turner* will likely prove insufficient, or will at best be a starting point. To prevent abuses of government power in particular rate cases, procedural protections will likely have to be made available to regulated speakers. In addition, given the possibility of abuse of the rate-setting power, the government could probably be required to meet a heightened standard—for example, by demonstrating that its requirements reflect traditional rate-setting principles and otherwise have no peculiarly harmful effect on speech.

Conclusion

We are in the midst of a far-reaching transformation of how information is produced and delivered. Until recently, over-the-air broadcasting was the nearly exclusive source of electronically delivered, widely distributed information, with cable television systems serving essentially as an adjunct delivery system dependent on broadcast programming. Now, a new information industry has emerged. Multiple outlets widely distribute voice, video, and text information products, including traditional print products, using a variety of technologies. Those sources deliver an expanding array of video programming and are poised to provide the next generation of interactive and customer-controlled information products.

These developments permit a dramatic expansion of First Amendment protections and an opportunity to reaffirm the essential elements of the First Amendment tradition. Together, they eliminate the bases for the social understanding that broadcasting (and perhaps other electronic media) are distinct from traditional speech and thus deserving of lesser First Amendment protections. The transformation of information production and delivery underscores that electronic media are not a unique information source, that nothing in the government's allocation of licenses justifies greater government regulation of speech, and that electronic service providers perform functions indistinguishable from those of speakers entitled to full legal protections. As the scope of the emerging media increases, so does the opportunity to increase First Amendment protections.

At the same time, the expanding sources and types of electronically delivered information pose difficult First Amendment issues for traditional antitrust and common-carrier regulation, as well as for new regulatory measures designed for the emerging information network. As traditionally regulated entities and entities often possessing market power begin to engage in activities protected by the First Amendment, regulations directed at them increasingly threaten First Amendment interests.

A return to traditional First Amendment principles also provides guidance for resolving this dilemma. As long as government can demonstrate that its regulations do not seek to shape the content of speech and directly pursues these legitimate objectives, it retains considerable latitude to regulate in pursuit of its antitrust and common-carrier objectives. Judicial scrutiny will be necessary to ensure that these regulations do not mask efforts to regulate content and do not otherwise unduly restrict the opportunities for speech. This process will be difficult and costly, and may subject vast reaches of traditional regulation to ongoing First Amendment challenges. The alternative is, however, more costly still.

Notes

Chapter One

1. Steve Brull, "New Sony President Aims at U.S. Data Highway," *International Herald Tribune*, March 29, 1995, p. 11.

2. See 47 U.S.C. §§ 301–33.

3. Ibid., §§ 201–08.

4. See, for example, *United States* v. *Paramount Pictures, Inc.*, 334 U.S. 131 (1948).

5. See *Inquiry into the Economic Relationship between Television Broadcasting and Cable Television, Report*, 71 F.C.C.2d 632 (1979); *Cable Television Syndicated Exclusivity Rules, Report*, 71 F.C.C.2d 951 (1979); *Notice of Proposed Rulemaking in Docket Nos. 20988 and 21284*, 71 F.C.C.2d 1004 (1979); *Amendment of Part 76 of the Commission's Rules and Regulations Concerning the Cable Television Certificate of Compliance Process, Report and Order*, 69 F.C.C.2d 697 (1978); see also *FCC* v. *Midwest Video Corp.*, 440 U.S. 689 (1979); *Home Box Office, Inc.* v. *FCC*, 567 F.2d 9 (D.C. Cir. 1977), cert. denied, 434 U.S 829 (1977).

6. See generally *Amendment of Section 64.702 of the Commission's Rules and Regulations, Final Decision*, 77 F.C.C.2d 384, modified, 84 F.C.C.2d 50 (1980); further modified, 88 F.C.C.2d 512 (1981) (hereafter *Computer II*); aff'd, *Computer & Communications Industry Ass'n* v. *FCC*, 693 F.2d 198 (D.C. Cir. 1982), cert. denied, 461 U.S. 938 (1983).

7. See 47 U.S.C. §§ 521–42; see also *United States* v. *Midwest Video Corp.*, 406 U.S. 649 (1972); *United States* v. *Southwestern Cable Co.*, 392 U.S. 157 (1968).

8. See *Computer II*.

9. See generally, for example, Nicholas Negroponte, *Being Digital* (New York: Alfred A. Knopf, 1995); Peter Huber, Michael K. Kellogg, and John Thorne, *The Geodesic Network II: 1993 Report on Competition in the Telephone Industry* (Washington, D.C.: The Geodesic Company, 1992); Walter G. Bolter, James W. McConnaughey, and Fred Kelsey, *Telecommunications Policy for the 1990s and Beyond* (Armonk, N.Y.:

M.E. Sharpe, 1990); Gerald R. Faulhaber, *Telecommunications in Turmoil: Technology and Public Policy* (Cambridge, Mass.: Ballinger, 1987); Ithiel de Sola Pool, *Technologies of Freedom* (Cambridge, Mass.: Belknap, 1983).

Chapter Two

1. See 47 U.S.C. §§ 201–28.

2. See, for example, *Southwestern Bell Tel. Co.* v. *FCC*, 19 F.3d 1475 (D.C. Cir. 1994); *National Ass'n of Regulatory Util. Comm'rs* v. *FCC*, 533 F.2d 601, 608–09 (D.C. Cir. 1976); see also 47 U.S.C. § 153(51) (enacted by Telecommunications Act of 1996, § 3).

3. See 47 U.S.C. §§ 152(b) (intrastate service), 153(h) (radio broadcasters), 541(c) (cable service providers).

4. Ibid., § 201(a).

5. Ibid., §§ 201(b), 202(a); see also, for example, *MCI Telecommunications Corp.* v. *FCC*, 917 F.2d 30 (D.C. Cir. 1990); *Ad Hoc Telecommunications Users Comm.* v. *FCC*, 680 F.2d 790 (D.C. Cir. 1982).

6. See 47 U.S.C. §§ 203(a), 203(c); see generally *MCI Telecommunications Corp.* v. *American Tel. & Tel. Co.*, 114 S. Ct. 2223 (1994); 47 U.S.C. § 16 (new "forbearance" power).

7. See 47 U.S.C. § 203(a), (c).

8. Ibid., §§ 204, 208.

9. Ibid., §§ 205, 214.

10. Ibid., § 154(i); *North American Telecommunications Ass'n* v. *FCC*, 772 F.2d 1282, 1292 (7th Cir. 1988).

11. Interstate Commerce Act, 24 Stat. 380 (1887); Hepburn Act, 34 Stat. 587 (1906).

12. See, for example, Thomas K. McCraw, *Prophets of Regulation: Charles Francis Adams, Louis D. Brandeis, James M. Landis, Alfred E. Kahn* (Cambridge, Mass.: Belknap, 1984); Lawrence L. Goodwyn, *The Populist Moment: A Short History of the Agrarian Revolt in America* (Oxford University Press, 1978).

13. See McCraw, *Prophets of Regulation*; see generally Richard B. Stewart, "The Reformation of American Administrative Law," *Harvard Law Review* 88 (June 1975), pp. 1667–1813; Stephen Breyer, *Regulation and Its Reform* (Harvard University Press, 1982).

14. See Collum Report, S. Rep. 46, 49 Cong. 1 sess. (1886).

15. Ibid.

16. See Kenneth A. Cox and William J. Byrnes, *The Common Carrier Provisions— A Product of Evolutionary Development*, in Max D. Paglin, ed., *A Legislative History of the Communications Act of 1934* (New York: Oxford University Press, 1989), pp. 25–60.

17. *Communications Act of 1934*, S. Rep. 781, 73 Cong. 2 sess. (1934).

18. Examples include the Civil Aeronautics Act of 1938, the Natural Gas Act of 1938, and the Motor Carrier Act of 1935.

19. *FCC* v. *Sanders Bros. Radio Stn.*, 309 U.S. 470, 474–75 (1940).

20. See 47 U.S.C. § 152(b).

21. See, for example, *Public Util. Comm'rs* v. *FCC*, 886 F.2d 1325 (D.C. Cir. 1989); *Illinois Bell Tel. Co.* v. *FCC*, 883 F.2d 104 (D.C. Cir. 1989).

22. See 47 U.S.C. § 253 (enacted by Telecommunications Act of 1996, § 101).

23. See U.S. Const., Art. VI; *Fidelity Federal Savings & Loan Ass'n* v. *de la Cuesta*, 458 U.S. 141 (1982).

24. See *Louisiana Public Serv. Comm'n* v. *FCC*, 476 U.S. 355 (1986); *California* v. *FCC*, 905 F.2d 1217 (9th Cir. 1990); see also *California* v. *FCC*, 39 F.3d 919 (9th Cir. 1994).

25. See *Smith* v. *Illinois Bell Tel. Co.*, 282 U.S. 133 (1930).

26. See generally 47 C.F.R. parts 32, 36. This subsidy could also be characterized as one flowing from greater users of long-distance service to lesser users.

27. States are increasingly adopting various types of incentive regulation, and even the FCC's price cap regulation of local exchange carriers has an important element of rate-of-return regulation (through the "sharing" element).

28. See, for example, *Prescription of Procedures for Separating and Allocating Plant Investment, Operating Expenses, Taxes and Reserves Between the Intrastate and Interstate Operations of Telephone Companies, Report and Order*, 16 F.C.C.2d 317 (1969); *American Tel. & Tel. Co. and the Associated Bell System Companies, Charges for Interstate and Foreign Communications Services, Memorandum Opinion and Order*, 3 F.C.C.2d 307 (1966); *Reservation Telephone Cooperative*, 59 R.R.2d 484 (1985).

29. See generally Martha Derthick and Paul J. Quirk, *The Politics of Deregulation* (Brookings, 1985).

30. See generally *United States* v. *Western Elec. Co.*, 552 F.Supp. 131, 160–63 (D.D.C. 1982), aff'd, *Maryland* v. *United States*, 460 U.S. 1001 (1983).

31. See *Lincoln Tel. & Tel. Co.* v. *FCC*, 659 F.2d 1092 (D.C. Cir. 1981); *MCI Telecommunications Corp.* v. *FCC*, 580 F.2d 590 (D.C. Cir. 1978), cert. denied, 439 U.S. 980 (1978); *MCI Telecommunications Corp.* v. *FCC*, 561 F.2d 365 (D.C. Cir. 1977), cert. denied, 434 U.S. 1040 (1978); see Jordan Jay Hillman, "Telecommunications Deregulation: The Martyrdom of the Regulated Monopolist," *Northwestern University Law Review* 79 (Dec. 1984/Feb. 1985), pp. 1183–1234.

32. See generally *National Ass'n of Regulatory Utility Comm'rs* v. *FCC*, 737 F.2d 1095 (D.C. Cir. 1984), cert. denied, 469 U.S. 1227 (1985); *MTS & WATS Market-Structure, Third Report and Order*, 93 F.C.C.2d 241 (1983).

33. See McCraw, *Prophets of Regulation*; Derthick and Quirk, *The Politics of Deregulation*.

34. Ibid.

35. See *Regulatory Policies Concerning Resale and Shared Use of Common Carrier Domestic Public Switched Network Services*, 83 F.C.C.2d 167 (1980); *Regulatory Policies Concerning Resale and Shared Use of Common Carrier Services and Facilities*, 60 F.C.C.2d 261 (1976), recon., 62 F.C.C.2d 588 (1977), aff'd, *AT&T* v. *FCC*, 572 F.2d 17 (2d Cir. 1977), cert. denied, 439 U.S. 875 (1978).

36. See *Computer III Remand Proceedings, Notice of Proposed Rulemaking*, 5 FCC Rcd. 5242 (1990); *Computer III Remand Proceedings: Bell Operating Company Safeguards and Tier 1 Local Exchange Company Safeguards, Report and Order*, 6 FCC

Rcd. 7571 (1991); see also *California* v. *FCC*, 4 F.3d 1505 (9th Cir. 1993) (and sources noted); *Amendment of Section 64.702 of the Commission's Rules and Regulations (Second Computer Inquiry), Final Decision*, 77 F.C.C.2d 384 (1980), recon., 84 F.C.C.2d 50 (1980), further recon., 88 F.C.C.2d 512 (1981) (hereafter, *Computer II*), aff'd, *Computer & Communications Industry Ass'n* v. *FCC*, 693 F.2d 198 (D.C. Cir. 1982), cert. denied, 461 U.S. 938 (1983).

37. See *MTS & WATS Market-Structure, Phase III*, 100 F.C.C.2d 860 (1985).

38. See *Policy and Rules Concerning Rates for Competitive Common Carrier Services and Facilities Authorizations Therefor, First Report and Order*, 85 F.C.C.2d 1 (1980), *Second Report and Order*, 91 F.C.C.2d 59 (1982), *Third Report and Order*, 48 Fed. Reg. 46,791 (1983), *Fourth Report and Order*, 95 F.C.C.2d 554 (1983), vacated, *AT&T* v. *FCC*, 978 F.2d 727 (D.C. Cir. 1992), *Fifth Report and Order*, 98 F.C.C.2d 1191 (1984), *Sixth Report and Order*, 99 F.C.C.2d 1020 (1985), rev'd, *MCI Telecommunications Corp.* v. *FCC*, 765 F.2d 1186 (D.C. Cir. 1985). At least with respect to tariff filing, and perhaps more broadly, these policies suffered significant judicial reversals; see, for example, *MCI Telecommunications Corp.* v. *American Telephone and Telegraph Co.*, 114 S. Ct. 2223 (1994), but the FCC has received greater powers in this respect. See 47 U.S.C. § 16 (enacted by Telecommunications Act of 1996, § 401).

39. See *Expanded Interconnection with Local Telephone Company Facilities, Report and Order and Notice of Proposed Rulemaking*, 7 FCC Rcd. 7369 (1992) (Special Access Order), recon., 8 FCC Rcd. 127 (1992), vacated in part and remanded, *Bell Atlantic Corp.* v. *FCC*, 24 F.3d 1441 (D.C. Cir. 1994); *Transport Rate Structure and Pricing, Report and Order and Further Notice of Proposed Rulemaking*, 7 FCC Rcd. 7006 (1992), recon., 8 FCC Rcd. 5370 (1993), petition for review pending sub nom., *Expanded Interconnection with Local Telephone Company Facilities, Transport Phase I, Second Report and Order and Third Notice of Proposed Rulemaking*, 8 FCC Rcd. 7374 (1993), petition for review pending; *Local Exchange Carriers' Rates, Terms, and Conditions for Expanded Interconnection for Switched Transport, Memorandum Opinion and Order*, 9 FCC Rcd. 817 (Common Carrier Bureau 1994).

40. See note 38.

41. See *Policy and Rules Concerning Rates for Dominant Carriers, Second Report and Order*, 5 FCC Rcd. 6786 (1990) (LEC Price Cap Order), recon., 6 FCC Rcd. 2637 (1991), further recon, 6 FCC Rcd. 4524 (1991), second further recon., 7 FCC Rcd. 5235 (1992), aff'd, *National Rural Telecom Ass'n* v. *FCC*, 988 F.2d 174 (D.C. Cir. 1993); *Policy and Rules Concerning Rates for Dominant Carriers, Report and Order and Second Further Notice of Proposed Rulemaking*, 4 FCC Rcd. 2873 (1989) (AT&T Price Cap Order); Kathleen B. Levitz, *Loosening the Ties that Bind: Regulating the Interexchange Services Market for the 1990s*, 2 FCC Rcd. 1495 (1987). Elements of rate-of-return regulation persisted under price cap regulation, especially for local exchange carriers.

42. See *Competition in the Interstate Interexchange Marketplace, Report and Order*, 6 FCC Rcd. 5880 (1991); *Second Report and Order*, 8 FCC Rcd. 3668 (1993).

43. See *AT&T Communications, Revisions to Tariff F.C.C. No. 12, Memorandum Opinon and Order on Remand*, 6 FCC Rcd. 7039 (1991), aff'd, *Competitive Telecommunications Ass'n* v. *FCC*, 998 F.2d 1058 (D.C. Cir. 1993).

44. See *Amendment of Section 64.702 of the Commission's Rules and Regulations, Final Decision*, 77 F.C.C.2d 384, recon., 84 F.C.C.2d 50 (1980), further recon., 88 F.C.C.2d 512 (1981), aff'd, *Computer and Communications Industry Ass'n* v. *FCC*, 693 F.2d 198 (D.C. Cir. 1982), cert. denied, *National Association of Regulatory Utility Commissioners et al.* v *FCC*, 461 U.S. 938 (1983); see also note 36.

45. See *Computer II; American Tel. & Tel. Co. (Docket No. 19129), Phase II, Final Decision and Order*, 64 F.C.C.2d 1 (1977); see also *Detariffing the Installation and Maintenance of Inside Wiring, Third Report and Order*, 7 FCC Rcd. 1334 (1992); *National Ass'n of Regulatory Utility Comm'rs* v. *FCC*, 880 F.2d 422 (D.C. Cir. 1989).

46. See Telecommunications Act of 1996, § 401.

47. See 47 U.S.C § 204 (as amended by the Telecommunications Act of 1996, § 402); see also Telecommunications Act of 1996, § 103 (amending the Public Utility Holding Company Act of 1935, 15 U.S.C. § 79).

48. See 47 U.S.C § 253 (enacted by the Telecommunications Act of 1996, § 101).

49. See 47 U.S.C § 254 (enacted by the Telecommunications Act of 1996, § 101).

50. See 47 U.S.C §§ 251–52 (enacted by the Telecommunications Act of 1996, § 101).

51. See 47 U.S.C §§ 271–76 (enacted by the Telecommunications Act of 1996, § 151).

52. See notes 36 and 39; see also *Filing and Review of Open Network Architecture Plans, Phase I, Memorandum Opinion and Order*, 4 FCC Rcd. 1 (1988), recon., 5 FCC Rcd. 3084 (1990); *Intelligent Networks, Notice of Proposed Rulemaking*, 8 FCC Rcd. 6813 (1993).

53. See note 36; see also *Separation of Costs of Regulated Telephone Service from Costs of Nonregulated Activities, Report and Order*, 2 FCC Rcd. 1298 (1987), recon., 2 FCC Rcd. 6283 (1987), further recon., 3 FCC Rcd. 6701 (1988), aff'd, *Southwestern Bell* v. *FCC*, 896 F.2d 1378 (D.C. Cir. 1990); 47 C.F.R. §§ 32.27, 64.901; *Amendment of Parts 32 and 64 of the Commission's Rules to Account for Transactions between Carriers and Their Unregulated Affiliates, Notice of Proposed Rulemaking*, 8 FCC Rcd. 8071 (1993); *Local Exchange Carriers' Permanent Cost Allocation Manuals for the Separation of Regulated and Nonregulated Costs*, 8 FCC Rcd. 3105 (1993).

54. See 47 U.S.C. §§ 272–76; note 36; see also *Automated Reporting Requirements for Certain Class A and Tier 1 Telephone Companies, Report and Order*, 2 FCC Rcd. 5770 (1987), recon., 3 FCC Rcd. 6375 (1988); *Revision of the Uniform System of Accounts and Financial Reporting Requirements for Class A and Class B Telephone Companies*, 60 R.R.2d 1111 (1986), recon., 2 FCC Rcd. 1086 (1987).

55. See 47 U.S.C. §§ 301–34.

56. See generally ibid., §§ 301–03, 307–11.

57. See, for example, ibid., §§ 310(b), 312(a)(7), 315, 317–18, 325.

58. See, for example, *National Ass'n for Better Broadcasting* v. *FCC*, 849 F.2d 665 (D.C. Cir. 1988); *Subscription Video, Report and Order*, 2 FCC Rcd. 1001 (1987).

59. The assumptions underlying and manifestations of this model are discussed below.

60. See *Policy Statement on Comparative Broadcast Hearings*, 1 F.C.C.2d 393 (1965). In the late 1980s and early 1990s, courts increasingly invalidated or called into question the FCC's selection criteria, on the grounds that they were unsup-

ported and thus arbitrary and capricious (see *Bechtel* v. *FCC*, 10 F.3d 875 (D.C. Cir. 1993)) or even unconstitutional (see *Lamprecht* v. *FCC*, 958 F.2d 382 (D.C. Cir. 1992)).

61. See 47 U.S.C. §§ 394, 396.

62. See *Report and Statement of Policy re Commission En Banc Programming Inquiry*, 44 F.C.C. 2303 (1960); *Infinity Broadcasting Corp., Memorandum Opinion and Order*, 2 FCC Rcd. 2705 (1987); *Policies and Rules Concerning Children's Television Programming; Revision of Programming and Commercialization Policies, Ascertainment Requirements, and Program Log Requirements for Commercial Television Stations, Report and Order*, 6 FCC Rcd. 2111 (1991), recon., 6 FCC Rcd. 5093 (1991). The Fairness Doctrine and other content-based regulations of broadcasting are also discussed later in the text.

63. See *Review of the Commission's Regulations Governing Television Broadcasting, Further Notice of Proposed Rulemaking*, 10 FCC Rcd. 3524 (1995); *Policy Statement on Comparative Broadcast Hearings*, 1 F.C.C.2d 393 (1965); 47 C.F.R. § 73.3555; *Implementation of Commission's Equal Employment Opportunity Rules*, 9 FCC Rcd. 6276 (1994).

64. See, for example, *Sixth Report and Order on Television Allocations*, 17 Fed. Reg. 3905 (May 2, 1952); John M. Kitross, *Television Frequency Allocation Policy in the United States* (New York: Arno, 1979); *Special Project, Television Service and the FCC, Texas Law Review* 46 (November 1968), p. 1100.

65. See 47 C.F.R. §§ 73.3555, 76.501; *FCC* v. *National Citizens Comm. for Broadcasting*, 436 U.S. 775 (1978).

66. 47 C.F.R. § 73.3555; see also Telecommunications Act of 1996, § 202.

67. Ibid.

68. See 47 U.S.C. §§ 309(i), (j); Department of Commerce, National Telecommunications and Information Administration, *U.S. Spectrum Management Policy: An Agenda for the Future*, Pub. 91-23 (Government Printing Office, 1992).

69. See *Revision of Programming and Commercialization Policies, Report and Order*, 98 F.C.C.2d 1076 (1984), recon., 104 F.C.C.2d 358 (1986), rev'd in part, *Action for Children's Television* v. *FCC*, 821 F.2d 741 (D.C. Cir. 1987).

70. See *Syracuse Peace Council* v. *Television Station WTVH, Memorandum Opinion and Order*, 2 FCC Rcd. 5043 (1987), aff'd, *Syracuse Peace Council* v. *FCC*, 867 F.2d 654 (D.C. Cir. 1989); see also *Inquiry into Section 73.1910 of the Commission's Rules and Regulations Concerning the General Fairness Doctrine Obligations of Broadcast Licensees, Report*, 102 F.C.C.2d 143 (1985).

71. See, for example, *Limitations on Commercial Time on Television Broadcast Stations, Notice of Inquiry*, 8 FCC Rcd. 7277 (1993); *Notice of Apparent Liability for a Forfeiture, Letter to Infinity Broadcasting Corp.*, FCC 94-26, 9 FCC Rcd. 1746 (1994); *Policies and Rules Concerning Children's Television Programming; Revision of Programming and Commercialization Policies, Ascertainment Requirements, and Program Log Requirements for Commercial Television Stations, Report and Order*, 6 FCC Rcd. 2111 (1991), recon., 6 FCC Rcd. 5093 (1991).

72. See, for example, *Evaluation of the Syndication and Financial Interest Rules, Second Report and Order*, 8 FCC Rcd. 3282 (1993); *Revision of Radio Rules and Policies, Report and Order*, 7 FCC Rcd. 2755 (1992), ibid., *Memorandum Opinion and*

Order and Further Notice of Proposed Rulemaking, 7 FCC Rcd. 6387 (1992); *Review of the Commission's Regulations Governing Television Broadcasting, Notice of Proposed Rulemaking*, 7 FCC Rcd. 4111 (1992); *Review of the Policy Implications of the Changing Video Marketplace, Notice of Inquiry*, 6 FCC Rcd. 4961 (1991); *Amendment of Section 73.3555 of the Commission's Rules, the Broadcast Multiple Ownership Rules, Second Report and Order*, 4 FCC Rcd. 1741 (1989), recon., 4 FCC Rcd. 6489 (1989).

73. See *Review of the Commission's Regulations Governing Television Broadcasting, Further Notice of Proposed Rulemaking*, 10 FCC Rcd. 3524 (1995); see also Seltzer & Levy, *Broadcast Television in a Multichannel Marketplace*, FCC Office of Plans and Policy, Working Paper 26, 6 FCC Rcd. 3996 (1991).

74. See *Review of the Commission's Regulations Governing Attribution of Broadcast Interests and Review of the Commission's Regulations and Policies Affecting Investment in the Broadcast Industry, Notice of Proposed Rulemaking*, 10 FCC Rcd. 3606 (1995).

75. See Telecommunications Act § 202 (f), (I) (amending 47 U.S.C. § 533).

76. See Telecommunications Act § 202 (a)–(d).

77. See Telecommunications Act §§ 203–04 (amending 47 U.S.C. §§ 307 (c), 309).

78. See Telecommunications Act § 201 (enacting 47 U.S.C. § 336).

79. See *Broadcasting & Cable*, 56 (August 15, 1994).

80. See 47 U.S.C. § 522(6).

81. Ibid., § 522(19).

82. See *Telephone Company-Cable Television Cross-Ownership Rules, Second Report and Order, Recommendation to Congress, and Second Further Notice of Proposed Rulemaking*, 7 FCC Rcd. 5781, 5820–22 (1992). In addition, the service providers' control over and selection of programming is required before the provider is "transmitting" video programming and other programming services. See *National Cable Television Ass'n v. FCC*, 33 F. 3d 66 (D.C. Cir. 1994).

83. See *Telephone Company-Cable Television Cross-Ownership Rules, Second Report and Order*, 7 FCC Rcd. at 5822.

84. See Telecommunications Act of 1996, § 301 (amending 47 U.S.C. § 522(6)(B)).

85. See 47 U.S.C. § 541(c).

86. See 47 U.S.C. §§ 651, 653; *Telephone Company–Cable Television Cross-Ownership Rules, Second Report and Order*, 7 FCC Rcd. at 5071–72.

87. Ironically, cable television's initial growth stemmed from FCC policies that dramatically restricted the number and scope of television broadcasting outlets, thus increasing demand for retransmitted signals. See *Amendment of Section 3.606 of the Commission's Rules and Regulations, Smith Report and Order*, 41 F.C.C. 148 (1952).

88. See, for example, *Second Report and Order in Dockets Nos. 14895, 15233, and 15971*, 2 F.C.C.2d 725 (1966), aff'd, *Black Hills Video Corp. v. FCC*, 399 F.2d 65 (8th Cir. 1968); see also *Carter Mountain Transmission Corp.v. FCC*, 32 F.C.C. 459 (1962), aff'd, 321 F.2d 359 (D.C. Cir. 1963).

89. See *United States v. Southwestern Cable Co.*, 392 U.S. 157 (1968); *United States v. Midwest Video Corp.*, 406 U.S. 649 (1972); *FCC v. Midwest Video Corp.*, 440 U.S. 689 (1979).

90. See, for example, *First Report and Order in Docket Nos. 14895 and 15233*, 38 F.C.C. 683 (1965); *Second Report and Order in Docket Nos. 14895, 15233, and 15971*, 2 FCC Rcd. 725 (1966), which severely limited the ability of cable operators to import television broadcast signals into the top 100 television markets; *Cable Television Report and Order*, 36 F.C.C.2d 143 (1972), recon., 36 F.C.C.2d 326 (1972), aff'd, *ACLU* v. *FCC*, 523 F.2d 1344 (9th Cir. 1975).

91. *Report and Order in Docket Nos. 20988 and 21284*, 79 F.C.C.2d 663 (1980); *Cable Television Syndicated Program Exclusivity Rules*, 71 F.C.C.2d 951 (1979); *Amendment of Part 76–CATV Certificate of Compliance Process*, 69 F.C.C.2d 697 (1978); *Motion Picture Association of America, Inc., Petition for Rulemaking, Memorandum Opinion and Order in RM- 2952*, 68 F.C.C.2d 57 (1978).

92. See 47 U.S.C. § 541–42.

93. See 47 U.S.C. §§ 532–34.

94. See, for example, ibid., §§ 531, 532.

95. See 47 C.F.R. §§ 73.658, 76.92-97; *Amendment of Parts 73 and 76 of the Commission's Rules Relating to Program Exclusivity in the Cable and Broadcast Industries, Report and Order*, 3 FCC Rcd. 5299 (1988), recon., 4 FCC Rcd. 2711 (1989).

96. See 47 C.F.R. §§ 76.92–97; *Amendment of Parts 73 and 76 of the Commission's Rules Relating to Program Exclusivity in the Cable and Broadcast Industries, Report and Order*, 3 FCC Rcd. 5299 (1988), recon., 4 FCC Rcd. 2711 (1989).

97. See *Quincy Cable TV, Inc.* v. *FCC*, 768 F.2d 1434 (D.C. Cir. 1985), cert. denied, 476 U.S. 1169 (1986); *Century Communications Corp.* v. *FCC*, 835 F.2d 292 (D.C. Cir. 1987).

98. For a survey of evidence supporting the conclusion that cable operators continue to exercise market power, see *Implementation of Section 19 of the Cable Television Consumer Protection and Competition Act of 1992: Annual Assessment of the Status of Competition in the Market for the Delivery of Video Programming, First Report*, 9 FCC Rcd. 7442 (1994). See also S. Rep. 92, Committee on Commerce, Science, and Transportation, 8–18, 102 Cong. 2 sess. (1991), which reported on evidence of cable television systems' market power.

99. See S. Rep. 92, p. 13.

100. Ibid., pp. 3–8, 20–23; *Cable Television Consumer Protection and Competition Act of 1992*, H.R. Rep. 628, 102 Cong. 2 sess. (GPO, 1992), pp. 30, 37.

101. See *Annual Assessment of the Status of Competition in the Market for the Delivery of Video Programming*, 9 FCC Rcd. 7442, 7570–71 (1994). The following are the seven largest owners of cable television systems and selected cable programming channels in which each has a significant financial interest: (1)Tele-Communications, Inc. (15.2 million subscribers): BET, TBS, Court TV, Discovery, Encore, Family Channel, QVC, E! Entertainment; (2) Time Warner (7.2 million subscribers): HBO, QVC, CNN, TBS, TNT, Cinemax, E! Entertainment, Comedy Central; (3) Continental Cablevision (3 million subscribers): CNN, TBS, QVC, TNT, Viewers' Choice, Home Shopping Network; (4) Comcast (2.9 million subscribers): CNN, TBS, Viewers' Choice, TNT, E! Entertainment, QVC; (5) Cablevision Systems Corp. (2.3 million subscribers): AMC, Bravo, SportsChannel, Court TV; (6) Cox Cable (1.8 million subscribers): Discovery Channel, Learning Channel, Viewers' Choice, E! Entertain-

ment; (7) Jones Intercable (1.3 million subscribers): CNN, TBS, TNT, Headline News. See "What Makes Top Seven MSOs Tick: Roadmap of How the Cable Highway Interconnects," *Advertising Age* (Apr. 11, 1994), p. S-10.

102. See, for example, *Cable Television Consumer Protection Act of 1991*, S. Rep. 92, pp. 24–32; see also *Cable Television Consumer Protection and Competition Act of 1992*, H.R. Rep. 628, pp. 38–44. These practices may have been rational and in perhaps most instances legal, but they nonetheless generated considerable political pressure for reform.

103. See 47 U.S.C. § 543(b); see generally *Implementation of Sections of the Cable Television Consumer Protection and Competition Act of 1992: Rate Regulation, Report and Order and Further Notice of Proposed Rulemaking*, 8 FCC Rcd. 5631 (1993) (hereafter *Report and Order*); *First Order on Reconsideration, Second Report and Order, and Third Further Notice of Proposed Rulemaking*, 9 FCC Rcd. 1164 (1993); *Third Report and Order*, 8 FCC Rcd. 8444 (1993); *Second Order on Reconsideration, Fourth Report and Order, and Fifth Notice of Proposed Rulemaking*, 9 FCC Rcd. 4119 (1994) (hereafter, *Fourth Report and Order*).

104. See *Implementation of Sections of the Cable Television Consumer Protection and Competition Act of 1992: Rate Regulation, Report and Order*, 8 FCC Rcd. 5631 (1993).

105. See ibid., *Fourth Report and Order,* 9 FCC Rcd. at 4136–37 (1994).

106. See 47 U.S.C. §§ 534–35; *Turner Broadcasting System, Inc.* v. *FCC*, 114 S. Ct. 2445 (1994).

107. See 47 U.S.C. § 533(f).

108. See *Implementation of Sections 11 and 13 of the Cable Television Consumer Protection and Competition Act of 1992, Horizontal and Vertical Ownership Limits, Second Report and Order*, 8 FCC Rcd. 8565 (1993); *Daniels Cablevision, Inc.* v. *United States*, 835 F.Supp. 1 (D.D.C. 1993).

109. See 47 U.S.C. § 548; see also *Implementation of Sections 12 and 19 of the Cable Television Consumer Protection and Competition Act of 1992, First Report and Order*, 8 FCC Rcd. 3359 (1993).

110. See 47 U.S.C. § 536; *Implementation of Sections 12 and 19 of the Cable Television Consumer Protection and Competition Act of 1992, Second Report and Order*, 9 FCC Rcd. 2642 (1993).

111. See 47 U.S.C. § 532(b); *Implementation of Sections of the Cable Television Consumer Protection and Competition Act of 1992: Rate Regulation*, 8 FCC Rcd. 5631, 5943–49 (1993).

112. See Telecommunications Act of 1996, § 301(b).

113. See Telecommunications Act of 1996, § 506 (amending 46 U.S.C. §§ 532(C) & 531(e)).

114. See Telecommunications Act of 1996, § 303 (amending 47 U.S.C. § 541(B)); see also Telecommunications Act of 1996, § 101 (enacting 47 U.S.C. § 253).

115. See Telecommunications Act of 1996, § 302 (enacting 47 U.S.C. §§ 651–53).

116. See 47 U.S.C. § 533(b).

117. See *Applications of Telephone Companies for Section 214 Certificates for Channel Facilities Furnished to Affiliated Community Antenna Television Systems,*

Final Report and Order, 21 F.C.C.2d 307 (1970), recon., 22 F.C.C.2d 746, aff'd, *General Telephone Co.* v. *United States* 449 F.2d 846 (5th Cir. 1971).

118. See 47 C.F.R. §§ 63.54–63.58 (1971).

119. See *Telephone Company–Cable Television Cross-Ownership Rules, Sections 63.54–63.58, Notice of Inquiry*, 2 FCC Rcd. 5092 (1987); ibid., *Further Notice of Inquiry and Notice of Proposed Rulemaking*, 3 FCC Rcd. 5849 (1988) (hereafter, *Further Notice of Inquiry*); ibid., *Further Notice of Proposed Rulemaking, First Report and Order, and Second Further Notice of Inquiry*, 7 FCC Rcd. 300 (1991) (hereafter, *First Report*), aff'd, *National Cable Television Ass'n* v. *FCC*, No. 91-1649, 33 F.3d 66 (1994) (D.C. Cir. 1994); *Second Report and Order, Recommendation to Congress, and Second Further Notice of Proposed Rulemaking*, 7 FCC Rcd. 5781 (1992) (hereafter, *Second Report*).

120. See *Telephone Company-Cable Television Cross-Ownership Rules*, §§ 63.54–63.58, *Further Notice of Inquiry*, 3 FCC Rcd. at 5865.

121. See *Telephone Company–Cable Television Cross-Ownership Rules, Second Report*, 7 FCC Rcd. at 5847–49. See generally *National Cable Television Ass'n* v. *FCC*, 33 F.3d 66 (1994); *Chesapeake & Potomac Tel. Co.* v. *United States*, 42 F.3d 181 (1994) (subsequent history omitted).

122. See *Telephone Company–Cable Television Cross-Ownership Rules, First Report*, 7 FCC Rcd. at 322–23.

123. See *Telephone Company–Cable Television Cross-Ownership Rules, Second Report*, 7 FCC Rcd. at 5820–23.

124. See generally ibid, 5820–23; *First Report*, 7 FCC Rcd. at 314–18.

125. See *Second Report*, 7 FCC Rcd. at 5802–23.

126. See generally *National Cable Television Ass'n* v. *FCC*, 33 F.3d 66 (1994).

127. See *Telephone Company–Cable Television Cross-Ownership Rules, Memorandum Opinion and Order on Reconsideration and Third Further Notice of Proposed Rulemaking*, 10 FCC Rcd. 244 (1995); see also *Fourth Further Notice of Proposed Rulemaking*, 10 FCC Rcd. 4617 (1995).

128. See *Application of New England Tel. & Tel. Co., Order and Authorization,* 10 FCC Rcd. 5346 (1995); *Application of BellSouth Telecommunications, Inc.*, File No. W-P-C 6977, *Order and Authorization* (released February 7, 1995); *Application of Chesapeake & Potomac Tel. Co. of Virginia, Order and Authorization*, 10 FCC Rcd. 2975.

129. See *US WEST, Inc.* v. *United States*, 48 F.3d 1092 (9th Cir., 1995), vacated and remanded (No. 95-315); *Chesapeake & Potomac Tel. Co.* v. *United States*, 42 F.3d 181 (4th Cir. 1994), vacated and remanded; *United States Tel. Ass'n* v. *United States*, No. 1:94CV01961 (D.D.C., Feb. 14, 1995); *GTE South, Inc.* v. *United States*, No. 94.1588-A (E.D. Va. Jan. 13, 1995); *NYNEX Corp.* v. *United States*, Civ. No. 93-323-P-C (D. Me., Dec. 8, 1994); *BellSouth Corp.* v. *United States*, No. CV 93-B-2661-S (N.D. Ala., Sept. 23, 1994); *Ameritech Corp.* v. *United States*, 867 F. Supp. 721 (N.D. Ill. 1994).

130. See, for example, *Chesapeake & Potomac Tel. Co.* v *United States*, 42 F.3d at 181; *US WEST, Inc.* v. *United States*, 48 F.3d at 1092.

131. See *Telephone Company–Cable Television Cross-Ownership Rules, Fourth Further Notice of Proposed Rulemaking,* 10 FCC Rcd. 4617 (1995). The FCC outlined its effort to allow and provide safeguards for telephone companies to provide video

programming, despite the continued existence of the statutory prohibition, as an exercise of its power to waive application of the prohibition.

132. Ibid., ¶¶ 9–17.

133. Ibid., ¶¶ 20–36.

134. Ibid., ¶¶ 37–39.

135. See Telecommunications Act of 1996, § 302(c).

136. See 47 U.S.C. § 651(a)(1) (enacted by Telecommunications Act of 1996, § 302 (a)).

137. See 47 U.S.C. § 651(a)(2) (enacted by Telecommunications Act of 1996, § 302 (a)).

138. See 47 U.S.C. § 651(a)(3) (enacted by Telecommunications Act of 1996, § 302 (a)).

139. See 47 U.S.C. § 652 (enacted by Telecommunications Act of 1996, § 302 (a)).

140. See 47 U.S.C. § 653(a)–(b) (enacted by Telecommunications Act of 1996, § 302 (a)).

141. See 47 U.S.C. §§ 651(b)–(c), 653(b) (enacted by Telecommunications Act of 1996, § 302 (a)).

142. See 47 U.S.C. § 653(c) (enacted by Telecommunications Act of 1996, § 302 (a)).

143. See *United States* v. *Western Elec. Co.*, 552 F. Supp. 131, 226 (D.D.C. 1982) ("Decree" or "MFJ" appended), aff'd, *Maryland* v. *United States*, 460 U.S. 1001 (1983); MFJ §§ II(D), VIII(C); see also *United States* v. *Western Elec. Co.*, 900 F.2d 283 (D.C. Cir. 1990).

144. See *United States* v. *Western Elec. Co.*, 552 F.Supp. at 131; MFJ §§ II(A), II(B).

145. See generally *United States* v. *Western Elec. Co.*, 552 F.Supp. at 135–40.

146. Department of Justice, *Competitive Impact Statement*, p. 4, *United States* v. *Western Elec. Co.*, Civ. No. 82-0192 (D.D.C., filed Feb. 5, 1982).

147. See, for example, *MCI Communications Corp.* v. *AT&T*, 708 F.2d 1081 (7th Cir. 1982), cert. denied, 464 U.S. 891 (1983).

148. See *United States* v. *Western Elec. Co.*, 552 F.Supp. at 226.

149. Department of Justice, *Competitive Impact Statement*, p. 6.

150. LATAs define the areas in which local rather than long-distance (or interexchange) telecommunications services are provided and were drawn to reflect residential communities of interest, taking into account local network efficiencies. *United States* v. *Western Elec. Co.*, 569 F.Supp. 990, 993–94 (D.D.C. 1983).

151. See MFJ § II(D).

152. Ibid., §§ II(A), II(B). Specifically, in the United States equal access requires a local exchange carrier to provide its customers the opportunity to presubscribe to an interexchange carrier and to reach that carrier by dialing simply 1, and to reach any interexchange carrier by dialing 10XXX, or some other short access code. Additionally, equal access requires a local exchange carrier to terminate calls coming into its system from an interexchange carrier.

153. See MFJ § I(D).

154. See *United States* v. *Western Elec. Co.*, 969 F.2d 1231 (D.C. Cir. 1992).

155. See MFJ § VIII(C); see also *United States* v. *Western Elec. Co.*, 900 F.2d 283 (D.C. Cir. 1990).

156. See *Opinion & Order, United States* v. *Western Elec. Co.,* No. 82-0192, (D.D.C. April 28, 1995).

157. See *Order, United States* v. *Western Elec. Co.*, No. 82-0192, (D.D.C. Oct. 24, 1994).

158. See, for example, *Order, United States* v. *Western Elec. Co.*, No. 82-0192, (D.D.C. June 26, 1995) (Pacific Telesis); ibid. (BellSouth); ibid. (NYNEX).

159. A waiver was necessary because AT&T sought to acquire McCaw's interests in cellular partnerships that were majority-owned by regional companies, thus rendering those interests the "stock or assets" of a Bell operating company, which the decree prohibited AT&T from acquiring without a waiver. See MFJ § I(D); *Order, United States* v. *Western Elec. Co.*, No. 82-0192 (D.D.C. Aug. 25, 1994).

160. See generally *United States* v. *Western Elec. Co.*, 900 F.2d 283 (D.C. Cir. 1990); see also *United States* v. *Western Elec. Co.*, 673 F.Supp. 525 (D.D.C. 1987) & 714 F.Supp. 1 (D.D.C. 1988), aff'd in part and remanded, 900 F.2d 283 (D.C. Cir. 1990).

161. See *United States* v. *Western Elec. Co.*, 900 F.2d 283 (D.C. Cir. 1990).

162. See *United States* v. *Western Elec. Co.*, 993 F.2d 1572 (D.C. Cir. 1993); see also *United States* v. *Western Elec. Co.*, 767 F.Supp. 308 (D.D.C. 1991), stay rev'd, 1991–92 Trade Cas. ¶ 69,610 (D.C. Cir. 1991), aff'd, 993 F.2d 1572 (D.C. Cir. 1993).

163. See Telecommunications Act of 1996, § 601(a).

164. Ibid; Conference Report, pp. 198–99.

165. See Telecommunications Act of 1996, § 601(a); 47 U.S.C. §153(33) & (35) (definitions of "affiliate" and "Bell operating company," enacted in Telecommunications Act of 1996, § 3).

166. See 47 U.S.C. § 251(g) (enacted by Telecommunications Act of 1996, § 151).

167. See 47 U.S.C. § 271(f) (enacted by Telecommunications Act of 1996, § 151).

168. See 47 U.S.C. § 271(a)–(b) (enacted by Telecommunications Act of 1996, § 151).

169. See 47 U.S.C. § 271(g) (enacted by Telecommunications Act of 1996, § 151).

170. See 47 U.S.C. § 273(a) (enacted by Telecommunications Act of 1996, § 151).

171. See, for example, 47 U.S.C. §§ 271(e), 272, 273(b)–(e), 274–75 (enacted by Telecommunications Act of 1996, § 151).

172. See 47 U.S.C. § 271(d)(3), 271(c), 251 (enacted by Telecommunications Act of 1996, §§ 101, 151).

173. See 47 U.S.C. § 271(d)(2) (enacted by Telecommunications Act of 1996, §. 151).

174. See Conference Report, p. 201.

Chapter Three

1. Note that broadcasting stations' importance as delivery systems is separate from the popularity of certain programming networks that also own stations and enter affiliations with stations.

2. See *Broadcasting & Cable*, August 15, 1994, p. 56; *Annual Assessment of the Status of Competition in the Market for the Delivery of Video Programming, Second Annual Report*, CS Docket No. 95-61, App. G (released December 11, 1995) (hereafter *Second Annual Report*).

3. See *Cable Television Consumer Protection Act of 1991*, S. Rep. 92, 102 Cong. 1 sess. (1991), p. 45; see also the sources cited therein, including *Must Carry, Hearing before the Subcommittee on Communications of the Senate Committee on Commerce, Science, and Transportation* (October 25, 1989), pp. 39, 80.

4. See *Evaluation of the Syndication and Financial Interest Rules, Second Report and Order* (hereafter *Second Report and Order*), 8 FCC Rcd. 3282, 3305 (1993).

5. Ibid. at 3305 n. 49, 3306.

6. See *Competition, Rate Deregulation, and the Commission's Policies Relating to the Provision of Cable Television Service, Report*, 5 FCC Rcd. 4962, 4984 (1990).

7. *Implementation of Section 19 of the Cable Television Consumer Protection and Competition Act of 1992, Annual Assessment of the Status of Competition in the Market for the Delivery of Video Programming, First Report*, 9 FCC Rcd. 7422, 7452 (1995).

8. See *Second Report and Order*, 8 FCC Rcd. at 3305.

9. See, for example, Barron, "Cable TV: The Big Picture," *New York Times*, April 10, 1994, §14, p. 1.

10. See *Motion for a Waiver of the Decree to Permit US WEST, Inc., to Provide Limited InterLATA Services and Engage in Limited Manufacturing Activities through Its Minority Partnership Investment in Time Warner Entertainment Company, L.P., United States* v. *Western Elec. Co.*, Civ. No. 82-0192 (D.D.C., filed Dec. 10, 1993).

11. The initial purchases, projected at approximately $2 billion, are principally for switching capable of providing traditional voice telephony. See "Cable Industry's Plans in Telephony Hinge on Federal Policies, Customer Reaction, Technical Developments," *Telecommunications Reports*, August 15, 1994, pp. 8–10.

12. See *Application of New Jersey Bell Tel. Co., Order and Authorization*, 9 FCC Rcd. 3677 (1994); *Application of Rochester Tel. Co., Order and Authorization*, 9 FCC Rcd. 2285 (1994); *Application of the Southern New England Tel. Co., Order and Authorization*, 9 FCC Rcd. 1019 (1993); *Application of US WEST Communications, Inc., Order and Authorization*, 9 FCC Rcd. 184 (1993); *Application of New York Tel. Co., Order and Authorization*, 8 FCC Rcd. 4325 (1993); *Application of the Chesapeake and Potomac Tel. Co., Order and Authorization*, 8 FCC Rcd. 2313 (1993).

13. See *Second Annual Report*, pp. 97–98.

14. See *Application of Chesapeake and Potomac Tel. Co., Order and Authorization*; see also *Application of Rochester Tel. Co., Order and Authorization*.

15. See *Application of New Jersey Bell Tel. Co., Order and Authorization*; *Application of US WEST, Inc., Order and Authorization*.

16. See *Telephone Company-Cable Television Cross-Ownership Rules, Sections 63.54–63.58, Second Report and Order, Recommendation to Congress, and Second Further Notice of Proposed Rulemaking*, 7 FCC Rcd. 5781 (1992) (petition for recon. pending, appeal pending); see also *National Cable Television Ass'n* v. *FCC*, 33 F.3d 66 (D.C. Cir., 1994). Approval for carriage of video programming presents different issues from delivery of programming owned by the carrier.

17. See *Second Annual Report*, ¶¶ 95–96.

18. See Telecommunications Act of 1996, § 302(b)(3).

19. See *Applications of Ameritech Operating Cos., Order and Authorization*, 10 FCC Rcd. 4101, 4105 (1995).

20. Ibid., 4105, 4106.

21. Ibid., 4104–07.

22. See *Applications of New England Tel. & Tel. Co.*, 10 FCC Rcd. 5346, 5348–49 (1995).

23. Ibid., 5348–51.

24. See 47 U.S.C. §§ 651–53 (enacted by Telecommunications Act of 1996, § 302).

25. See "Pacific Bell Unveils Plan to Deploy Broadband Local Distribution Network to 5.5 Million Homes by Year 2000," *Telecommunications Reports*, November 15, 1993, pp. 1–3.

26. "U.S. West Announces Plans to Deploy Broadband Network across Its Service Territory," *Telecommunications Reports*, February 8, 1993, pp. 6–8.

27. See "Bell Atlantic Picks AT&T, GI, BBT to Supply Full-Service Network; Deployment Set for 1995," *Telecommunications Reports*, May 23, 1994, pp. 11–12.

28. See "GTE Unveils Plans to Provide Video Services in 66 Markets within Next 10 Years," *Telecommunications Reports*, May 30, 1994, pp. 9–10.

29. See "SNET to Spend $4.5 Billion on Connecticut's Info Superhighway," *Telecommunications Reports*, January 17, 1994, p. 30.

30. See 47 U.S.C. §§ 651–53 (enacted by Telecommunications Act of 1996, § 302).

31. See *Comments of Satellite Broadcasting and Communications Ass'n, 1994 Video Competition Inquiry*, CS Docket No. 94-48. Satellite-delivered pay television service, principally offered through cable television stations, commenced in 1976. See *Leapfrog Rules—Cable Television*, 57 F.C.C.2d 625 (1976).

32. See *Comments of Satellite Broadcasting and Communications Ass'n*, p. 3.

33. Ibid.; see also *Comments of Home Box Office, 1994 Video Competition Inquiry*, CS Docket No. 94-48, p. 8.

34. See *United States* v. *Primestar Partners, L.P.*, 58 Fed. Reg. 33,948 (June 22, 1993); see also *New York* v. *Primestar Partners, L.P., Complaint*, 93 Civ. 3868 (S.D.N.Y. June 9, 1993).

35. See *Comments of Primestar Partners, L.P., 1994 Video Competition Inquiry*, Docket No. 94-48, pp. 5–6.

36. "Primestar Tests Retail Distribution," *Satellite Week*, 17, no. 11 (March 13, 1995), p. 3.

37. Ibid., *Second Annual Report*, ¶51.

38. James F. Peltz, "Hughes' DirecTV Already a Rival to Cable Technology: But the Direct-to-Home Satellite Service Is Still Far from the Subscriber Level It Needs to Break Even," *Los Angeles Times*, March 10, 1995, p. D 1. See *Comments of DirecTV, 1994 Video Competition Inquiry*, Docket No. 94-48, pp. 1–2, 14–15.

39. *Second Annual Report*, ¶51.

40. See "USSB's Customer Satisfaction Hits 88 Percent, Survey Shows," *Satellite Week*, 18, no. 13, March 27, 1995, p. 5.

41. *Second Annual Report*, ¶51.

42. Ibid.; see also Jonathan Takiff, "Small Dish Mania: How DSS Is Bringing Digital Sizzle to Satellite Television," *Video Magazine*, 19, no. 1 (April, 1995), p. 46;

Bill Beck, "One Hot Dish: The RCA Digital Satellite System Is the Best-Selling New Consumer Electronics Product in History," *Indiana Business Magazine*, 39, no. 3 (March 1995), p. 8.

43. For a description of these systems and their relation to cable television systems and regulation of cable television, see *FCC* v. *Beach Communications, Inc.*, 113 S. Ct. 2096 (1993); see also *Beach Communications, Inc.* v. *FCC*, 965 F.2d 1103 (D.C. Cir. 1992), rev'd, 113 S. Ct. 2096 (1993).

44. See *Notice of Inquiry, 1994 Video Competition Proceeding*, Docket 94-48, 17; *Comments of Home Box Office*, 9.

45. See *Second Annual Report*, ¶106; *Comments of Home Box Office, Inc., 1994 Video Competition Inquiry*, CS Docket 94-48, 9.

46. See *1990 Cable Television Report*, 5 FCC Rcd. 5013 n. 141, 5014–16; *Comments of Wireless Cable Ass'n, 1994 Video Competition Proceeding*, Docket 94-48, 6.

47. See *Second Annual Report*, ¶69.

48. *Comments of Wireless Cable Ass'n, 1994 Video Competition Proceeding*, CS Docket No. 94-48, 3.

49. Ibid., 3, 13; see also 47 U.S.C. §§ 548, *Amendment of Parts 21, 43, 74, 78, and 84 of the Commission's Rules Governing Use of the Frequencies in the 2.1 and 2.5 GHz Bands Affecting: Private Operational-Fixed Microwave Service, Multipoint Distribution Service, Multichannel Multipoint Distribution Service, Instructional Television Fixed Service, and Cable Television Relay Service, Report and Order*, 5 FCC Rcd. 6410 (1990).

50. See *Comments of Cellularvision of New York, L.P., 1994 Video Competition Inquiry*, CS Docket 94-48, 1; *Notice of Inquiry*, CS Docket 94-48, at 12; see also *Rulemaking to Amend Part 1 and Part 21 of the Commission's Rules to Redesignate the 27.5-29.5 GHz Frequency Band and to Establish Rules and Policies for Local Multipoint Distribution Service, Notice of Proposed Rulemaking, Order, Tentative Decision, and Order on Reconsideration*, 8 FCC Rcd. 557 (1993) (recon. petitions pending).

51. See *Notice of Inquiry, 1994 Video Competition Proceeding*, CS Docket 94-48, at 12–13; *Rulemaking to Amend Part 1 and Part 21 of the Commission's Rules, Second Notice of Proposed Rulemaking*, 9 FCC Rcd. 1394 (1994).

52. See "AT&T, New Jersey Utility to Test Interactive System," *Telecommunications Reports*, (January 23, 1995), p. 10.

53. See, for example, *Communications Act of 1994*, S. Rep. 367, pp. 10–11, 103 Cong. 2 sess. (GPO, 1994).

54. See Telecommunications Act of 1996, § 103 (amending The Public Utility Holding Company Act of 1935, 15 U.S.C. § 79ff).

55. Those services include interactive text and video services (which allow a subscriber through two-way communication to gain information from databases and other sources), video-on-demand (which also employs two-way communications to allow subscribers to choose among libraries of video programming), and services that allow subscribers to initiate and produce video communications.

56. See, for example, Edmund L. Andrews, "*HDTV for Profit is Pushed,*" *New York Times,* March 2, 1994, p. D1.

57. See *Implementation of Section 309(j) of the Communications Act—Competitive Bidding, Fifth Report and Order*, 59 Fed. Reg. 37,566 (July 22, 1994); *Amendment of*

Parts 0, 1, 2, and 95 of the Commission's Rules to Provide Interactive Video and Data Services, Report and Order, 7 FCC Rcd. 1630 (1992).

58. See *Amendment of Part 76, Subpart J, Section 76.501 of the Commission's Rules and Regulations to Eliminate the Prohibition on Common Ownership of Cable Television Systems and National Television Networks, Report and Order,* 7 FCC Rcd. 6156, 6162–63 (1992), recon., 8 FCC Rcd. 1184 (1993).

59. See n. 8.

60. See 47 U.S.C. §§ 534–35.

61. See *Review of the Commission's Regulations Governing Television Broadcasting, Further Notice of Proposed Rulemaking,* MM Docket No. 91-221, 10 FCC Rcd. 3524, 3597 (1995), App. C (released Jan. 17, 1995). The document details a study of leisure that compared 1970 and 1988 household activities; Harold L. Vogel, *Entertainment Industry Economics: A Guide for Financial Analysis,* 2d ed. (Cambridge University Press, 1990).

62. Ibid., ¶¶ 24–30 (detailing basis of FCC conclusion); see also Jonathan D. Levy and Peter K. Pitsch, "Statistical Evidence of Substitutability Among Video Delivery Systems," in E. Noam, ed., *Video Media Competition: Regulation, Economics, and Technology* (Columbia University Press, 1985), pp. 56–92. Related evidence arises in studies addressing pricing in the market for delivery of advertising. See *Review of the Commission's Regulations Governing Television Broadcasting, Further Notice of Proposed Rulemaking,* 10 FCC Rcd. 3524, 3571 (1995); see also Bruce M. Owen and Steve S. Wildman, *Video Economics* (Harvard University Press, 1992); Barry J. Seldon and Chulho Jung, "Derived Demand for Advertising Messages and Substitutability among the Media," *Quarterly Review of Economics and Finance,* 33 (Spring 1993), pp. 71–86.

63. See *Review of the Commission's Regulations Governing Television Broadcasting, Further Notice of Proposed Rulemaking,* 10 FCC Rcd. 3524, 3536–37 (1995); *Implementation of Section 19 of the Cable Television Consumer Protection and Competition Act of 1992, Annual Assessment of the Status of Competition in the Market for the Delivery of Video Programming, First Report,* 9 FCC Rcd. 7442, 7492 (1994).

64. Ibid., 7493.

65. See *Amendment of Part 76, Subpart J, Section 76.501 of the Commission's Rules and Regulations to Eliminate the Prohibition on Common Ownership of Cable Television Systems and National Television Networks, Report and Order,* 7 FCC Rcd., 6163 (1992).

66. *Evaluation of the Syndication and Financial Interest Rules, Second Report and Order,* 8 FCC Rcd., 3282, 3304 (1993).

67. By 1993 advertisers' expenditures for cable television were $2.564 billion; they were $10.209 billion for network television advertising (and $17.811 billion for spot and syndicated television advertising). During the same period, newspaper advertising declined slightly, to $32.025 billion. See *Review of the Commission's Regulations Governing Television Broadcasting, Further Notice of Proposed Rulemaking,* 10 FCC Rcd. 3524, 3598 (1995).

68. See, for example, ibid; *Amendment of Part 76, supra,* 7 FCC Rcd. 6156 (1992); *Evaluation of the Syndication and Financial Interest Rules, Second Report and Order,* 8 FCC Rcd. 8270 (1993); *Amendment of Section 73.3555 of the Commission's Broad-*

cast Multiple Ownership Rules, Second Report and Order, 4 FCC Rcd. 1741 (1989), recon., 4 FCC Rcd. 6489 (1989).

69. See *Review of the Syndication and Financial Interest Rules, Sections 73.659–73.663, Report and Order,* FCC 95-382, n. 52 (released Sept. 6, 1995).

70. See *Review of the Prime Time Access Rule, Section 73.658(k), Report and Order,* ¶27 (released July 31, 1995).

71. Ibid., ¶7.

72. Ibid., ¶8.

73. The Communications Act embodies this division directly. "Common carriers" regulated pursuant to Title II do not include broadcasters. See 47 U.S.C. § 153(h); *FCC v. Midwest Video Corp.,* 440 U.S. 689 (1979). Providers of cable service cannot for that service be regulated as common carriers. See 47 U.S.C. § 541(c).

74. Early cable television systems were known as community antenna television, or CATV. See *Amendment of Parts 21, 74, and 91 to Adopt Rules and Regulations Relating to the Distribution of Television Broadcast Signals by Community Antenna Television Systems, Second Report and Order,* 2 F.C.C.2d 725 (1966), aff'd, *Black Hills Video Corp.* v. *FCC,* 399 F.2d 65 (8th Cir. 1968).

75. See, for example, 47 U.S.C. §§ 531–32, 533(f)(1)(B), 534–35.

76. See 47 U.S.C. § 532; *Implementation of Sections of the Cable Television Consumer Protection and Competition Act of 1992, Rate Regulation, Report and Order and Further Notice of Proposed Rulemaking,* 8 FCC Rcd. 5631, 5933–61 (1993); see also 47 U.S.C. § 533(f)(1); *Implementation of Sections 11 and 13 of the Cable Television Consumer Protection and Competition Act of 1992, Horizontal and Vertical Ownership Limits, Second Report and Order,* 8 FCC Rcd. 8565 (1993). The commercial leased access provisions have widely been perceived as ineffective. See *Competition, Rate Deregulation, and the Commission's Policies Relating to the Provision of Cable Television Service, Report,* 5 FCC Rcd. 4962, 4973–76 (1990).

77. These developments underlie the joint venture between Time Warner and US WEST to provide "full service networks," which would upgrade cable systems, integrate them with wireless communications systems, link them to centralized sources of interactive services and programming, and eventually integrate them into the landline telecommunications network. See n. 10 (and accompanying text); *Time Warner Entertainment Co., L.P. and US WEST Communications, Inc., Petition for Waiver of Section 63.54 of the Commission's Rules,* 8 FCC Rcd. 7106 (1993); see also *Expanded Interconnection with Local Telephone Company Facilities (Transport Phase II), Third Report and Order,* 9 FCC Rcd. 2718 (1994).

78. See 47 U.S.C. § 548; *Implementation of Sections 12 and 19 of the Cable Television Consumer Protection and Competition Act of 1992, Development of Competition and Diversity in Video Programming Distribution and Carriage, First Report and Order,* 8 FCC Rcd. 3359 (1993); see also *Showtime Networks, Inc.* v. *FCC,* 932 F.2d 1 (D.C. Cir. 1991); *Eastern Microwave, Inc.* v. *Doubleday Sports, Inc.,* 691 F.2d 125 (2d Cir. 1982).

79. See, for example, *Competition in the Interstate Interexchange Marketplace, Report and Order,* 6 FCC Rcd. 5880 (1991); ibid., *Memorandum Opinion and Order on Reconsideration,* 7 FCC Rcd. 2677 (1992); ibid., *Second Report and Order,* 8 FCC Rcd. 3668 (1993).

80. See *Telephone Company–Cable Television Cross-Ownership Rules, Sections 63.54–63.58, Second Report and Order, Recommendation to Congress, and Second Further Notice of Proposed Rulemaking,* 7 FCC Rcd. 5781 (1992).

81. See "NBC-Microsoft Alliance Targets Online Srvices, CD-ROM Products Now, Interactive TV Later," *Telecommunications Reports,* May 22, 1995, pp. 13–14.

82. See 47 U.S.C. §§ 251–53. Considerable unbundling of and access to the local telephone network is under consideration in New York and Illinois, and federal and local regulatory responses to plans submitted by Ameritech, Rochester Telephone Co., and NYNEX may advance those developments. For a survey that emphasizes emerging competition in local telephony, see Peter W. Huber, Michael Kellogg, and John Thorne, *The Geodesic Network II: 1993 Report on Competition in the Telephone Industry* (Washington, D.C.: The Geodesic Company, 1992); compare ETI/Hatfield Assoc., *The Enduring Local Bottleneck: Monopoly Power and the Local Exchange Carriers* (1994) (sponsored by AT&T Corp., MCI Communications Corp., and the Competitive Telecommunications Association). These studies differ on whether LECs will continue to exercise market power that may harm competition in related markets, but both address the provision of the delivery of information products in those related markets.

83. Ibid.

84. See, for example, ibid.; *Application of New Jersey Bell Tel. Co., Order and Authorization,* 9 FCC Rcd. 3677 (1994); *Application of US WEST Communications, Inc., Order and Authorization,* 9 FCC Rcd. 184 (1993).

85. See *Evaluation of the Syndication and Financial Interest Rules, Second Report and Order,* 8 FCC Rcd. 3282 (1993).

86. Ibid., 3337–42.

87. See *Comments of National Cable Television Ass'n, Inc., 1994 Video Competition Proceedings,* CS Docket 94-48, 23.

88. See *Cable Television Consumer Protection Act of 1991,* S. Rep. 92, 102 Cong. 1 sess. (GPO, 1991), 21, 27.

89. Telecommunications Act of 1996, § 202.

90. See *Amendment of Section 64.702 of the Commission's Rules and Regulations, Final Decision,* 77 F.C.C.2d 384 (1980) recon., 84 F.C.C.2d 50 (1980), further recon., 88 F.C.C.2d 512 (1981), aff'd, *Computer & Communications Industry Ass'n* v. *FCC,* 693 F.2d 198 (D.C. Cir. 1982), cert. denied, 461 U.S. 938 (1983).

91. Ibid.

92. See *California* v. *FCC,* 39 F.3d 919 (9th Cir. 1994), cert. denied, 115 S. Ct. 1427 (1995); see also *Computer III Remand Proceedings, Report and Order,* 5 FCC Rcd. 7719 (1990) (and sources noted); *Computer III Remand Proceedings: Bell Operating Company Safeguards and Tier 1 Local Exchange Company Safeguards, Report and Order,* 6 FCC Rcd. 7571 (1991) (and sources noted).

93. See *United States* v. *Western Elec. Co.,* 767 F.Supp. 308, 332 (D.D.C. 1991), aff'd, 993 F.2d 1572 (D.C. Cir. 1993).

94. See 47 U.S.C. § 653 (enacted by Telecommunications Act of 1996, § 302).

95. See *Telephone Company–Cable Television Cross-Ownership Rules, Sections 63.54–63.58, Second Report and Order, Recommendation to Congress, and Second Further Notice of Proposed Rulemaking,* 7 FCC Rcd. 5781 (1992).

96. See, for example, Geraldine Fabrikant, "MCA Chiefs Fail to Sway Matsushita," *New York Times*, October 20, 1994, p. D1.

97. Examples include AT&T's purchase of McCaw Communications and the joint wireless ventures between US WEST and Airtouch Communications (formerly Pacific Telesis's wireless operations), as well as between Bell Atlantic and NYNEX. Those last four companies may venture together in providing wireless services, possibly with MCI's participation. See "Bell Atlantic, Nynex Shift Cellular Talks," *Wall Street Journal*, October 20, 1994, p. A3. Sprint has joined with major owners of cable television systems to secure spectrum for advanced wireless communications services through the auction process and, presumably, to develop and provide wireless services jointly.

98. See, for example, Fabrikant, "MCA Chiefs Fail."

99. Prominent examples include the unsuccessful TCI/Bell Atlantic (approximately $33 billion) and Southwestern Bell/Cox Cable Communications ventures (approximately $4.9 billion), as well as the $2.5 billion interest assumed by US WEST in Time Warner Entertainment.

100. For example, British Telecommunications has recently acquired a $4.3 billion interest in MCI. See "MCI, BT Close $4.3 Bilion Deal, Begin 'Concert' Alliance," *Telecommunications Reports*, October 3, 1994, p. 23.

101. See *Second Annual Report*, ¶35.

102. See "Telecommunications Mergers Eclipse Drug Industry in 1994 Activity," *Communications Daily*, January 3, 1995, p. 1.

103. Ibid., p. 2.

104. See chapter 1.

105. William Glaberson, "Media Business; Press Notes," *New York Times*, October 10, 1994, p. D5.

106. This venture included Cox Newspapers, Inc., Gannett Co., Knight-Ridder, Inc., Hearst Corp., Times Mirror Co., Tribune Co., Advanced Publications, Inc., and the Washington Post Co. See P. Reilly, "Eight Publishers Announce Venture for On-Line News," *Wall Street Journal*, April 20, 1995, p. B3.

107. See "NBC-Microsoft Alliance."

Chapter Four

1. See 47 C.F.R. § 73.3555; *FCC* v. *National Citizens Comm. for Broadcasting*, 436 U.S. 775 (1978); see also *Computer III Remand Proceedings: Bell Operating Company Safeguards and Tier 1 Local Exchange Company Safeguards*, 6 FCC Rcd. 7571 (1991), vacated in part, *California* v. *FCC*, 39 F.3d 919 (9th Cir. 1994).

2. See generally chapter 2.

3. See Telecommunications Act of 1996, § 101 (enacting 47 U.S.C. §§ 251–53).

4. See Telecommunications Act of 1996, § 151 (enacting 47 U.S.C. §§ 271–76).

5. See Telecommunications Act of 1996, § 151 (enacting 47 U.S.C. §§ 271, 274).

6. See Telecommunications Act of 1996, § 302 (enacting 47 U.S.C. §§ 651, 653).

7. The "carriage" inheres in any electronic transmission that delivers content, but the existence of that function as a service offering largely reflects regulatory requirements as well as the transmitters' structuring of service. When access to an unaffiliated entity is mandated in a manner that allows it a direct commercial relation with end users, the separate transmission function by the entity controlling the transmission facilities may be deemed carriage. Thus telephone companies and other common carriers are presumed and required to provide this service, while broadcasters are presumed not to (but, apart from regulatory protections, are able to do so). Compare 47 U.S.C. § 201 with 47 U.S.C. § 153(h). Cable system operators function much as traditional broadcasters for the portions of the programming that they select, but they, too, are "carrying" programming originated elsewhere. They function more as traditional offerers of carriage service for those channels they must make available to unaffiliated entities. See 47 U.S.C. §§ 531–32, 534–35. That cable operators' "own" programming is often secured on a per-subscriber rate for a particular channel offering, or a per-channel payment by an unaffiliated programmer, reflects the blurring between the roles. The regulation of "open video systems" acknowledges the combined broadcast and carriage components of broadband distribution systems. See 47 U.S.C. §§ 651, 653.

8. See generally *Implementation of Section 19 of the Cable Television Consumer Protection and Competition Act of 1992, Annual Assessment of the Status of Competition in the Market for the Delivery of Video Programming, Second Annual Report,* CS Docket No. 95-61 (released December 11, 1995).

9. Particularly for telephony, the phenomenon outlined here and related network developments have been addressed extensively in Peter W. Huber, Michael Kellogg, and John Thorne, *The Geodesic Network II: 1993 Report on Competition in the Telephone Industry* (Washington, D.C.: The Geodesic Company, 1992); and George Calhoun, *Wireless Access and the Local Telephone Network* (Boston: Artech House, 1992). The discussions in these works are directed in part to establishing decreasing existence or at least relevance of local carriers' bottleneck monopoly, but are important as well for the separate issue of the challenge to regulatory structure addressed here. As noted below, the decrease of market power, and the ability to employ that power anticompetitively, cannot necessarily be inferred from this multiplicity of delivery routes, especially for the most advanced, interactive video services.

10. See, for example, *Review of the Commission's Regulations Governing Television Broadcasting, Further Notice of Proposed Rulemaking,* 10 FCC Rcd. 3524 (1995).

11. See generally 47 U.S.C. §§ 153, 307–09.

12. This is so at least as long as telephone companies structure their offerings to avoid having them fall within the definition of "cable system" and to avoid being characterized themselves as a "cable operator." See *National Cable Television Ass'n* v. *FCC*, 33 F.3d 66 (D.C. Cir. 1994).

13. See 47 U.S.C. §§ 153, 201–05.

14. Ibid., § 203; *MCI Telecommunications Corp.* v. *American Tel. & Tel. Co.*, 114 S. Ct. 2223 (1994).

15. See, for example, 47 U.S.C. § 543.

16. See *California* v. *FCC*, 39 F.3d 919 (9th Cir. 1994); see also *Computer III Remand Proceedings: Bell Operating Company Safeguards and Tier 1 Local Exchange Company Safeguards, Report and Order,* 6 FCC Rcd. 7571 (1991); *Amendment of §*

64.702 of the Commission's Rules and Regulations, Report and Order (Third Computer Inquiry), 104 F.C.C.2d 958 (1986).

17. See *Amendment of Parts 0, 1, 2, and 95 of the Commission's Rules to Provide Interactive Video and Data Services, Report and Order*, 7 FCC Rcd. 1630 (1992).

18. See 47 U.S.C. §§ 651, 653; see also *Telephone Company–Cable Television Cross-Ownership Rules, Second Report and Order, Recommendation to Congress, and Second Further Notice of Proposed Rulemaking*, 7 FCC Rcd. 5781 (1992); ibid., *Memorandum Opinion and Order on Reconsideration and Third Further Notice of Proposed Rulemaking*, 10 FCC Rcd. 244 (1994).

19. See *Review of the Commission's Regulations Governing Television Broadcasting, Notice of Proposed Rulemaking*, 7 FCC Rcd. 4111 (1992); ibid., *Further Notice of Proposed Rulemaking*, 10 FCC Rcd. 3524 (1995).

20. See 47 U.S.C. § 653; *Telephone Company–Cable Television Cross-Ownership Rules, Fourth Further Notice of Proposed Rulemaking*, 10 FCC Rcd. 4617 (1995).

21. See, for example, *Review of the Commission's Regulations Governing Attribution of Broadcast Interests & Review of the Commission's Regulations and Policies Affecting Investment in the Broadcast Industry, Notice of Proposed Rulemaking*, 10 FCC Rcd. 3606 (1995); *Review of the Commission's Regulations Governing Television Broadcasting, Further Notice of Proposed Rulemaking*, 10 FCC Rcd. 3524 (1995).

22. The Sherman and Clayton acts (26 Stat. 209 and 69 Stat. 283), principally, embody and establish this generally applicable regulation of competition.

23. See chapter 5.

24. See, for example, *Otter Tail Power Co.* v. *United States*, 410 U.S. 366 (1973); *MCI Communications Corp.* v. *AT&T*, 708 F.2d 1081, 1132 (7th Cir. 1981), cert. denied, 464 U.S. 891 (1983). The "essential facility" in antitrust doctrine is discussed later in the text.

25. See generally *Implementation of Section 19 of the Cable Television Consumer Protection and Competition Act of 1992, Annual Assessment of the Status of Competition in the Market for the Delivery of Video Programming, Second Report*, CS Dock. 95-61 (released December 11, 1995).

26. See, for example, *United States* v. *Western Elec. Co.*, 900 F.2d 283 (D.C. Cir. 1990). The extent of the continuing local bottleneck remains subject to considerable debate. See *Memorandum in Support of Motion of Bell Atlantic Corporation, BellSouth Corporation, NYNEX Corporation, and Southwestern Bell Corporation to Vacate the Decree, United States* v. *Western Elec. Co.*, No. 82-0192 (D.D.C., filed July 6, 1994).

27. See 47 C.F.R. § 22.901–02.

28. See, for example, *Evaluation of the Syndication and Financial Interest Rules, Second Report and Order*, 8 FCC Rcd. 3283 (1993), recon., 8 FCC Rcd. 8270 (1993), petition for review dismissed, *Capital Cities/ABC, Inc.* v. *FCC*, 29 F.3d 309 (7th Cir. 1994). See also comments received in response to *Price Cap Performance Review for AT&T, Notice of Inquiry*, 7 FCC Rcd. 5322 (1992), and *Public Notice*, 8 FCC Rcd. 7581 (1993) (requesting comments on *Motion for Reclassification of American Telephone & Telegraph Company as a Nondominant Carrier, Policies and Rules Concerning Rates for Competitive Common Carrier Services and Facilities Authorizations Therefor*, CC Docket No. 79-252 (filed September 22, 1993)).

29. Because it is far from certain how or whether competition for these services will develop, it is as likely that, in any particular locale, these services will be provided by only local telephone companies *or* cable television systems.

30. See generally Robert W. Crandall, *After the Breakup: The U.S. Telecommunications Industry in a More Competitive Era* (Brookings, 1991).

31. See 47 U.S.C. § 254 (enacted by Telecommunications Act of 1996, § 101); see also Communications Act of 1994, § 1822, 103 Cong. 2 sess., §§ 101–04 (September 14, 1994); cf. *Antitrust and Communications Reform Act of 1994*, H.R. 3626, 103 Cong. 2 sess., §§ 301, 303 (GPO, 1994).

32. Direct rather than "hidden" redistribution could eliminate the need for either broad regulatory requirements placed on carriers to provide service widely (or universally) or specific requirements placed on carriers to favor certain information providers or consumers. See, for example, *Antitrust and Communications Reform Act of 1994*, § 303; Communications Act of 1994, § 103. Designating specific beneficiaries in this manner particularly invites political capture.

33. Already, groups claiming to represent consumers and members of minority groups have challenged initial proposals to test, market, and offer video dialtone services. The NAACP and Consumer Federation of America have accused the regional companies of "electronic redlining" in video dialtone applications by "bypass[ing] many lower-income and/or minority communities in their initial deployment of video dial tone"—a "discriminatory practice" they assert "amounts to a denial of a service which may be essential to the economic and social livelihood of the community that is redlined." "Interest Groups Accuse Telcos of 'Electronic Redlining,'" *Telecommunications Reports*, May 30, 1994, pp. 18–19.

34. The continuing need for oversight of interconnection and the forms such regulation might take (especially in increasingly competitive markets) is the subject of extensive debate. See generally E. Noam, *Interconnecting the Network of Networks* (AEI Press, forthcoming).

35. See generally Richard B. Stewart, "The Reformation of American Administrative Law," *Harvard Law Review*, 88 (June 1975), pp. 1667, 1670–76; James M. Landis, *The Administrative Process* (Westport, Conn.: Greenwood Press, 1938).

36. The objective might be characterized as making the administrative process less like a free-ranging mini-legislature and more like a specialized version of the Department of Justice's antitrust division (albeit one that is more directly accountable and charged with a more specific mandate formed by a consistent competitive theory).

37. Congress has, for example, repeatedly intervened in regulatory proceedings addressing sensitive areas of broadcast policy, especially for matters involving preferences afforded to members of minority groups, the access and charges levied on political candidates, and carriage of broadcast signals.

38. See 28 U.S.C. §§ 2342, 2344; 5 U.S.C. §§ 704-06; *Chevron U.S.A. Inc.* v. *Natural Resources Defense Council*, 467 U.S. 837 (1984); *Motor Vehicle Manuf. Ass'n* v. *State Farm Mutual Automobile Ins. Co.*, 463 U.S. 29 (1983).

39. The Clinton administration had in speeches suggested that certain advanced services be regulated pursuant to a new and additional "Title VII" of the Communications Act. Legislation designed to revise the Communications Act did not include this or any similar proposal. Crafting a new regulatory regime for advanced services would

address certain of the difficulties with overlapping and conflicting requirements imposed through common-carrier and cable television regulation, as well as the cable-telco bar. That additional regulatory regime would likely suffer from several disadvantages not contained within the comprehensive regulation suggested here. First, a new section of the Communications Act would exacerbate the line-drawing problems that already exist for advanced services (for both cable and common-carrier regulation) and would possibly result in an additional set of regulatory requirements. Second, it is unlikely that Title VII could apply to local telephone and cable television companies without adopting measures to open networks, prevent cross-subsidy, and ensure nondiscrimination—which would require borrowing from or replicating the regulatory tools touted here. Third, an additional Title VII would perpetuate the assumption of distinct services requiring distinct regulatory regimes and likely fail to address the competitive issues that cross industry boundaries. Finally, creating a new Title VII would ensure the continued operation of outdated regulatory regimes and prevent the more widespread revision and deregulation of each that recent developments support.

40. See 47 U.S.C. § 152(b).

41. See 47 U.S.C. § 253; see also Telecommunications Act of 1996, § 601 (c)(1) (preemption).

42. See 47 U.S.C. §§ 252, 271.

43. See 47 U.S.C. § 253 (enacted by Telecommunications Act of 1996, 101).

44. See ibid; see generally William J. Baumol & Gregory Sidak, *Toward Competition in Local Telephony* (Cambridge, Mass., and Washington, D.C.: MIT Press and American Enterprise Institute, 1994).

45. The Telecommunications Act of 1996 limited the ability of states to bar entry into local telephone services, and increased the FCC's power to preempt such barriers, but the legislation at the same time preserves state regulatory power through fairly open-ended grants of power and may in certain respects increase states' power by charging them with resolving disputes between local carriers and other service providers over the availability and terms of interconnection. See Telecommunications Act of 1996, § 101 (47 U.S.C. §§ 251–53).

46. See 47 U.S.C. §§ 201–05, 214.

47. See *Policy and Rules Concerning Rates for Competitive Common Carrier Services and Facilities Authorizations Therefor, First Report and Order*, 85 F.C.C.2d 1 (1980); ibid., *Second Report and Order*, 91 F.C.C.2d 59 (1982).

48. See Telecommunications Act of 1996, § 401.

49. As noted above, the FCC itself pursued this course in deeming enhanced services and inside wiring to be beyond Title II jurisdiction and now has additional powers in this respect. See 47 U.S.C. § v.0.

50. See 47 U.S.C. § 153(51) (enacted by Telecommunications Act of 1996, § 3).

51. See generally *Application of Chesapeake & Potomac Tel. Co. of Virginia, Order and Authorization*, 10 FCC Rcd. 2975 (1995); *Telephone Company–Cable Television Cross-Ownership Rules, Fourth Further Notice of Proposed Rulemaking,* 10 FCC Rcd. 9617 (1995).

52. Cf. 47 U.S.C. § 612.

53. Certain "leased-access" regulations attempt to integrate an aspect of common-carrier functions into cable television systems, but those requirements have proven

ineffective and would in any event allow access to consumers only for those few providers that could be carried on the limited designated channels. The FCC has also attempted to increase access either by mandating that certain programmers be carried (as through the "must-carry" provisions favoring broadcasters) or through limitations on cable systems' carriage of affiliated programming. None of these requirements creates any general ability to gain access to consumers but rather simply reshuffles which programmers gain access and which will be excluded. The "open video system" regulations appear initially to present the same difficulty. See 47 U.S.C. §§ 651, 653.

54. See 47 U.S.C. § 522(6).

55. See *National Cable Television Ass'n* v. *FCC*, 33 F.2d 66 (D.C. Cir. 1994).

56. See Conference Report, p. 169; see 47 U.S.C. § 301(a).

57. See 47 U.S.C. §§ 543(a)(2) and 543(l)(1); see also Telecommunications Act of 1996, § 301(b).

58. See Telecommunications Act of 1996, § 301(b).

59. See 47 U.S.C. §§ 541–44.

60. See Telecommunications Act of 1996, § 303 (amending 47 U.S.C. § 541(b)).

61. Local authorities do control essential rights of way over public properties, and exercises of local power are often required to ensure construction of a comprehensive delivery system. These powers may justify narrowly tailored conditions attached to grants of benefits that protect the locality's interests in public property, but hardly justify the broad regulations that local franchising authorities are allowed to impose that are entirely unrelated to land use interests.

62. See chapter 5.

63. See, for example, *Telephone Company–Cable Television Cross-Ownership Rules, Memorandum Opinion and Order on Reconsideration and Third Further Notice of Proposed Rulemaking*, 10 FCC Rcd. 244 (1994).

64. See 47 U.S.C. § 651(a) (enacted by Telecommunications Act of 1996, § 302).

65. See 47 U.S.C. § 653.

66. See 47 U.S.C. § 652 (enacted by Telecommunications Act of 1996, § 302).

67. See *Computer III Remand Proceedings: Bell Operating Company Safeguards and Tier 1 Local Exchange Company Safeguards*, 6 FCC Rcd. 7571 (1991), vacated in part, *California* v. *FCC*, 39 F.3d 919 (9th Cir. 1994); see also *Amendment of Section 64.702 of the Commission's Rules and Regulations, Second Computer Inquiry, Final Decision*, 77 F.C.C.2d 384, recon., 84 F.C.C.2d 50, aff'd, *Computer & Communications Industry Ass'n* v. *FCC*, 693 F.2d 198 (D.C. Cir. 1982).

68. See, for example, 47 C.F.R. § 64.901–05; *Separation of Costs of Regulated Telephone Service from Costs of Nonregulated Activities*, 2 FCC Rcd. 1298 (1987); see also 47 C.F.R. § 32.27.

69. Cf. *United States* v. *Western Elec. Co.*, 552 F.Supp. 131 (D.D.C. 1982), aff'd, *Maryland* v. *United States*, 460 U.S. 1001 (1983); *United States* v. *Western Elec. Co.*, 900 F.2d 283 (D.C. Cir. 1990).

70. See *United States* v. *Western Elec. Co.*, 900 F.2d 283 (D.C. Cir.), cert. denied, 498 U.S. 911 (1990).

71. See MFJ § VIII(C); see also MFJ § VII.

72. See *Motion of Bell Atlantic Corporation, BellSouth Corporation, NYNEX Corporation, and Southwestern Bell Corporation to Vacate the Decree, United States* v. *Western Elec. Co.*, No. 82- 0192 (D.D.C., filed July 6, 1994).

73. See 47 U.S.C. § 271(d).

74. Ibid.

75. See 47 U.S.C. § 271(d).

76. See 47 U.S.C. §§ 271, 251–52.

77. See 47 U.S.C. § 274.

78. See 47 U.S.C. §§ 251, 271.

79. See R. H. Coase, "The Federal Communications Commission," *Journal of Law and Economics*, 2 (October 1959), pp. 1–40. Coase developed and generalized the ideas set forth in this article into what popularly became known as the Coase Theorem. See R. H. Coase, *The Firm, The Market, and the Law* (University of Chicago Press, 1988), pp. 10–11, 157–58, in which he traces the origin of "the problem of social cost."

80. There may, however, be some government interest in seeing that the spectrum is in fact usefully employed. There is also little reason to believe that market incentives will generally fail to produce this result.

81. As discussed in greater detail below, there is no legal basis for regulating all sources of information, including that communicated through print, wireline communications, and using the spectrum, and there is in any event neither the political will nor a clear policy basis for that course.

82. A later section more generally addresses policy and legal objections to government regulation of broadcast content, and specifically addresses and seeks to rebut the argument that the increase in information sources, and the difficulty of distinguishing broadcast information from other information sources, actually justifies broader government regulation of all information sources.

83. See Telecommunications Act of 1996, § 201 (enacting 47 U.S.C. § 336).

84. Before the auctions the auction of spectrum for new uses had been expected to generate $10 billion over five years, but the principal auctions for broadband PCS spectrum generated $12.1 billion in early 1995 alone. In addition, the enormous sums paid to transfer television stations between private parties in large part reflect the value of the license rather than the value added by the license holder.

85. See Telecommunications Act of 1996, §§ 201–04.

Chapter Five

1. See, for example, *Red Lion Broadcasting Co.* v. *FCC*, 395 U.S. 367 (1969); *National Broadcasting Co.* v. *United States*, 319 U.S. 190 (1943).

2. Antitrust actions and other government measures were occasionally directed against the motion picture industry. See, for example, *United States* v. *Paramount Pictures, Inc.*, 334 U.S. 131 (1948). Copyright and defamation laws applied to print products, and particular laws governed use of the mails.

3. Certain classes of speech are often accorded lesser First Amendment protection. For example, defamatory speech, obscenity, certain incitements to imminent unlawful

action, "fighting words," and certain proposals for commercial transactions have been subjected to regulation based on the content of the communications. See, for example, *Gertz* v. *Robert Welch, Inc.*, 418 U.S. 323 (1974); *Brandenburg* v. *Ohio*, 395 U.S. 444 (1969); *Chaplinsky* v. *New Hampshire*, 315 U.S. 568 (1942); *Virginia State Board of Pharmacy* v. *Virginia Citizens Consumer Council*, 425 U.S. 748 (1976); *Miller* v. *California*, 413 U.S. 15 (1973).

4. See, for example, *Miami Herald Pub. Co.* v. *Tornillo*, 418 U.S. 241 (1974); *New York Times Co.* v. *Sullivan*, 376 U.S. 254 (1964).

5. A limited exception arguably exists for regulation of indecent speech broadcast into the home in a form available to minors (see below). Regulation of indecent speech is not, however, the rationale invoked or available to justify the extensive regulation of broadcast licensees and other electronic communications designed to alter the balance of and speakers generating the particular messages communicated electronically.

6. See *First National Bank of Boston* v. *Bellotti*, 435 U.S. 765 (1978); *New York Times Co.* v. *Sullivan*, 376 U.S. 254 (1964).

7. See, for example, *Ward* v. *Rock against Racism*, 491 U.S. 781 (1989) (and cases cited); see generally Geoffrey R. Stone, "Content Regulation and the First Amendment," *William and Mary Law Review*, 25 (Winter 1983), pp. 189–252; Paul B. Stephan III, "The First Amendment and Content Discrimination," *Virginia Law Review*, 68 (February 1982), pp. 203–51; Daniel A. Farber, "Content Regulation and the First Amendment: A Revisionist View," *Georgetown Law Journal*, 68 (February 1980), pp. 727–63; John Hart Ely, "Flag Desecration: A Case Study in the Roles of Categorization and Balancing in First Amendment Analysis," *Harvard Law Review*, 88 (May 1975), pp. 1482–1508.

8. *R.A.V.* v. *City of St. Paul*, 112 S. Ct. 2538, 2542 (1992).

9. See, for example, *Sable Communications* v. *FCC*, 492 U.S. 115, 126 (1989).

10. See, for example, *Ward* v. *Rock Against Racism*, 491 U.S. 781 (1989).

11. See, for example, ibid.; *Clark* v. *Community for Creative Non-Violence*, 468 U.S. 288 (1984); *United States* v. *Albertini*, 472 U.S. 675 (1985).

12. *Smith* v. *Daily Mail Publ. Co.*, 443 U.S. 97, 103 (1979).

13. *Brandenburg* v. *Ohio.*, 395 U.S. 444 (1969).

14. *First National Bank of Boston* v. *Bellotti*, 785; see also *Thomas* v. *Collins*, 323 U.S. 516, 545 (1944) (Jackson, J., concurring); "The very purpose of the First Amendment is to foreclose public authority from assuming a guardianship of the public mind through regulating the press, speech, and religion."

15. *Buckley* v. *Valeo*, 424 U.S. 1, 48–49 (1978).

16. See, for example, *Miami Herald Pub. Co.* v. *Tornillo*, 418 U.S. 241 (1974).

17. See generally C. Edwin Baker, "Scope of the First Amendment Freedom of Speech," *U.C.L.A. Law Review*, 25 (June 1978), pp. 964–1040; Martin H. Redish, "The Value of Free Speech," *University of Pennsylvania Law Review*, 130 (January 1982), pp. 591–645; Harry H. Wellington, "On Freedom of Expression," *Yale Law Journal*, 88 (May 1979), pp. 1105–42; Thomas I. Emerson, *The System of Freedom of Expression* (Random House, 1970).

18. *Riley* v. *National Fed'n of the Blind*, 487 U.S. 781, 790–91 (1988).

19. *First Nat'l Bank of Boston* v. *Bellotti*, 435 U.S. at 781.

20. Reflecting these principles, "The constitutional right of free expression is . . . intended to remove governmental restraints from the arena of public discussion, putting the decision as to what views shall be voiced largely into the hands of each of us, in the hope that use of such freedom will ultimately produce a more capable citizenry and more perfect polity." *Cohen* v. *California*, 403 U.S. 15, 24 (1971).

21. See n. 73; *Connick* v. *Myers*, 461 U.S. 138 (1983).

22. See nn. 7–13.

23. See *Red Lion Broadcasting Co.* v. *FCC*, 395 U.S. 367 (1969).

24. See *Columbia Broadcasting System, Inc.* v. *Democratic Nat'l Comm.*, 412 U.S. 94, 110–11 (1973); *Syracuse Peace Council* v. *Television Station WTVH*, 2 FCC Rcd. 5043, 5058 n.2 (1987), recon., 3 FCC Rcd. 2035 (1988), aff'd, *Syracuse Peace Council* v. *FCC*, 867 F.2d 654 (D.C. Cir. 1989); *Fairness Report*, 48 F.C.C.2d 1 (1974), recon., 58 F.C.C.2d 691 (1976), aff'd, *National Citizens Comm. for Broadcasting* v. *FCC*, 567 F.2d 1095 (D.C. Cir. 1977), cert. denied, 436 U.S. 926 (1978).

25. See 47 C.F.R. § 73.1930 (1970); see also *Red Lion Broadcasting Co.* v. *FCC*, 395 U.S. 367 (1969); *cf. Letter to Nicholas Zapple*, 23 F.C.C.2d 707 (1970).

26. *Red Lion Broadcasting Co.* v. *FCC*, 395 U.S. at 371–75. A conservative radio commenter had attacked the book. Some observers have suggested that this use of the Fairness Doctrine was part of a more general effort by the Kennedy Administration and its supporters to chill criticism by conservative radio critics. See Fred W. Friendly, *The Good Guys, The Bad Guys, and the First Amendment: Free Speech vs. Fairness in Broadcasting* (Vintage Books, 1977); Marc A. Franklin, *Cases and Materials on Mass Media Law* (Mineola, N.Y.: Foundation Press, 1987).

27. See *Red Lion Broadcasting Co.* v. *FCC*, 395 U.S. at 376, 388–89, 396–400.

28. Ibid., 387–89.

29. Ibid., 390.

30. Ibid., 391.

31. Ibid., 389.

32. *Telecommunications Research & Action Ctr.* v. *FCC*, 801 F.2d 501, 508 (D.C. Cir. 1986) (Bork, J., joined by Scalia, J.), reh'g en banc denied, 806 F.2d 1115 (D.C. Cir. 1986), cert. denied, 107 S. Ct. 3196 (1987).

33. See, for example, R. H. Coase, "The Federal Communications Commission," *Journal of Law and Economics*, 2 (1959); pp. 1–40; Mark S. Fowler and Daniel L. Brenner, "A Marketplace Approach to Broadcast Regulation," *Texas Law Review*, 60 (1982), pp. 207–57.

34. See *FCC* v. *League of Women Voters of California*, 468 U.S. 364, 376 n.11 (1984); *Red Lion Broadcasting Co.* v. *FCC*, 395 U.S. at 396–400.

35. See *Syracuse Peace Council*, 2 FCC Rcd., n. 25; see also *Inquiry into Section 73.1910 of the Commission's Rules and Regulations Concerning the General Fairness Doctrine Obligations of Broadcast Licensees, Report*, 102 F.C.C.2d 143 (1985).

36. See 47 U.S.C. §§ 309(a), (g).

37. See *Revision of Programming and Commercialization Policies, Report and Order*, 98 F.C.C.2d 1076, 1098–1101 (1984), recon., 104 F.C.C.2d 358 (1986), rev'd in part, *Action for Children's Television* v. *FCC*, 821 F.2d 741 (D.C. Cir. 1987).

38. See, for example, 47 C.F.R. §§ 73.660–61.

39. See 47 U.S.C. §§ 317, 508; 47 C.F.R. § 73.1212.

40. See 18 U.S.C. § 1307; 47 C.F.R. § 73.1211; see generally *United States* v. *Edge Broadcasting Co.*, 113 S. Ct. 2696 (1993).

41. See 18 U.S.C. § 1464; *Action for Children's Television* v. *FCC*, 58 F. 3d 654 (D.C. Cir. 1995), cert. denied, 116 S.Ct. 701 (1996).

42. See 47 U.S.C. § 73.658; *National Ass'n of Independent Television Producers and Distributors* v. *FCC*, 516 F.2d 526 (2d Cir. 1975); *Mt. Mansfield Television, Inc.* v. *FCC*, 442 F.2d 470 (2d Cir. 1971); see also *Evaluation of the Syndication and Financial Interest Rules, Memorandum Opinion and Order*, 8 FCC Rcd. 8270 (1993).

43. See 47 U.S.C. § 315; *Codification of the Commission's Political Programming Policies, Report and Order*, 7 FCC Rcd. 678 (1991), recon., 7 FCC Rcd. 4611 (1992); see also *Arkansas AFL-CIO* v. *FCC*, 11 F.3d 1430 (8th Cir. 1993) (en banc).

44. See, for example, *Policy Statement on Comparative Broadcast Hearings*, 1 F.C.C.2d 393 (1965). The commission's selection criteria have met with increasing judicial hostility, principally on the ground that they are arbitrary and capricious because without any evidentiary basis. See *Bechtel* v. *FCC*, 10 F.3d 875 (D.C. Cir. 1993).

45. Ibid.; *Metro Broadcasting, Inc.* v. *FCC*, 497 U.S. 547 (1990), overruled in part, *Adarand Constructors, Inc.* v. *Pena*, 115 S. Ct. 2097 (1995); *Statement of Policy on Minority Ownership of Broadcasting Facilities*, 68 F.C.C.2d 979, 980-81 (1978).

46. See, for example, *Policy Statement on Comparative Broadcast Hearings*; *Amendment of Sections 73.35, 73.240, and 73.636 of the Commission Rules Relating to Multiple Ownership of Standard, FM, and Television Broadcast Stations, First Report and Order*, 22 F.C.C.2d 306 (1970), recon., 28 F.C.C.2d 662 (1971); see also *Amendment of Section 73.3555 of the Commission's Rules, the Broadcast Multiple Ownership Rules, Second Report and Order*, 4 FCC Rcd. 1741, recon., 4 FCC Rcd. 6489 (1989).

47. See *Turner Broadcasting System, Inc.* v. *FCC*, 114 S. Ct. 2445 (1994). *Turner* held that the lesser standard of judicial protection currently applicable to broadcasting did not apply to cable television operators, but the Court in *Turner* declined to reconsider *Red Lion*'s validity. The author participated in *Turner* on behalf of certain broadcaster appellees.

48. See 47 U.S.C. § 315(c)(1); *Letter of January 24, 1994, to Storer Cable*, 9 FCC Rcd. 813 (1994); *Licensees and Cable Operators Reminded of Lowest Unit Charge Obligations*, 4 FCC Rcd. 3823 (1988).

49. See 47 U.S.C. § 531. Even if this conclusion were not proven true, cities' implementation of carriage requirements for public, educational, and governmental channels would be vulnerable to First Amendment challenge if the franchise agreement favored particular speakers (especially incumbent politicians) on the ground that they were able to present especially valuable messages, or if they otherwise embodied content-based preferences.

50. See *Communications Act of 1994,* S. 1822, 103 Cong. 2 sess., § 103 (GPO, 1994); cf. *National Communications Competition and Information Infrastructure Act of 1994,* H.R. 3636, 103 Cong. 2 sess., § 103 (GPO, 1994).

51. "Spectrum scarcity" does not apply to wireline delivery systems because they do not employ the spectrum to deliver information, and does not apply to switched wireless systems, especially if they are operated on a common-carrier basis, because switching removes the capacity constraint identified in *Red Lion.*

52. A legal regime may reflect ideology in the sense of responses issuing from a shared outlook, or conception of values and operation of events, based in turn on a

commonly shared and explained set of relevant historical events and distinctions justifying the legal or other response. See, for example, Bernard Bailyn, *The Ideological Origins of the American Revolution* (Cambridge, Mass.: Belknap Press, 1967). This interplay between social understanding of fact, subject to challenge or reappraisal, and legal or other coordinated social response also underlies much of the recent revival of pragmatism. See, for example, Richard Rorty, *The Consequences of Pragmatism* (University of Minnesota Press, 1982).

53. FCC policies contributed significantly both to the development of the national television networks and, especially, to the limited number of television stations available to serve particular communities. Assigning a single owner to each station further constricted the variety of video programming and other uses of broadcasting facilities. See generally Note, "UHF and the FCC: The Search for a Television Allocations Policy," *University of Florida Law Review*, 28 (Winter 1976), pp. 399–438; "Special Project, Television Service and the FCC," *Texas Law Review*, 46 (November 1968), p. 1100; Note, "The Darkened Channels: UHF Television and the FCC," *Harvard Law Review*, 75 (June 1962), pp. 1578–1607.

54. Regulations particularly limited the uses and availability of cable television systems until the mid- to late 1970s. See, for example, *Amendment of Parts 21, 74, and 91 to Adapt Rules and Regulations Relating to the Distribution of Television Broadcast Signals by Community Antenna Television Systems, Second Report and Order*, 2 F.C.C.2d 725 (1966), aff'd, *Black Hills Video Corp. v. FCC*, 399 F.2d 65 (8th Cir. 1968); *Amendment of Part 74, Subpart K, of the Commission's Rules and Regulations Relative to Community Antenna Television Systems, Cable Television Report and Order*, 36 F.C.C.2d 143, recon., 36 F.C.C.2d 326 (1972), aff'd, *ACLU v. FCC*, 523 F.2d 1344 (9th Cir. 1975).

55. The FCC was charged with broad powers to allocate licenses in the public interest and to attach conditions to achieve that purpose; see, for example, 47 U.S.C. §§ 303, 307, 309; *National Broadcasting Co. v. United States*, 319 U.S. 190 (1943); *FCC v. Pottsville Broadcasting Co.*, 309 U.S. 134 (1940). In addition, the Communications Act limits the license grant to ensure that no full ownership interest passes from ultimate government control. See 47 U.S.C. §§ 301, 307. The "license" granted, as the term suggests, a temporary interest in and authorization to occupy the government's property subject to the conditions set forth by the government.

56. See 47 U.S.C. § 326.

57. *Red Lion Broadcasting Co. v. FCC*, 395 U.S. at 386–95.

58. Ibid., 394 (emphasis added).

59. For example, the most popular programming delivered over cable systems continues to be network television programming, and many cable networks deliver programming that initially aired on television networks.

60. A television network such as Fox or CBS bundles programming, some self-produced and some acquired, for presentation as the network's product. A cable television network such as Home Box Office operates similarly.

61. The networks own and operate television stations in major markets, but their programming is predominantly distributed through independently owned affiliates. In fact, a network is defined for most purposes according to this programming function, which could exist entirely separately from the ownership of television stations. See 47

C.F.R. § 73.662(f) (1994); *Evaluation of the Syndication and Financial Interest Rules, Second Report and Order,* 8 FCC Rcd. 3282, 3331–35 (1993). Similarly, many cable networks are not owned by owners of cable television systems.

62. That element of control may be reflected through, for example, an affiliation agreement, a syndication barter arrangement, or allocation of a cable system's channel to programming from a particular source.

63. See *Red Lion Broadcasting Co.* v. *FCC,* 395 U.S. at 387–92.

64. In addition, "network" programming originates from a variety of sources, particularly Hollywood studios.

65. See *Policy Statement on Comparative Broadcast Hearings,* 1 F.C.C.2d 393 (1965).

66. See 47 U.S.C. § 309(i); see also, for example, *Cellular Lottery Decision,* 98 F.C.C.2d 175 (1984); *Florida Cellular Mobile Communications Corp.* v. *FCC,* 28 F.3d 191, 193 (D.C. Cir. 1994); *Singleton* v. *FCC,* 952 F.2d 1444, 1446–47 (D.C. Cir. 1992); *Pappas* v. *FCC,* 807 F.2d 1019 (D.C. Cir. 1986).

67. See 47 U.S.C. § 309(j); *Implementation of Section 309(j) of the Communications Act—Competitive Bidding, Second Report and Order,* 9 FCC Rcd. 2348 (1994); ibid., *Third Report and Order,* 9 FCC Rcd. 2941 (1994), recon., *Third Memorandum Opinion and Order and Further Notice of Proposed Rulemaking,* 10 FCC Rcd. 175 (1995); ibid., *Fourth Report and Order,* 59 Fed. Reg. 24,947 (May 13, 1994); ibid., *Fifth Report and Order,* 59 Fed. Reg. 37,566 (July 22, 1994).

68. See *Implementation of Section 309(j) of the Communications Act—Competitive Bidding, Third Report and Order;* ibid., *Fifth Report and Order.*

69. See 47 U.S.C. § 336 (enacted by Telecommunications Act of 1996, § 201).

70. See, for example, *Red Lion Broadcasting Co.* v. *FCC,* 395 U.S. at 386.

71. See, for example, *Leathers* v. *Medlock,* 499 U.S. 439, 444 (1991); *Los Angeles* v. *Preferred Communications, Inc.,* 476 U.S. 488, 494 (1986); *Miami Herald Publ. Co.* v. *Tornillo,* 418 U.S. at 257–59.

72. See *Telecommunications Deregulation and Competition Act of 1995,* S. 652, 104 Cong. 1 sess., § 143.

73. See, for example, *Miller* v. *California,* 413 U.S. 15 (1973).

74. See *Alliance for Community Media* v. *FCC,* 56 F.3d 105 (D.C. Cir. 1995)(en banc), cert. granted sub nom., *Denver Area Educational Telecommunications Consortium Inc.* v. *FCC,* 116 S. Ct. 471 (U.S. November 13, 1995).

75. See *FCC* v. *Pacifica Foundation,* 438 U.S. 726 (1978).

76. See *Sable Communications* v. *FCC,* 492 U.S. 115 (1989).

77. See 47 U.S.C. § 223(a) (amended by Telecommunications Act of 1996, § 502).

78. Ibid.

79. See 47 U.S.C. §§ 531(e), 532(c)(2) (enacted by Telecommunications Act of 1996, § 506).

80. See 47 U.S.C. § 223(d) (amended by Telecommunications Act of 1996, § 502).

81. See 47 U.S.C. § 303(w) (amended by Telecommunications Act of 1996, § 551(b)); Telecommunications Act of 1996, § 551(e).

82. Telecommunications Act of 1996, § 561.

83. See Telecommunications Act of 1996, §§ 551(c)–(d), 552.

84. See Cass R. Sunstein, *Democracy and the Problem of Free Speech* (New York: Free Press, 1993), pp. 107–13

85. Ibid., pp. 67–92.

86. Previous sections have sought to establish that no such justification exists.

87. See Thomas G. Krattenmaker and Lucas A. Powe Jr., *Regulating Broadcast Programming* (MIT Press and American Enterprise Institute, 1995); *Syracuse Peace Council* v. *Television Station WTVH*; *Inquiry into Section 73.1910 of the Commission's Rules and Regulations Concerning the General Fairness Doctrine Obligations of Broadcast Licensees*, 102 F.C.C.2d 143 (1985).

88. Cf., for example, Brief for Intervenor-Appellees Consumer Federation of America, National Council for Senior Citizens, International Association of Machinists and Aerospace Workers, AFL-CIO, and the Office of Communication of the United Church of Christ, *Turner Broadcasting System, Inc.* v. *FCC*, No. 93-44 (November 9, 1993).

89. See Sunstein, *Democracy and the Problem of Free Speech,* pp. 74, 82.

90. See *FCC* v. *Midwest Video Corp.*, 440 U.S. 689, 701 (1979) (common carriage exists when carrier "makes a public offering . . . whereby all members of the public who choose to employ such facilities may communicate or transmit intelligence of their own design and choosing."); *National Ass'n of Regulatory Utility Comm'rs* v. *FCC*, 533 F.2d 601, 608 (D.C. Cir. 1976) (Wilkey, J.); *National Ass'n of Regulatory Utility Comm'rs* v. *FCC*, 525 F.2d 630 (D.C. Cir.), cert. denied, 425 U.S. 992 (1976).

91. See, for example, *MTS and WATS Market Structure, Phase III Report and Order*, 100 F.C.C.2d 860 (1985); *United States* v. *Western Elec. Co.*, 552 F.Supp. 131 (D.D.C. 1982), aff'd, *Maryland* v. *United States*, 460 U.S. 1001 (1983).

92. See 47 U.S.C. §§ 201–05, 208.

93. See, for example, *Lorain Journal Co.* v. *United States*, 342 U.S. 143 (1951); *United States* v. *Paramount Pictures, Inc.*, 334 U.S. 131 (1948); *Associated Press* v. *United States*, 326 U.S. 1 (1945).

94. See *Red Lion Broadcasting Co.* v. *FCC*, 395 U.S. 367 (1969); *Metro Broadcasting, Inc.* v. *FCC*, 497 U.S. 547 (1990), overruled in part, *Adarand Constructors, Inc.* v. *Pena*, 115 S. Ct. 2097 (1995); 47 U.S.C. §§ 301–33 (Title III of the Communications Act).

95. See *Turner Broadcasting System, Inc.* v. *FCC*, 114 S. Ct. 2445 (1994).

96. See, for example, *Minneapolis Star & Tribune Co.* v. *Minnesota Comm'r of Revenue*, 460 U.S. 575 (1983).

97. *Thomas* v. *Collins*, 323 U.S. 516, 545 (1945) (Jackson, J., concurring).

98. See, for example, *Williamson* v. *Lee Optical of Oklahoma, Inc.*, 348 U.S. 483 (1955).

99. See, for example, *Citizen Publ. Co.* v. *United States*, 394 U.S. 131 (1969); *Lorain Journal Co.* v. *United States*, 342 U.S. 143 (1951); *FTC* v. *Superior Court Trial Lawyers Ass'n*, 493 U.S. 411 (1990); *Associated Press* v. *United States*, 326 U.S. 1 (1975).

100. *Associated Press* v. *United States*, 326 U.S. at 20; see also *Citizen Publ. Co.* v. *United States*, 394 U.S. at 139–40; *Lorain Journal Co.*, 342 U.S. at 155–56.

101. See, for example, *Otter Tail Power Co.* v. *United States*, 410 U.S. 366 (1973); *United States* v. *Terminal R.R. Ass'n of St. Louis*, 224 U.S. 383 (1912); *Aspen Highlands Skiing Corp.* v. *Aspen Skiing Co.*, 738 F.2d 1509 (10th Cir. 1984), aff'd on other

grounds, 472 U.S. 585 (1985); *MCI Communications Corp.* v. *AT&T*, 708 F.2d 1081, 1132 (7th Cir.), cert. denied, 464 U.S. 891 (1983).

102. See, for example, *United States* v. *Western Elec. Co.*, 552 F.Supp. 131 (D.D.C. 1982), aff'd, *Maryland* v. *United States*, 460 U.S. 1001 (1983); *MCI Communications Corp.* v. *AT&T*, 708 F.2d at 1132.

103. *Lorain Journal Co.* v. *United States*, 342 U.S. 143 (1981); see also *Associated Press* v. *United States*, 326 U.S. 1 (1945).

104. See, for example, *Citizen Publ. Co.* v. *United States*, 394 U.S. 131 (1969).

105. See, for example, *Associated Press* v. *United States*, 326 U.S. 1 (1945); *United States* v. *Paramount Pictures, Inc.*, 334 U.S. 131 (1948).

106. See *Arkansas Writers' Project, Inc.* v. *Ragland*, 481 U.S. 221 (1987); *Minneapolis Star & Tribune Co.* v. *Minnesota Comm'r of Revenue*, 460 U.S. 575 (1983); *Grosjean* v. *American Press Co.*, 297 U.S. 233 (1936).

107. See, for example, *Landmark Communications, Inc.* v. *Virginia*, 435 U.S. 829 (1978).

108. *FCC* v. *National Citizens Comm. for Broadcasting*, 436 U.S. 775 (1978).

109. Ibid., at 800 n.18.

110. *Turner Broadcasting System, Inc.* v. *FCC*, 114 S. Ct. 2445 (1994).

111. *Cable Television Consumer Protection and Competition Act of 1992*, P. L. 102-385, §§ 4 & 5.

112. See 47 U.S.C. §§ 534, 535.

113. See, for example, *Turner Broadcasting System, Inc.* v. *FCC*, 114 S. Ct. at 2462–68, 2475–76 (O'Connor, J., dissenting).

114. Ibid., at 2456, 2468–69, 2470–72. On remand for further factual inquiry, the District Court again upheld the must-carry requirements, and the Supreme Court is reviewing that decision. See *Turner Broadcasting* v. *FCC*, 910 F. Supp. 734 (D.D.C. 1995), prob. juris. noted, 116 S. Ct. 907 (February 20, 1996).

115. Ibid., 2458–64.

116. Ibid., at 2476 (O'Connor, J., dissenting: "I agree with the Court that some speaker-based restrictions—those genuinely justified without reference to content—need not be subject to strict scrutiny").

117. Ibid., 2469.

118. Ibid., 2458.

119. Ibid.

120. Ibid., 2470–72.

121. See Brief for Appellant Time Warner Entertainment, L.P., *Turner Broadcasting System, Inc.* v. *FCC*, No. 93-44 (Nov. 9, 1993); Brief for Appellant National Cable Television Ass'n, ibid.; Brief for Appellants Discovery Communications, Inc., and The Learning Channel, Inc., ibid.; Brief for Appellant Daniels Cablevision, Inc., ibid.

122. See, for example, Brief for Appellant Time Warner Entertainment, pp. 28–31; Brief for Appellant National Cable Television Ass'n, pp. 23–27; Brief for Appellants Discovery Communications, Inc., and The Learning Channel, p. 32; see also Brief of United States Tel. Ass'n. et al., *Turner Broadcasting System, Inc.* v. *FCC*, No. 93-44, 22 and n. 26.

123. These groups identified and relied on the "essential First Amendment right . . . [of the public] to receive information" and "an equally important First Amendment right

to receive access to the widest possible dissemination of information." Brief for Interve-
nor-Appellees Consumer Federation of America, National Council of Senior Citizens,
International Association of Machinists and Aerospace Workers, AFL-CIO, and the
Office of Communication of the United Church of Christ, *Turner Broadcasting System,
Inc.* v. *FCC*, No. 93-44, 14.

124. See Brief for the Federal Appellees, *Turner Broadcasting System, Inc.* v. *FCC*,
No. 93-44 (relying on *Red Lion* v. *FCC*).

125. Ibid., 16–36.

126. See Brief of Appellee National Ass'n of Broadcasters, *Turner Broadcasting
System, Inc.* v. *FCC*, No. 93-44, 17–19, 49; Brief of Appellee Association of Independent Television Stations, Inc., ibid., 34.

127. See *Smith* v. *Goguen*, 415 U.S. 566 (1974); *Shuttlesworth* v. *City of Birming-
ham*, 394 U.S. 147 (1969); *Freedman* v. *Maryland*, 380 U.S. 51 (1965).

128. For this reason, the proponents of this theory reiterated their support for the
Fairness Doctrine as well. See Brief for Intervenor-Appellees Consumer Federation of
America et al., 15 n. 7.

129. The consumer groups cited only broadcasting cases to support their claim of a
"'paramount' [First Amendment] right to receive information." See Brief for Intervenor-Appellees Consumer Federation of America et al., 11 (citing *Columbia Broadcasting System, Inc.* v. *FCC*, 453 U.S. 367, 395–96 (1981); *Columbia Broadcasting System,
Inc.* v. *Democratic National Comm.*, 412 U.S. 94 (1973); *Red Lion Broadcasting Co.* v.
FCC, 395 U.S. 367 (1969)). In addition, much of the interest groups' argument fails to
distinguish between a governmental interest in providing or ensuring the provision of
information to the public (which justifies a broad range of educational measures,
commercial restrictions, and limitations directly incident to operation of governmental
programs) and doing so in a manner that restricts rather than supplements private actors'
speech.

130. See Brief for Federal Appellees, *Turner Broadcasting System, Inc.* v. *FCC*, No.
93-44, 16–21.

131. This disjunction between the speech-balancing interest identified in *Red Lion*
and antitrust analysis produces even more profound difficulties. In any context where
distribution is expensive (whether it is electronic or otherwise), the views of those who
cannot afford delivery costs will be excluded—whether or not any market power exists.
In contrast, it may be exceptionally difficult and in many cases impossible to identify the
views excluded by a monopolist in control of distribution facilities (especially if market
power is reflected in monopoly pricing, but not full exclusion).

132. For similar reasons, both strict scrutiny and intermediate scrutiny are employed
to review measures alleged to reflect race or gender discrimination. Such scrutiny is
designed to determine whether and ensure that the government is pursuing a legitimate
object (for example, remedying racial discrimination) rather than impermissible ones
(such as fostering stereotypes or allocating goods according to race). See, for example,
Richmond v. *J. A. Croson Co.*, 488 U.S. 469, 493–95, 498–502 (1989); *Wygant* v.
Jackson Bd. of Educ., 476 U.S. 267 (1986); see *generally* John H. Ely, *Democracy and
Distrust: A Theory of Judicial Review* (Harvard University Press, 1980).

133. The *Turner* decision held that "the requirement of narrow tailoring is satisfied
'so long as the . . . regulation promotes a substantial government interest that would be

achieved less effectively absent the regulation.'" *Turner Broadcasting System, Inc.* v. *FCC*, 114 S. Ct. at 2469 (quoting *Ward* v. *Rock Against Racism*, 491 U.S. 781, 799 (1989)). The government must also demonstrate the substantiality of the risk to the asserted government interest in the particular circumstances and the efficacy of the regulation. Ibid., 2470; the government "must demonstrate that the recited harms are real, not merely conjectural, and that the regulation will in fact alleviate those harms in a direct and material way."

134. Ibid., at 2469.

135. See *United States* v. *O'Brien*, 391 U.S. 367 (1968). *Turner* directly applied the test contained in *O'Brien*, 391 U.S. at 377, as modified in *United States* v. *Albertini*, 472 U.S. 675, 689 (1985), and *Ward* v. *Rock Against Racism*, 491 U.S. at 799. See *Turner Broadcasting System, Inc.* v. *FCC*, 114 S. Ct. at 2469.

136. Measures that regulate the "time, place, and manner" of speech are valid "provided that they are justified without reference to the content of the regulated speech, that they are narrowly tailored to serve a significant governmental interest, and that they leave open ample alternative channels for communication of information." *Clark* v. *Community for Creative Non-Violence*, 468 U.S. 288, 293 (1984). The Court has held that this standard is equivalent to that set forth in *United States* v. *O'Brien*, 391 U.S. at 689. See *Clark* v. *Community for Creative Non-Violence*, 468 U.S. at 298.

137. See *United States* v. *O'Brien*, 391 U.S. at 689.

138. See *Clark* v. *Community for Creative Non-Violence*, 468 U.S. at 293, 298.

139. See *Ward* v. *Rock against Racism*, 491 U.S. at 799; see also *Clark* v. *Community for Creative Non-Violence*, 468 U.S. at 293.

140. See *Turner Broadcasting System, Inc.* v. *FCC*, 114 S. Ct. at 2459.

141. *Leathers* v. *Medlock*, 111 S. Ct. 1438, 1447 (1991).

142. See chapter 3, above. *Turner* expressly declined to address the continuing validity of broadcasting regulation.

143. See *Turner Broadcasting System, Inc.*, 114 S. Ct. at 2476 (O'Connor, J., dissenting)(citing 1992 Cable Act §§ 2(a)(6), 2(a)(8)(A), 2(a)(10), 2(a)(11)(statements of legislative purpose), 47 U.S. C. §§ 534 (h)(1)(C)(ii), 534(H)(2)(B).

144. See 47 U.S.C. § 535.

145. See generally 47 U.S.C. §§ 390–94, addressing assistance for public communications facilities, National Endowment for Children's Educational Television, and 47 U.S.C. §§ 396–99B, addressing public broadcasting stations and the Corporation for Public Broadcasting.

146. See *Turner Broadcasting System, Inc.* v. *FCC*, 114 S. Ct. at 2469–71.

147. Ibid., 2472.

148. See, for example, *Metro Broadcasting, Inc.* v. *FCC*, 497 U.S. at 547; *Walters* v. *National Ass'n of Radiation Survivors*, 473 U.S. 305, 331 n.12 (1985); *Rostker* v. *Goldberg*, 453 U.S. 57, 72–73 (1981); *Columbia Broadcasting System, Inc.* v. *Democratic National Comm.*, 412 U.S. 94, 102 (1973); see also *Rust* v. *Sullivan*, 111 S. Ct. 1759, 1767 (1991).

149. *Turner Broadcasting System, Inc.* v. *FCC*, 114 S. Ct. at 2469.

150. The dissenters in *Turner* understood these asserted interests in this manner. See *Turner Broadcasting System, Inc.* v. *FCC*, 114 S. Ct at 2477–78 (O'Connor, J., dissenting).

151. See, for example, *FCC* v. *National Citizens Comm. for Broadcasting*, 436 U.S. 775, 800 n.18 (1978); *Associated Press* v. *United States*, 326 U.S. 1, 20 (1945).

152. See, for example, *Citizen Publ. Co.* v. *United States*, 394 U.S. 131, 139–40 (1969); *Lorain Journal Co.* v. *United States*, 342 U.S. 143, 155–56 (1951); *National Broadcasting Co.* v. *United States*, 319 U.S. 190, 226–27 (1943); *Associated Press* v. *United States*, 326 U.S. at 20.

153. See, for example, *Buckley* v. *Valeo*, 429 U.S. 1, 48–49 (1976): "The concept that government may restrict the speech of some elements of our society in order to enhance the relative voice of others is wholly foreign to the First Amendment"; see also *R.A.V.* v. *St. Paul*, 112 S. Ct. 2538, 2545 (1992): "The government may not regulate based on hostility—or favoritism—toward the underlying message expressed."

154. See, for example, *Lorain Journal Co.* v. *United States*, 342 U.S. 143 (1951); *Citizen Publ. Co.* v. *United States*, 394 U.S. 131 (1969); *Associated Press* v. *United States*, 326 U.S. 1 (1945).

155. See *Turner Broadcasting System, Inc.* v. *FCC*, 114 S. Ct. at 2469–70.

156. Ibid (relying on *United States* v. *Southwestern Cable Co.*, 392 U.S. 157 (1968); *Capital Cities Cable, Inc.* v. *Crisp*, 467 U.S. 691 (1984); *United States* v. *Midwest Video Corp.*, 406 U.S. 649 (1972) (plurality opinion)).

157. This analysis sets to one side the exceptionally rare cases in which a content-based restriction may survive strict judicial scrutiny.

158. See *Hurley* v. *Irish-American Gay, Lesbian and Bisexual Group of Boston*, 115 S. Ct. 2338, 2347–49 (1995).

159. For example, the 1992 Cable Act imposed limits on cable operators designed to foster competition but that were recognized as more stringent than those required by antitrust doctrine. See *Implementation of Sections 11 and 13 of the Cable Television Consumer Protection and Competition Act of 1992, Horizontal and Vertical Ownership Limits, Cross-Ownership Limitations, and Anti-Trafficking Provisions, Notice of Proposed Rulemaking and Notice of Inquiry*, 8 FCC Rcd. 210, 216 (1993). But see *Daniels Cablevision, Inc.* v. *United States*, 835 F.Supp. 1 (D.D.C. 1993), which declared unconstitutional subscriber limitations imposed on cable operators pursuant to the 1992 Cable Act.

160. See *Ward* v. *Rock Against Racism*, 491 U.S. at 799; *Turner Broadcasting System, Inc.* v. *FCC*, 114 S. Ct. at 2469.

161. See *Turner Broadcasting System, Inc.*, 114 S. Ct. at 2469.

162. Cf. *Daniels Cablevision, Inc.* v. *United States*, 835 F.Supp. 1 (D.D.C. 1993) (1992 Cable Act's provisions regarding "access" to satellite broadcasting delivery systems and limits on cable operators' scope of service violate the First Amendment).

163. The extent to which local carriers continue to exercise market power over local facilities, and the form of necessary regulation, is subject to robust debate. Cf. *United States* v. *Western Elec. Co.*, 900 F.2d 283 (D.C. Cir. 1990); *United States* v. *Western Elec. Co.*, 673 F.Supp. 525 (D.D.C. 1987), aff'd in part, remanded in part, ibid., *with Memorandum of Bell Atlantic Corporation, BellSouth Corporation, NYNEX Corporation, and Southwestern Bell Corporation in Support of Their Mo-*

tion to Vacate the Decree, United States v. *Western Elec. Co.*, No. 82-0192 (filed July 6, 1994).

164. See *Cable Television Consumer Protection Act of 1991*, S. Rep. 92, 102 Cong. 1 sess. (GPO 1991), pp. 8–13.

165. Ibid., 23–32 (and sources noted); 47 U.S.C. §§ 534–35, 548; *United States* v. *Western Elec. Co.*, 552 F.Supp. 131 (D.D.C. 1982), aff'd, *Maryland* v. *United States*, 460 U.S. 1001 (1983); *Amendment of Section 64.702 of the Commission's Rules and Regulations (Second Computer Inquiry), Final Decision*, 77 F.C.C.2d 384 (1980) (hereafter, *Computer II*), recon., 84 F.C.C.2d 50 (1980), further recon., 88 F.C.C.2d 512 (1981), aff'd, *Computer & Communications Industry Ass'n* v. *FCC*, 693 F.2d 198 (D.C. Cir. 1982), cert. denied, 461 U.S. 938 (1983).

166. See 47 U.S.C. § 201(a); cf. 49 U.S.C. § 1(4) (1970).

167. See, for example, *Otter Tail Power Co.* v. *United States*, 410 U.S. 366 (1973); *MCI Communications Corp.* v. *AT&T*, 708 F.2d 1081, 1132 (7th Cir.), cert. denied, 464 U.S. 891 (1983).

168. For example, interconnection obligations imposed on the predominant local exchange carrier are essential to the prominent deregulatory plans proposed by carriers themselves, in which they would coordinate their network with networks of their competitors to increase potential competition and, in return, receive significant regulatory benefits. See *Pleading Cycle Established for Comments on Ameritech's Petition for Declaratory Ruling and Related Waivers to Establish a New Regulatory Model for the Ameritech Region, Public Notice*, 8 FCC Rcd. 2964 (1993); *Pleading Cycle Established for Comments on Petition for Waiver Filed by Rochester Telephone Corporation*, 8 FCC Rcd. 4216 (1993).

169. See, for example, *Bell Atlantic Tel. Co.* v. *FCC*, 24 F.3d 1441 (D.C. Cir. 1994); *Expanded Interconnection with Local Telephone Company Facilities, Report and Order and Notice of Proposed Rulemaking*, 7 FCC Rcd. 7369 (1992), recon., 8 FCC Rcd. 127, further recon., 8 FCC Rcd. 7341 (1993), vacated in part, remanded, ibid.; *Local Exchange Carriers' Rates, Terms, and Conditions for Expanded Interconnection for Switched Transport, Memorandum Opinion and Order*, 9 FCC Rcd. 817 (Common Carrier Bureau 1994); *Local Exchange Carriers' Rates, Terms, and Conditions for Expanded Interconnection for Special Access, Order Designating Issues for Investigation*, 8 FCC Rcd. 6909 (Common Carrier Bureau 1993).

170. 47 U.S.C. §§ 251–61 (enacted by Telecommunications Act of 1996, § 101).

171. See, for example, *Eastman Kodak Co.* v. *Image Technical Services, Inc.*, 112 S. Ct. 2072 (1992); *Jefferson Parish Hosp. Dist. No. 2* v. *Hyde*, 466 U.S. 2 (1984); *United States Steel Corp.* v. *Fortner Enterprises, Inc.*, 429 U.S. 610 (1977).

172. See, for example, *Computer III Remand Proceedings: Bell Operating Company Safeguards and Tier 1 Local Exchange Company Safeguards, Notice of Proposed Rulemaking and Order*, 6 FCC Rcd. 174 (1990); see also *Amendment of Section 64.702 of the Commission's Rules and Regulations (Third Computer Inquiry), Report and Order*, 104 F.C.C.2d 958 (1986), recon., 2 FCC Rcd. 3035 (1987), further recon., 3 FCC Rcd. 1135 (1988).

173. See 47 U.S.C. § 251(g); *MTS and WATS Market Structure, Phase III, Report and Order*, 100 F.C.C.2d 860 (1985); *United States* v. *Western Elec. Co.*, 552 F.Supp. at 227 (MFJ § II(B)), aff'd, *Maryland* v. *United States*, 460 U.S. 1001 (1983).

174. See, for example, 47 U.S.C. §§ 201(a), 531–32.

175. Ibid., §§ 534–35; *Turner Broadcasting System, Inc.* v. *FCC*, 114 S. Ct. at 2445.

176. Ibid., § 202(a).

177. Ibid., § 202(a); *MCI Telecommunications Corp.* v. *FCC*, 917 F.2d 30 (D.C. Cir. 1990); *Ad Hoc Telecommunications Users Comm.* v. *FCC*, 680 F.2d 790 (D.C. Cir. 1982).

178. See 47 U.S.C. §§ 534–35; *Turner Broadcasting System, Inc.* v. *FCC*, 114 S. Ct. at 2445.

179. See *Turner Broadcasting System, Inc.* v. *FCC*, 114 S. Ct. at 2469–72.

180. Of course, even if an interconnection, access, unbundling, or nondiscrimination regulation were shown to reflect either of these general, content-neutral objectives, the *Turner* analysis would still require a sufficient evidentiary showing that the regulation directly advances the government interest and does not unduly restrict speech.

181. See *Chesapeake & Potomac Tel. Co.* v *United States*, 42 F.3d 181 (4th Cir. 1995), cert. granted, 115 S. Ct. 2608 (1995), vacated, 116 S. Ct. 1036 (1996).

182. See Telecommunicatons Act of 1996, § 202(i).

183. See Telecommunications Act of 1996, § 202(f); 47 C.F.R. § 76.501; *Amendment of Part 76, Subpart J, Section 76.501 of the Commission's Rules and Regulations to Eliminate the Prohibition on Common Ownership of Cable Television Systems and National Television Networks, Report and Order*, 7 FCC Rcd. 6156 (1992), recon., 8 FCC Rcd. 1184 (1993).

184. Cross-ownership by cable system operators in SMATV or MMDS services serving a common area is prohibited. See 47 U.S.C. § 533(a)(amended by Telecommunications Act of 1996, § 202(i)); 47 C.F.R. § 21.912; *Implementation of Sections 11 and 13 of the Cable Television Consumer Protection and Competition Act of 1992, Horizontal and Vertical Ownership Limits, Cross-Ownership Limitations and Anti-Trafficking Provisions, Report and Order and Further Notice of Proposed Rulemaking*, 8 FCC Rcd. 6828 (1993).

185. See 47 C.F.R. § 73.3555(d)(3); see also *FCC* v. *National Citizens Committee for Broadcasting*, 436 U.S. 775 (1978).

186. See *United States* v. *Western Elec. Co.*, 552 F.Supp. 131 (D.D.C. 1982), aff'd, *Maryland* v. *United States*, 460 U.S. 1001 (1983); *United States* v. *Western Elec. Co.*, 767 F.Supp. 308, 332 (D.D.C. 1991), aff'd, 993 F.2d 1572 (D.C. Cir. 1993). A decree catch-all restriction on the Bell Operating Companies and a prohibition on AT&T's provision of electronic publishing were also removed. See *United States* v. *Western Elec. Co.*, 673 F.Supp. 525, 597–99 (D.D.C. 1987); *United States* v. *Western Elec. Co.*, 1989-2 Trade Cas. ¶ 68,673 (D.D.C. 1989).

187. See, for example, *Computer II,* 77 F.C.C.2d 384 (1980), recon., 84 F.C.C.2d 50 (1980), further recon., 88 F.C.C.2d 512 (1981), aff'd, *Computer & Communications Industry Ass'n* v. *FCC*, 693 F.2d 198 (D.C. Cir. 1982), cert. denied, 461 U.S. 938 (1983); *Computer III Remand Proceedings: Bell Operating Company Safeguards and Tier 1 Local Exchange Company Safeguards, Report and Order*, 6 FCC Rcd. 7571 (1991) (petitions for review pending); see also *Separation of Costs of Regulated Telephone Service from Costs of Nonregulated Activities, Amendment of Part 31, the Uniform System of Accounts for Class A and Class B Telephone Companies to Provide for Nonregulated Activities and to Provide for Transactions between Telephone Com-*

panies and Their Affiliates, Report and Order, 2 FCC Rcd. 1298 (1987), recon., 2 FCC Rcd. 6283 (1987), modified, 3 FCC Rcd. 6701 (1988), aff'd, *Southwestern Bell Corp.* v. *FCC,* 896 F.2d 1378 (D.C. Cir. 1990).

188. See 47 U.S.C. § 533(f); *Implementation of Sections 11 and 13 of the Cable Television Consumer Protection and Competition Act of 1992,* 8 FCC Rcd. 6828 (1993).

189. See 47 C.F.R. § 73.3555. In addition, regulations have governed the sources of and interests that may be taken in network programming. See *Evaluation of the Syndication and Financial Interest Rules, Second Report and Order,* 8 FCC Rcd. 3282 (1993); see also 47 C.F.R. §§ 659–60; *Schurz Communications* v. *FCC,* 982 F.2d 1043 (7th Cir. 1992).

190. See *FCC* v. *National Citizens Comm. for Broadcasting,* 436 U.S. 775 (1978); *National Broadcasting Co.* v. *United States,* 319 U.S. 190 (1943).

191. Ibid.

192. See *US WEST, Inc.* v. *United States,* 855 F.Supp. 1184 (W.D. Wash. 1994), aff'd., 48 F.3d 1092 (9th Cir. 1994), vacated and remanded, 116 S. Ct. 1037 (1996); *Chesapeake & Potomac Tel. Co.* v. *United States,* 830 F.Supp. 909 (E.D. Va. 1993) (subsequent history omitted).

193. See *US WEST, Inc.* v. *United States,* 48 F.3d at 1184; *Chesapeake & Potomac Tel. Co.* v. *United States,* 42 F.3d 181 (4th Cir., 1994), cert. granted, 115 S. Ct. 2608 (1995), vacated 116 S. Ct. 1036 (1996); *NYNEX Corp.* v. *United States,* 1994 WL 779761 (D. Me., 1994); *Ameritech Corp.* v. *United States,* 867 F.Supp. 721 (N.D. Ill. 1994); *BellSouth Corp.* v. *United States,* 868 F.Supp. 1335 (N.D. Ala. 1994). Local telephone companies also invoked the First Amendment in their challenge to the prohibition on their provision of information services contained in the consent decree governing the divestiture of the Bell System. See Brief of the Bell Company Appellants Regarding Information Services, Nos. 87-5388 et al. (D.C. Cir., filed April 17, 1989); see also *United States* v. *Western Elec. Co.,* 900 F.2d 283 (D.C. Cir.), cert. denied, 498 U.S. 911 (1990).

194. See, for example, *FCC* v. *National Citizens Comm. for Broadcasting*; 436 U.S. 775 (1978); *United States* v. *Western Elec. Co.,* 552 F.Supp. 131 (D.D.C. 1982), aff'd, *Maryland* v. *Western Elec. Co.,* 460 U.S. 1001 (1983)

195. See, generally, *Telephone Company–Cable Television Cross-Ownership Rules, Fourth Further Notice of Proposed Rulemaking,* 10 FCC Rcd. 4617 (1995).

196. Most FCC regulation of telecommunications carriers, including rate regulation, reflects the FCC's Title II powers over common carriers. See 47 U.S.C. §§ 201–05; *Virgin Islands Tel. Corp.* v. *FCC,* 989 F.2d 1231 (D.C. Cir. 1993); *AT&T* v. *FCC,* 836 F.2d 1386 (D.C. Cir. 1988). The rate powers are, however, potentially more expansive. See, for example, *New England Tel. & Tel. Co.* v. *FCC,* 826 F.2d 1101 (D.C. Cir. 1987), cert. denied, 490 U.S. 1039 (1989).

197. See 47 U.S.C. §§ 543–44 (enacted 1992).

198. See *Policy and Rules Concerning Rates for Dominant Carriers, Report and Order and Second Further Notice of Proposed Rulemaking,* 4 FCC Rcd. 2873 (1989), recon., 6 FCC Rcd. 665, *Second Report and Order,* 5 FCC Rcd. 6786 (1990), recon., 6 FCC Rcd. 2637 (1991), aff'd, *National Rural Telecommunications Ass'n* v. *FCC,* 988

F.2d 174 (D.C. Cir. 1993); see also *Price Cap Performance Review for AT&T*, 8 FCC Rcd. 6968 (1993).

199. See 47 U.S.C. § 543; *Implementation of Sections of the Cable Television Consumer Protection and Competition Act of 1992, Rate Regulation, Memorandum Opinion and Order and Further Notice of Proposed Rulemaking*, 8 FCC Rcd. 5585 (1993); ibid., *Report and Order and Further Notice of Proposed Rulemaking*, 8 FCC Rcd. 5631 (1993); ibid., *First Order on Reconsideration, Second Report and Order, and Third Further Notice of Proposed Rulemaking*, 9 FCC Rcd. 1164 (1993); ibid., *Third Report and Order*, 8 FCC Rcd. 8444 (1993).

200. See, for example, *Minneapolis Star & Tribune Co.* v. *Minnesota Comm'r of Revenue*, 460 U.S. 575 (1983).

201. Cable television rate regulation has been defended successfully on this basis. See *Daniels Cablevision, Inc.* v. *United States*, 835 F.Supp. 1 (D.D.C. 1993). See *Time Warner Entertainment* v. *FCC*, 56 F.3d 151 (D.C. Cir. 1995).

Index

Administrative issues: antitrust issues, 84, 90; First Amendment issues, 142; MFJ, 109–10; railroad industry and, 17; regulation and rulemaking, 14, 81, 84–86, 90–92, 108; telecommunications, 18–19, 23. *See also* Federal Communications Commission

Administrative Procedure Act, 92

ADSL. *See* Asymmetrical digital subscriber line service

Airline industry, 20

American Telephone and Telegraph (AT&T), 40, 80, 175n159. *See also* Bell System

Ameritech, 47, 48

Antitrust issues: Bell System, 14, 38, 41, 42, 80, 108, 109; broadcasting, 113–14, 115; characteristics of, 84; cross-ownership, 141, 160; essential facilities, 83, 143, 156, 158; First Amendment and, 139–62; information industry, 108, 145, 151; mass media, 140; motion picture industry, 4; regulations and, 81, 84; satellite service, 53–54; telephone service provision of video services, 104–05. *See also* Monopoly issues

AT&T. *See* American Telephone and Telegraph

Asymmetrical digital subscriber line (ADSL) service, 47–48

Bell Atlantic, 47–48, 49, 80

Bell System: "Baby Bells," 7, 22–23, 37, 47–53, 65; competition and, 19–20, 23, 39–40; consent decree, 14, 38–40, 41, 63, 72, 84, 107–10, 156, 159, 175n159;

information services, 41, 63, 201n193; interexchange and long-distance services, 41–42; rates, 20; regulation and oversight of, 19, 21, 22, 37–43, 72, 107–10; Telecommunications Act of *1996*, 14, 37, 41–43; video programming, 47–48

Bell Telephone Laboratories, 38

Blockbuster Entertainment, 65–66

Broadcast stations and media: advertising, 58; cable television and, 28–29, 56–58, 78; competition in, 110–11, 113, 127; early regulations, 3, 4, 10; facilities, 113; First Amendment and, 9–10, 26, 112, 117, 119, 126, 121, 128–29, 130–63; general characteristics, 3, 44–46, 56, 57, 58–59, 113; interactive services, 57, 114–15; ownership, 25; programming, 127–28; public interest issues, 110–15, 119, 123, 125, 128; regulation of, 15, 16, 24–27, 58, 71, 76–77, 78, 79, 80, 110–15, 121, 123, 124–26, 127, 128–62; satellites, 61; technological advances, 57, 61; television, 7, 58–59; video programming, 56–58. *See also* Information services; Licenses; Networks; Radio; Television

Business issues: antitrust issues, 84; changes in information transmission, 1–2; competitive issues, 7–8, 79; corporate power, 11, 138; facility use and development, 73, 86; joint ventures, 68, 182n97; mergers and acquisitions, 65–66, 67t, 84; regulations, 7–8, 79, 84; telecommunications requirements, 21

Cable Acts of *1984, 1992*: definition of video programming, 28; Federal Communication

203

Commission and, 29; regulations of, 14, 27–32, 33, 57, 100, 101–02, 144, 198*n*159
Cable television. *See* Television, cable
Carlin, George, 134
Carriage service. *See* Common carrier issues
CATV. *See* Community antennae television
CBS Records, 65
Chicago Tribune, 68
Columbia Records, 65
Common carrier issues: cable television and, 77; definition of "common carrier," 16, 194*n*90; competition, 77; First Amendment issues, 140, 158, 191*n*49; integration carriage service with distribution of information products, 59–68, 73; overlap of functions, 45, 74, 154, 182*n*7; regulations, 4, 8, 13, 15–23, 28, 72, 77, 93–98, 154–55; telecommunications, 139–40; telephone company provision of video; programming, 33–35, 36; universal service, 88
Communications Act of *1934*: Federal Communications Commission and, 21; general characteristics, 15–18, 42–43; licenses, 192*n*55; nondiscrimination requirements, 157; regulatory authority of, 18; section 214, 34, 36; telecommunication regulation, 13, 23; Title II, 4, 16, 17–18, 21, 23, 35, 36, 37, 73, 80, 94, 95–98, 100, 103, 104; Title III, 3, 24, 36, 45, 73, 77; Title VI, 27, 35, 80, 103, 104; "Title VII," 185*n*39. *See also* Cable Acts
Communications, electronic, 4, 60–61. *See also* Broadcast stations and media; Satellite systems; Telephone; Television
Communications, switched: broadband, 127–28; cable television and, 5, 47, 60, 61–62; general characteristics, 3; programming of, 127; regulations, 3–4, 100; technological advances, 5, 62, 99, 100; telephone service and, 61–62
Communications, wire-based, 117, 124
Communications, wireless: First Amendment issues, 117; local multipoint distribution service, 55–56; multipoint multichannel distribution service (MMDS), 55; personal communication services, 61; power of, 125; regulations, 13, 125; telephone company provision of video programming, 104. *See also* Broadcast media; Radio; Telephone; Television; Satellite systems and service

Community antennae television (CATV), 28. *See also* Television, cable
Competition: Bell System, 19–20, 23, 39–40; broadcast and cable systems, 28–29, 110–11; cable and telephone systems, 20–21, 32, 37, 72, 78, 95, 102, 103–07; in communications, 11; cross-ownership issues, 160; early regulations, 4, 8, 14; facilities and, 74, 83, 97–98, 105; First Amendment issues, 139–62; in the New Deal era, 18; private industry and, 79; regulations, 14, 15, 19–23, 74, 78, 79, 85, 94, 102, 103, 184*n*22; technological advances, 79–80; Telecommunications Act of *1996*, 22–23; universal service, 87; video programming, 126–27
Computer industry: information network and transmission, 2, 4, 6–7, 13, 21, 67, 74, 76; personal computers, 4–5; regulation of, 4
Constitution, 18, 142. *See also* First Amendment; Supreme Court rulings
Consumer electronic industry, 2
Copyright issues. *See* Intellectual property
Corporations. *See* Business issues
Cross-ownership rules: First Amendment issues, 141; restrictions, 25, 26, 158–61; Telecommunications Act of 1996

Databases, 5, 62, 67, 76
Digital satellite system (DSS). *See* Satellite systems and service
Digital technologies, 57, 67–68
Direct-to-home (DTH) satellite service. *See* Satellite systems and service
DirecTV, 54
DSS (Digital satellite system). *See* Satellite systems and service
DTH (Direct-to-home satellite service). *See* Satellite systems and service

Electric utilities, 22, 56

Fairness Doctrine: abuses of, 137, 190n26; broadcasting and, 121–24; Federal Communications Commission and, 25, 26; First Amendment and, 26, 121–22
FCC v. *National Citizens Committee for Broadcasting*, 143
Federal Communications Commission (FCC): advanced information services, 79; Bell System and, 19, 37, 109; benchmark rates, 31; broadcasting, 112, 123; cable regulations, 101, 102; competition and, 20–21, 90–91, 97–98; deregulation, 29, 62–63, 91; early regulations, 3–4, 14,

192*n*53, 192*n*54; establishment of, 16; Fairness Doctrine, 121, 123; judicial oversight of, 92–93; licensee selection, 24–25, 111; programming, 25, 26; role and authority of, 16–17, 18–19, 22, 24, 80–81, 90–92, 96–98, 134–35, 192*n*55; spectrum auctions, 57; Telecommunications Act of *1996*, 22, 96, 134–35; telephone company provision of video programming, 32–36, 104–05; Title II (Communications Act of *1934*), 16, 201*n*196; universal service and, 87. *See also* Administrative issues

First Amendment issues: antitrust issues, 139–62; broadcasting, 9–10, 26, 112, 117, 119, 126, 121, 128–29, 130–39, 144–63; cable systems, 29, 160; competition, 139–62; cross-ownership restrictions, 158–59; electronic media, 116–39; Fairness Doctrine and, 26; interconnection, unbundling, access, and nondiscrimination requirements, 157–58; Libertarian model, 119–24; offensive speech, 133–36, 188*n*3, 189*n*5; products and product integration, 63, 66–68, 82; rates, 161–62; regulations and, 4, 10, 82, 85, 103, 112, 118, 120, 163; telephone company provision of video programming, 32, 35; traditional doctrine, 9–10, 118, 131, 136–39, 142–43, 151, 152, 189*n*14, 189*n*20; *Turner Broadcasting System* v. *FCC*, 144–49

Fox Broadcasting Company, 59

Franchises. *See* Licenses

General Electric (GE), 65
Government, role of. *See* Federal Communications Commission; Regulation
Greene, Harold, 40, 41, 80, 108
GTE, 48, 49

Hauser systems, 39
Hepburn Act of 1906, 17
Hollywood, 62

ICA. *See* Interstate Commerce Act
ICC. *See* Interstate Commerce Commission
"Information superhighway," 2, 86. *See also* Internet
Information services: advertising, 179*n*67; antitrust issues, 108, 145, 151; Bell operating companies, 39, 41; changes in, 1–3, 4–6, 45, 67–68, 69, 74, 75, 76, 88–89, 126–27, 140–41, 162–63; cross-ownership issues, 159–60; First Amendment issues, 116–18, 131–33, 135–36, 141; gateway

services, 63; integration of delivery systems and information products, 62–66, 94, 117–18, 140–41; integration with carriage service, 59–62, 97; mass media, 140; packaged, 3, 45, 75, 117, 127; performing arts, 68; press and media, 121; provision and delivery, 45–59, 68, 74–75, 112; regulation of, 6, 71–115, 146–53, 188*n*81; universal service, 87–89

Intellectual property, 4, 6
Interactive systems, 5, 57
Interactive video and data service (IVDS), 57
Internet, 5, 75, 76. *See also* "Information superhighway"
Interstate Commerce Act (ICA; *1887*), 17–18, 20
Interstate Commerce Commission (ICC), 17
IVDS. *See* Interactive video and data service

Judicial system: administrative oversight, 92–92, 108, 150; judicial proceedings, 84, 85; regulation of competition, 108–09

Kahn, Alfred, 20

Libertarian values: electronic communications and, 11; First Amendment doctrines and, 10, 82, 119–24, 136–39, 149; Telecommunications Act of *1996*, 134–35
Licenses: broadcasting, 110, 111, 113, 114, 122, 123, 124; cable television, 29, 32, 102; cross-ownership restrictions, 159; Federal Communications Commission and, 3, 24, 25–26; fees for, 27, 77–78, 113, 130, 188*n*84; franchising, 102; public trust issues, 125, 129–30, 192*n*55; regulation of, 25–26, 113, 129–30, 187*n*61; spectrum scarcity rationale, 122, 123, 124–26, 191*n*51; Telecommunication Act of *1996*, 27, 36, 63
LMDS (Local multipoint distribution service). *See* Communications, wireless
Local multipoint distribution service (LMDS). *See* Communications, wireless
Lorain Journal Co. v. *United States*, 143

Market power: Bell System, 109; cable television, 29, 146; facilities and, 83–84, 89–90, 143, 155; local telephone service, 95; newspapers, 143; regulations and, 10, 70, 77, 91, 149, 155, 158; telecommunications carriers, 140
Matsushita Electronics, 65
McCaw Communications, 40, 80, 175*n*159

MCA, 65
MCI, 19, 20
MFJ (Modification of Final Judgment), 71,
72, 84, 108–09. *See also* Bell system
Microsoft Corporation, 61, 68, 75
Minority issues, 25, 26
MMDS (Multipoint multichannel
distribution service). *See* Communications,
wireless
Monopoly issues: access requirements, 156;
Bell System, 38, 40; cable television, 29,
78; local telephone companies, 61;
technological change, 83; unbundling,
156. *See also* Antitrust issues
Motion picture industry, 3, 4, 6
Multipoint multichannel distribution service
(MMDS). *See* Communications, wireless
Municipal and local authority. *See* Regulation

National Broadcasting Company (NBC), 61,
65, 68
National Telecommunications and
Information Administration (NTIA), 26
NBC. *See* National Broadcasting Company
Networks: cable television and, 29; as
carriers or broadcasters, 73; First
Amendment issues, 128–29; "full service,"
62, 180*n*77; programming of, 26, 29, 45,
62, 73, 128–29, 192*n*60, 192*n*61;
regulations, 80; television and, 7
New Deal, 18, 92, 125
Nobuyki Idei, 1
NTIA. *See* National Telecommunications
and Information Administration
NYNEX, 47, 48, 49. *See also* Bell System

Obscenity. *See* First Amendment

Pacific Bell, 49. *See also* Bell System
Pacific Telesis, 47, 48. *See also* Bell System
Paramount, 65–66
Personal communications services (PCS), 61
Plants, delivery: broadband, 49, 53, 63,
127–28; copper, 47–48; fiber-optic, 48;
satellite, 53–54
Political issues: broadcasters, 114; cable
rates, 101; campaigns and candidates, 124;
Fairness Doctrine, 137; Federal
Communications Commission, 92, 109,
110; local regulators, 102; regulations and,
8, 85, 87; rent-seeking and protections, 82,
85; universal service, 88
Print media: electronic distribution, 67–68,
71–72, 76; First Amendment and, 9,
66–67; newspapers, 143

Programming. *See* Video programming;
individual services
Public interest issues, 24–25, 27, 41
Publishing industry, 2, 6

Radio: mobile services and, 5; regulations, 8,
15, 77; Telecommunications Act of *1996*,
27; transmissions, 24
Rates: cable television, 29, 30–31, 32;
regulation of, 16, 101, 161–62;
telecommunications, 19, 20, 21. *See also*
Tariffs
RCA, 65
Red Lion Broadcasting Co. v. *FCC*, 122–23,
124, 126, 128, 147, 190*n*26
Regulation: cable television, 27–32, 99–104;
changes in, 8–9, 14–15, 20, 21;
common-carrier, 4, 8, 13, 15–23, 28, 72,
77; competition and, 19–23, 28–29, 70, 76;
costs of, 82, 86–87; deregulation, 29,
62–63, 83, 108, 113–14; disparities
between developing networks and
traditional regimes, 71–95, 124–25, 131,
139–41, 147; early policies, 3–4, 6, 8, 13,
14, 76, 79; First Amendment issues,
141–62; general characteristics of, 3, 8,
15, 44–45, 69–72, 94–95, 141; incentive
regulation, 21, 161, 166*n*27, 167*n*41; local,
102–03; models of, 13, 86–93, 111;
narrow tailoring, 147–48, 150, 152,
196*n*133, 197*n*136; railroads and, 4, 13,
17, 155; reforms of, 69–115; social costs
of, 82; state and local, 18, 29, 72–73,
94–95, 110, 166*n*27; technological
advances and, 79; telecommunications,
16–23, 99–104; universal service, 87. *See
also* Administrative issues;
Communication Act of *1934*;
Telecommunications Act of *1996*;
individual services
Regulations, specific: distribution of
programming, 31; interconnection,
unbundling, access and nondiscrimination,
154–58, 185*n*33, 196*n*132, 199*n*168,
200*n*180; must carry provisions, 31, 36,
144–45, 150–52, 153, 186*n*53; open video
systems, 36, 49, 53, 73, 80, 104, 105;
syndicated exclusivity, 29; video dialtone,
33–34, 48, 49, 103, 104. *See also* Antitrust
issues; Fairness Doctrine

Satellite Master Antenna Television Systems
(SMATV). *See* Satellite systems and
service
Satellite systems and service: development
of, 4, 5, 25, 53, 60–61; digital satellite

systems, 54; direct-to-home satellite service, 53; Primestar, 53–54; programming, 54, 61, 73–74, 127; regulation of, 4, 25, 77, 80; Satellite Master Antenna Television Systems, 54–55

Sherman Act, 151, 184n22

Single-mast antenna television systems (SMATV). *See* Television

SMATV (Satellite Master Antenna Television Systems; single-mast antenna television systems). *See* Satellite systems and service; Television

Social issues, 10–11, 137, 151. *See also* Broadcast stations and media; Licenses

Sony Corporation, 1, 65

Southern New England Telephone, 53

Southwestern Bell, 39. *See also* Bell System

Sunstein, Cass, 137

Supreme Court rulings: cable television, 28–29, 144–49; Communications Act of *1934*, 19; cross-ownership issues, 159; information industry, 142–54; "indecent" speech, 134; telephone company provision of video programming, 35. *See also FCC* v. *National Citizens Committee for Broadcasting; Lorain Journal Co.* v. *United States; Red Lion Broadcasting Co.* v. *FCC; Turner Broadcasting System* v. *FCC*

Stations, television and radio. *See* Broadcast stations and media

Stern, Howard, 133

Switched communications. *See* Communications, switched

Tariffs: review and filing schemes, 16, 17, 95–96; Telecommunications Act of *1996*, 22. *See also* Rates

TCI, 80

Technology. *See* Broadcast stations and media; Plants, delivery; Satellite systems and service

Telecommunications: common carriage in, 139–40; First Amendment and, 10; regulation of, 16–19, 21–22, 44–45, 79, 94, 155, 161; technological advances in, 44–45, 98. *See also* Communications, switched; Radio; Television; Satellite services

Telecommunications Act of *1996*: Bell System consent decree, 14, 37, 41–43, 72; broadcasters, 149–50; cable television, 31–32, 101; competition and, 109, 156; cross-ownership, 27, 72; deregulation, 22; electric utilities, 56; Federal Communications Commission, 96; First

Amendment issues, 134–35; licenses, 27, 114, 130; local telephone services, 94, 156; as a missed opportunity, 6, 8, 15, 72, 96, 101, 110; rates, 102; state and local regulators, 94, 102, 186n45; telecommunications service, 97, 100; telephone provision of video services, 14, 32, 36–37, 48, 49, 53, 104; television, 149–50; two-way services, 28

Telephone service: cellular, 26, 40, 83; competition and competitive pressures, 20–21, 61, 65; cross-subsidies, 34; deregulation, 63; information and database services, 61, 62; *800*-number services, 5, 61, 76; regulations, 13, 16, 63, 71; Telecommunications Act of *1996*, 32, 36–37, 53; video dialtone services, 62, 71, 72, 103. *See also* Bell System

Telephone service, local: equal access, 20–21, 39, 156, 174n152; cable television and, 1, 32–37, 53, 77, 78, 99, 159–60; competition, 21, 22, 23, 62, 72, 75, 78, 105–07; facilities of, 75, 78, 83, 105; First Amendment issues, 160; information services, 7, 41, 63, 159; open video systems, 63; regulatory issues, 8, 18–19, 20–21, 72–73, 77, 87–88, 94, 102–06; rates, 21, 106; services, 63, 75, 78, 127; subsidies, 88; universal service, 87–88; video services and, 14, 32–37, 47–53, 73, 80, 102–10. *See also* Bell System; Communications, switched

Telephone service, interstate and long distance: Bell operating companies, 39; equal access, 20–21; facilities for, 83; competition in, 20; regulatory issues, 18–9, 20

Television: commercial independent stations, 59; public, 7, 149–50; rating code, 134; regulations and, 7; single-mast antenna systems (SMATV), 30; stations, 7; Telecommunications Act of *1996*, 27. *See also* Broadcast media; Networks

Television, cable: advertising, 58; antitrust and First Amendment issues, 144–49; broadcasting and, 28–29, 57–58, 60, 78, 127; deregulation, 63; facilities, 73, 83, 105; growth and development of, 4, 5, 7, 25, 28, 46, 58, 60, 65, 83, 170n87; ownership, license, and franchise issues, 29, 30, 31, 32, 62–63, 64t, 66, 171n101; programming, 30–31, 32, 46–47, 57–58, 60, 140, 159, 192n59, 192n60; rates, 101–02, 161; regulations, 4, 13–14, 25, 27–32, 60, 71, 72, 77, 78, 98–106, 150, 161, 186n53; services of, 27–28, 30, 78,

83, 127; technological advances and, 60, 78, 83, 98; Telecommunications Act of *1996*, 31–32, 53, 63; telecommunications functions and, 1, 5, 28, 32, 60, 61–62, 77, 98, 101, 103–07, 176*n*11. *See also* Cable Acts; Video programming
Time Inc., 65–66
Time-Warner Entertainment cable systems, 39, 40, 47, 180*n*77
Title II, III, VI, VII. *See* Communications Act of *1934*
Turner Broadcasting System v. *FCC:* access requirements, 157, 158; cross-ownership restrictions, 158–59, 160, 161; effects of, 124, 142, 149; further proceedings, 150; narrow tailoring, 152, 196*n*133; refinement of antitrust principle, 144–49, 153–54; regulations, 154–55, 162
Two-way signaling and services, 23

United Paramount Network, 59
United States Satellite Broadcasting Company (USSB), 54
USSB. *See* United States Satellite Broadcasting Company

US WEST, 39, 40, 47, 49, 180*n*77. *See also* Bell System

Viacom, 65
Video programming: cable television systems and, 27–28, 46–47, 83; competition in, 126–27; definition of, 101; delivery systems, 74–75, 101, 103; financial interests in, 62–63; open video systems, 36, 63; outlets for, 45–46; provision of, 45–59; range of services, 73; regulation of, 127; telephone company provision of, 14, 32–37, 47–53, 73, 80, 102–10; video dialtone services, 62, 71, 72, 103

Waivers. *See* Bell System
Warner Communications, 65–66. *See also* Time-Warner Entertainment cable systems
WB network, 59
Western Electric Company, 38. *See also* Bell System
Wire. *See* Plant, delivery
Wireless transmission, 24. *See also* Communications, wireless